SEX DEGREES
OF **SEPARATION**

SEX DEC

OF SEPA

San Francisco

GREES
ARATION

The Ultimate Guide to Celebrity Relationships   by Irad Eyal

Chronicle Books

CHRONICLE BOOKS
SAN FRANCISCO

Sin-dex

Sidebars

Introduction

News travels fast these days, and it's nearly impossible to keep up with the important events that rock our world: namely, which celebrities hooked up, broke up, texted a booty call (pg. 92), or paid off a $250,000 poker debt with sexual favors (pg. 88). The kind of news that matters.

The press and paparazzi do an admirable job of breaking stories (God bless them), but as scholars of romance, we have only so much time at the airport or dentist's office to process all of the mind-bending, head-spinning details. What the world needs now is a comprehensive guide that helps it all make sense—a hidden map of the heart that links celebrities in a glorious, sticky web of love. You're holding that sticky web right now.

This book is the culmination of modern society's great hope to know everything there is to know about the mating habits of our favorite stars. More importantly, it reveals what you've always suspected: that all celebrities are closely connected by an incestuous network of romantic relationships, or, as our trademark puts it, *Sex Degrees of Separation*. And that means every celebrity (note: except Danny DeVito and Rhea Perlman, monogamous and loving it).

There are a lot of surprises between the covers. You'll find out Mark Wahlberg (pg. 27) was convicted of attempted murder and that David Schwimmer (pg. 66) has never married, possibly because his mom was Elizabeth Taylor's divorce lawyer. You'll learn how Lindsay Lohan (pg. 93) hooked up in rehab and hear Bijou Phillips's (pg. 145) complaint about losing her virginity to Evan Dando (pg. 62) (hint: it involves tongue).

There's also a wealth of well-reported dramas you may have forgotten: Paris Hilton's (pg. 89) feuds, Alyssa Milano's (pg. 95) on-screen sexual awakening, Ben Affleck's (pg. 80) stripper romp with Christian Slater (pg. 22) *and* his wife.

But the one thing you've never seen before is the bird's-eye view of the sexual landscape of Hollywood. You'll find connections you never dreamed possible. Here are just a few of the sex degrees of separation you'll discover:

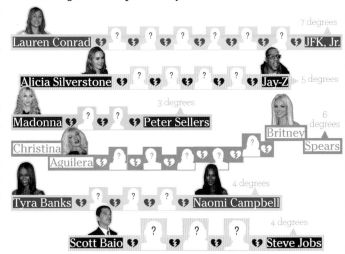

Sex Degrees of Separation is a source of gossip you can rely on—every fact is verified and every relationship is real. So flip through the pages, explore, and find your own sweet trails of romance or sick twisted sex degrees. And take inspiration from civilians Riley Giles (pg. 93), Tracy McShane (pg. 33), and Connie Angland (pg. 142)—with a little luck and hard work, even *you* could bed a celebrity. Hey, maybe you'll be in the next edition.

Glenn Close

Close has mastered the role of the sinister psycho in films like *Dangerous Liaisons* (keep her away from your girlfriend), *Fatal Attraction* (keep her away from your bunny), and *101 Dalmatians* (keep her away from your puppies).

The dates for each relationship are right here, along with an icon that reveals just how serious it was.

🔒 married
🔓 divorced
8 engaged
𝔅 broken engagement
♥ dating
💔 broken up

While working on *Biloxi Blues*, Harrelson started dating Neil Simon's daughter, and the couple got married as a goof in Tijuana. Her father became concerned that Harrelson might be gunning for his fortune, so he must have been relieved when the couple got a summary dissolution a few months later.

Nancy Simon
Neil Simon's daughter

💔 1991

1991

Woody Harrelson

Harrelson's father, Charles, was a contract killer convicted of murdering a Texas judge. Woody played the airhead bartender Woody on *Cheers* for eight seasons, and then he went off to make movies, including his Oscar-nominated turn as *Hustler* publisher Larry Flynt in 1996.

💔 1985

🔒 1985 🔒 2008–

Despite his statement to Barbara Walters that he didn't believe in the institution of marriage and that "you can't really say you're gonna have and hold someone 'til death do you part, because you don't know," Woody came around after twenty years of dating his ex-assistant. They sealed the deal in 2008.

Laura Louie
Woody Harrelson's assistant

The lines indicate a relationship between the two celebrities. Check out the relationship descriptions and follow the lines to learn more about who is connected a few sex degrees away.

Close dated the younger Harrelson when he was but a child pouring drinks behind the bar on *Cheers*. They met while working on a Los Angeles stage play (yes, they exist) called *Brooklyn Laundry*.

The lines leading off the page with these big photos mean the drama continues right on the next page.

2° to Al Pacino ▶
3° to Jennifer Grey ▶
4° to John F. Kennedy, Jr. ▶
Penelope Anne Miller NEXT ▶

When Shields and Harrelson began dating, Shields's mother, Teri, was livid. "I just cannot understand my daughter. I mean, the man is way beneath her standing. She could have any man in the world, but now she says she's in love and that's that," she said.

💔 1988

Brooke Shields p. 115 ▶

Follow these lines to the next celebrity by turning to the indicated page.

Daryl Hannah

Hannah played the hot acrobatic robot Pris in 1982's *Blade Runner*, followed by her role as the scaly-but-sexy mermaid in *Splash* (opposite Tom Hanks). Since 2006 she's been working on a documentary to end sexual slavery, inspired by her own experience of being lured to Las Vegas and narrowly escaping at age seventeen.

Kennedy was there for Hannah after she was beaten up by her boyfriend, and the two embarked on a relationship. At least one biographer has alleged that Kennedy was sleeping with the actress at the time of his death.

◀ p. 115 Brooke Shields

Helen Hunt

Sweet Helen of the sitcom *Mad About You* was typecast as a drug fiend in early childhood roles, first as the marijuana smoker in *The Facts of Life* and then as a PCP user in the after-school special *Desperate Lives*.

Jan Tarrant
Acting coach

In 2001, the world (and Pacino's girlfriend Diane Keaton, pg. 141) found out that he had a two-year-old daughter with Strasberg Institute acting teacher Tarrant. Surprise!

1988–1989

Amy Poehler

Poehler joined *Saturday Night Live* in 2001 and her first episode was broadcast after the unfunny 9/11 attacks. She was brilliant as Hillary Clinton opposite Tina Fey's Sarah Palin in a 2008 parody.

Arnett and Poehler have spent more time together on screen than off. She played his "accidental" wife on *Arrested Development*, and they starred as incestuous ice-skating siblings in *Blades of Glory*.

◀ BACK Woody Harrelson

◀ p. 131 Beverly D'Angelo   1997–2003 ❣

Pacino started dating D'Angelo when she auditioned for *Sea of Love* while he was still involved with his on-and-off girlfriend of seven years, Lyndall Hobbs. D'Angelo provided what Hobbs couldn't—fantastic impressions of Patsy Cline (she played her in *Coal Miner's Daughter*) and kids—twins, in fact.

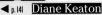

◀ p. 141 Diane Keaton   1972–1991 ❣

Al Pacino

After being nominated for iconic performances in *Serpico*, *The Godfather*, *Dog Day Afternoon*, and *Glengarry Glen Ross*—and losing—Pacino inexplicably won an Oscar for his "Hoo-ahh!" portrayal of a blind asshole in *Scent of a Woman*. He's never been married but has three children with two girlfriends.

"[Pacino] wanted to make love every minute of the day and night," said long-time girlfriend Hobbs, just not always with her, as affairs with Penelope Ann Miller (pg. 11) and Jan Tarrant proved.

Lyndall Hobbs
Australian director

❣ 1991–1997

❣ 1993

Carolyn Bessette
Personal shopper for Calvin Klein

Bessette worked as a saleswoman at the New York Calvin Klein store when she met Kennedy. They were married in a small, secret ceremony in 1996 to avoid the media spotlight to which she never grew accustomed.

2° to Vanilla Ice
3° to Kate Hudson
5° to Demi Moore

Madonna p.103

||

1996–1999 🔒

1989–1994 💔

1989 💔

💔 1988

💔 1993

💔 1988

Janice Dickinson p.139 ▶

John F. Kennedy, Jr.

JFK Jr. was a successful journalist (he founded *George* magazine), a mediocre lawyer (it took him three tries to pass the New York bar), and a lousy pilot. Named the "Sexiest Man Alive" by *People* magazine in 1988, the son of John F. Kennedy lived and loved in the spotlight.

Parker said, "John was really beautiful. He was sort of beyond being a sexual person... Extremely American handsome boy-man." Sounds like she liked the guy.

Sarah Jessica Parker NEXT ▶

2003– 🔒

Broderick and Hunt dated briefly after monkeying around on the set of 1987's *Project X*. (And yes, we know their characters were supervising chimpanzees, not monkeys.)

1987–1988 💔

Sarah Jessica Parker NEXT ▶

Will Arnett
Arnett couldn't get a break in Hollywood—he starred in four pilots that were either canceled or rewritten minus his character. But one last audition got him the role of GOB in *Arrested Development* with Jason Bateman, and his career finally took off.

Matthew Broderick
When Broderick hooked up his modem to play Global Thermonuclear War in 1983's *WarGames*, it was the start of his movie career and the Internet era. He was the first choice to play Alex P. Keaton on *Family Ties* but chose to focus on film, and the role went to Michael J. Fox (pg. 88) instead.

1997– 🔒

📞 1987–1988

1994–1995 🔒
1985 💔

Jennifer Grey p.115

Miller had this to say after dating Pacino on the set of *Carlito's Way*: "Al is a very passionate person and he brought out a certain ... passion in me. It's not a secret and I'm not ashamed of it."

Penelope Ann Miller

The star of 1992's *The Gun in Betty Lou's Handbag*, whom Teri Garr once called "Cantaloupe Ann Miller," has many claims to fame—she's the only actress to have starred with all three *Godfather* fellas, Brando (pg. 146), De Niro (pg. 55), and Pacino, and she taught Arnold Schwarzenegger how to kiss on the set of *Kindergarten Cop*.

1993 💔

Miller and Broderick romanced while working on the stage version of *Biloxi Blues* in 1985. While she claimed he was her "first real love," that didn't stop her from scoring with understudy Woody Harrelson as well (she described him as "fun, but it wasn't serious").

💔 1985–1986

Broderick and Grey were briefly engaged after meeting on the set of *Ferris Bueller's Day Off* (she played his sister). They were vacationing in Ireland when Broderick crashed their car into a vehicle in the opposite lane, killing two people. He faced prison time but got off on a lesser charge.

Parker began dating Cage when they costarred in *Honeymoon in Vegas*, and she claimed he was "a wonderful traveling companion," as anyone would be who jumps out of planes dressed as Elvis.

Kristen Zang p.72

Cage's proposal to Zang in Central Park on her nineteenth birthday, with a pink diamond engagement ring and fountain backdrop, was a lot more romantic than when he dumped her to marry Patricia Arquette soon after. "I found out about it in a phone call," said Zang.

Brooke Shields p.115

Lisa Marie Presley
Elvis Presley's daughter

Cage and Lisa Marie tied the knot on the twenty-fifth anniversary of Elvis Presley's death in a secret ceremony in Hawaii and split 108 days later. Their divorce proceedings lasted five times longer than their marriage.

◄ BACK **JFK Jr.**

1997– 🔒 1988 💔 1992–1993

Sarah Jessica Parker

The show was canceled after one season, but *Square Pegs* (in which she played a thoughtful nerd) launched Parker's career and led to her starring role in *Sex and the City*. In 2008, she did the undoable—she had her signature chin mole removed.

◄ BACK **Matthew Broderick**

After eleven years of marriage, Broderick broke the illusion of this picture-perfect couple when he allegedly started seeing a twenty-five-year-old youth counselor (whatever that is) in 2008 while Parker was filming *Sex and the City: The Movie* in Los Angeles. But they reconnected, at least enough to have cute twins through a surrogate in 2009.

💔 1984–1991

Downey Jr. blames his addictions for ruining his relationship with Parker, who had never seen cocaine before they started dating. "I liked to drink, and I had a drug problem, and that didn't jibe with Sarah Jessica, because it was the furthest thing from what she is."

1992–1993 💔   💍 1992–1994 2002 💔

Nicolas Cage

To hide his ties to uncle Francis Ford Coppola, Cage changed his name from Nicolas Coppola to Cage. That didn't stop him from appearing in his uncle's *Rumble Fish* after landing his signature drowsy-eyed role in 1983's *Valley Girl*.

LaPier married Van Damme in Thailand in 1994, but the romance didn't last. In the divorce, she claimed that he was a drug addict and had kicked her in the chest, rupturing her breast implants.

Robert Downey Jr.
Oscar-winning American actor

Thomas Jane

Originally resistant to playing a superhero when offered the lead in *The Punisher*, Jane relented when he realized that the character was an "antihero." He didn't know the movie would be an anti-success. He stars in HBO's *Hung*.

They were engaged for four years before getting married, but Arquette filed for divorce in 2008 after Jane was clocked driving his Maserati 119 mph while drunk. She stopped the split, and they planned to renew their vows in 2009.

2006– 🔒

Patricia Arquette

The middle sibling of the Arquettes, Patricia got her start in *A Nightmare on Elm Street 3: Dream Warriors*. She continued to take on supernatural roles in the 1999 film *Stigmata* and the TV series *Medium*. She probably does not actually have supernatural powers, though.

🔒 1995–2000

Darcy LaPier
Hawaiian Tropic model and accomplished barrel racer

When Cage was trying to woo Arquette, she made him prove his love by sending him on a scavenger hunt for impossible-to-find items like J. D. Salinger's autograph (which Cage procured). They got married and separated after nine months but kept up appearances for four years before finalizing their divorce.

At the time, they were both icons of virginity, and no one was convinced that they were actually together. That didn't stop Shields from insisting that "to call it platonic makes it seem less than it is." Which is?

1983–1985

1994–1996 🔒

The marriage between Jackson and the daughter of Elvis Presley was always shrouded in suspicion, coming around the same time Jackson was accused of sexually molesting a thirteen-year-old boy. Presley insisted that they weren't faking and were "sexually active," which is not what you should say when trying to seem normal!

1975

Michael Jackson

Jackson's love life was as mysterious and controversial as his pixie face. In his last years, the pop star who wanted to be Peter Pan appeared to avoid romantic relationships in order to concentrate on his kids, who were present when he died of an anesthetic overdose in 2009.

According to Jackson, his first girlfriend was twelve-year-old O'Neal who tried to seduce him in 1975 when she "touched the button on [his] shirt to open it." Tatum remembered things differently saying, "[Michael] has a very vivid imagination." Who you gonna believe?

1975

2002

Tatum O'Neal

Despite the Culkins, Fannings, and Breslins, Tatum O'Neal remains the youngest Oscar winner ever for her performance with her dad, Ryan (pg. 56), in 1974's *Paper Moon*. Her father gave her the typical messed-up Hollywood childhood featuring drugs, alcohol, and orgies.

Alec Baldwin NEXT ▶

John McEnroe

McEnroe turned tennis into a full-contact sport in the 1980s, serving up more expletives than, well, serves. After his sports star dimmed, McEnroe tried to break into television with a spectacularly unsuccessful CNBC talk show *McEnroe*. You cannot be serious!

McEnroe hated the media attention swirling around his marriage to Tatum and said, "Suddenly, wherever I went, it felt like a spectacle." And if there's one thing McEnroe doesn't like, it's being a spectacle.

🔒 1984–1993

1995

Gladys Portugues
Professional bodybuilder

Van Damme and his female counterpart, bodybuilder Gladys Portugues, were married and divorced, then remarried in 1999 after his split from Darcy LaPier. "I love the woman. I came back," he said.

1987–

1994–1997

1995

1997

1994

Jean Claude Van Damme

Van Damme's decades of martial arts training were supplemented by five years of ballet, which may have helped define his signature move in 1988's *Bloodsport*—doing the splits and punching his opponent in the nuts.

Princess Stephanie
Princess of Monaco

Lowe and Princess Stephanie exchanged friendship rings, but it wasn't long before the princess was frolicking shirtless on a beach with another man. That's how they roll in Europe.

1986–1987

Rob Lowe

Lowe was part of the 1980s "Brat Pack" after a break-out role in *The Outsiders* but he broke truly new ground with one of the first commercially available sex tapes that documented his romp with two women (one of whom turned out to be sixteen) during the 1988 Democratic National Convention.

Kylie Minogue p.67 ▼

Van Damme and Minogue had a torrid affair during the filming of *Streetfighter*—the only high point of the Australian-filmed, universally panned movie.

♂ 1981–1987

Lowe and his *Outsiders* costar Gilbert were a longtime item until Lowe decided to upgrade from an actress to a princess. After his relationship with princess Stephanie fizzled, he reconnected with Gilbert and proposed, though the engagement was short-lived.

Melissa Gilbert p.131 ▼

Nicole Seidel
Lawyer

This couple met in a New York restaurant when loud-talking Baldwin came over to her table and asked if he was bothering her and she said, "Yes!"

◀ p. 142 Jeff Goldblum

For Goldblum, one Davis was not enough and he dated Kristin briefly in 2002.

2002

2003–2007

1983

Vanity was the lead in Prince's girl group Vanity 6. These days, Denise K. Smith, as she is known, is a born-again Christian.

Vanity p.47 ▲

Ron Snyder-Britton
Makeup artist

When this couple divorced, Snyder-Britton got the mansion, but they couldn't decide how to divvy up their ten dogs, multiple cats, and half dozen birds. When Basinger married Alec Baldwin, Snyder-Britton offered him this now-prophetic warning: "She's a devil woman who'll disturb any man. I don't envy [you]."

You had to wonder why Baldwin, who once said George W. Bush's reelection was as damaging as 9/11, got together with Turner, who would campaign for Sarah Palin in 2008. They went as far as getting engaged but called it off after the wedding invitations had already been sent.

1980

Alec Baldwin

Alexander Rae Baldwin III can get serious (*Glengarry Glen Ross*, *The Hunt for Red October*) and seriously funny (*Beetlejuice*, *30 Rock*). And over the course of his career he's seriously screwed up as well (recall the leaked "rude little pig" voicemail to daughter Ireland).

Kristin Davis

Best known for her uptight *Sex and the City* character, Charlotte, Davis actually got her first big TV role on *Melrose Place*, but her character, Brooke, was so despised that she was written out after one season.

Prince

The delirious singer who partied like it was 1999 and drove his little red corvette in the purple rain skyrocketed to fame in the 1980s with an enigmatic persona that oozed sexuality.

Janine Turner
American actress who played Maggie on *Northern Exposure*

2001   2002

1990–2000

1990–2000

1989

The official reason cited for this breakup was schedule conflicts, but the 9/11 attacks on Baldwin and Davis's home city might have contributed to the split.

◀ BACK Tatum O'Neal

This storybook romance ended in the king of all bad divorces, followed by an even more insane custody battle for daughter Ireland. Basinger compared Baldwin to Saddam Hussein. He called her a "black widow." And that was just the start.

Prince incorporated Basinger into his medley-single "Scandalous Sex Suite," which featured the lyrics "2night why don't we skip all the foreplay, mama, And just get down here on the floor?" Basinger's brother had to snatch her from Prince's mansion because he feared the singer had a "weird sexual hold" on her.

Fox and Williams eloped in 1999 and had daughter Sasha in 2000. He said, "I was on the road ten months out of the year, so our communication was tested." And by tested he may be referring to the *National Enquirer* photos of him kissing another woman published in 2004.

1999–2004

2006–2008

Sharon Stone p.22 ▼

Sly Fox said, "I think we all should be so lucky and fortunate to be in a romance with Sharon Stone."

Rick Fox

Fox played for the Celtics and Lakers before retiring from basketball to focus on his acting career. He appeared in *Oz*, *One Tree Hill*, *Dirt*, and *Ugly Betty* (thanks to his ex-wife, Vanessa Williams).

Vanessa Williams

Williams was the first African American Miss America when she was crowned in 1983, but her reign ended abruptly when nude photos of her in lesbian scenarios were sold to *Penthouse* by shameless photographer Tom Chiapel.

Banks and Fox ended their relationship quickly, but not before Banks introduced him to her friend Vanessa Williams, whom he went on to marry.

1998

Basinger met Peters on the set of *Batman* and quickly filed for divorce from her makeup artist husband Ron Snyder-Britton to get with the ex-hairdresser turned movie mogul. In the divorce filings, Snyder-Britton accused her of getting with two other *Batman* artists—Michael Keaton (pg. 155) and Prince.

Jon Peters p. 118 ▲

Singleton and Busia met on the set of his 1997's film *Rosewood*, got pregnant with daughter Hader, married (he reportedly answered his phone during the ceremony), and divorced twelve days after the child was born.

1996–1997

Akosua Busia

Busia is the daughter of Ghana's ex–prime minister Kofi Abrefa Busia and a princess of the Ashanti empire, which ruled West Africa from the 1700s until colonization. She played Jewel in *The Color Purple*.

1995

John Singleton

A year after graduating from USC, south-central Los Angeles native Singleton made his directorial debut at age twenty-four with *Boyz n the Hood* and was honored as the youngest person (and the only African American ever) to be nominated for an Oscar for best director.

Singleton briefly dated Long (his second *Fresh Prince of Bel Air* girlfriend) after splitting with his first, Tyra Banks. Long had a role in Singleton's breakout feature, *Boyz n the Hood*, years before.

Nia Long
American actress

When confronted by another woman who was into Webber at a New York nightclub, Long threw down with fists flying and scared the rival away.

1993–1995

1980–1988

1988

Kim Basinger

Basinger starred in *Katie: Portrait of a Centerfold*, then as a prostitute in *From Here to Eternity*. She played one of Sean Connery's (pg. 55) Bond girls, did her first *Playboy* spread to promote the film in 1983, and mixed things up with *9½ Weeks* and an Oscar-winning performance in *L.A. Confidential*—as a prostitute. Typecasting?

Singleton cast Banks in his film *Higher Learning* (her feature debut), but she joked that he wasn't affectionate enough during the shoot. "I just felt like he should have rubbed my head after every take ..." said Banks.

Chris Webber

Despite being 1993's number one NBA draft pick, C-Webb never led a team to the championship, and he'll be remembered for getting arrested for marijuana possession twice in 1998 (once while coming through U.S. Customs from Puerto Rico).

1993–1995

Banks devoted an entire episode of her talk show to the subject of "Professional Athletes and the Women Who Love Them" and shed tears, saying "I was with my boyfriend for a long time ... I couldn't stay ..."

John Utendahl
Investment banker

2007–

Despite her protests to the contrary, Banks's desire to be closer to Utendahl might explain why she moved her slate of TV shows from Los Angeles to New York.

Tyra Banks

Banks broke barriers for body baring as the first African American to appear on the covers of *Sports Illustrated* and the Victoria's Secret catalog in 1997. Since then she's launched the hit TV series *America's Next Top Model*, and her talk show competes with the likes of Oprah Winfrey.

2001–2004

1996

Seal NEXT ▶

Tyler Perry

Perry blew the white man's mind when his movie, *Diary of a Mad Black Woman*, grossed ten times its budget at the box office. He built his brand with successful sitcoms, more movies, and a best-selling book.

1998

2006

When Day-Lewis decided to end his on-off relationship with Adjani for good, he sent her a fax. In the spectrum of bad breakup methods, faxing ranks right below a text message and right above a brick with a note thrown through a window.

1994–1995

Day-Lewis and Roberts were rumored to be getting cozy when they were set to star in *Shakespeare in Love*, but they ditched the project when the film was stuck in development hell and didn't get back together until after her divorce from Lyle Lovett.

Kiedis met O'Conner in 1989, describing her as "this super ridiculously hot bald Irish girl with a magical voice . . ." She wasn't exactly letting me all the way in her door . . . it was the most wonderful nonsexual relationship I'd ever had."

After she ripped up a picture of the pope on *Saturday Night Live*, the scorn she endured was so overwhelming that O'Connor attempted suicide while touring with boyfriend Peter Gabriel.

Peter Gabriel
English musician

1991

Daniel Day-Lewis

Oscar winner Daniel Day-Lewis is renowned for staying in character throughout a production. He forced crew members to carry him in a wheelchair on *My Left Foot*, and nearly died of pneumonia while working on *Gangs of New York* because they "didn't have antibiotics in those days."

Maybe he lurked backstage at fashion shows, because Seal always found a way to meet the models. His relationship with Banks was brief and a few years later Seal said, "I had a course in the meaning of love: what it meant to me and what I wanted from life."

1990 **Sinead O'Connor**
Irish singer

1996

◄ BACK Tyra Banks

1996–

Day-Lewis met Miller while visiting her father, Arthur Miller (yes, that Arthur Miller), at his home in 1996. They have two children together.

Rebecca Miller
Film director

Jenny McCarthy

She started out as a *Playboy* model but has expanded her talents to hosting, acting, and battling scientists about the risks of vaccinations. Despite this busy career she still found time to make out with porn star Jenna Jameson (pg. 39) and admitted to cheating on her first husband with both men and women.

When they made their relationship public in 2006, Carrey was photographed strolling Malibu in McCarthy's one-piece bathing suit. Carrey has said that they have no plans to get married, "but we're never getting divorced, which is fantastic."

2005–

2000

Jim Carrey

Stretchy-faced Carrey has laughed numerous women into the sack during his successful career; one can only imagine what his "O" face looks like.

Melissa Womer
Comedy Store waitress

1987–1994

Renee Zellweger
p.125

Lauren Holly
Holly has starred in countless films and television series, but she will always be known for her "Nice pair of hooters you got there" role in *Dumb and Dumber*.

1996–1997

After falling for his *Dumb and Dumber* costar Lauren Holly, Carrey began divorce proceedings to end his marriage to his already estranged wife, Womer. In 2003, Womer went back to court to ask for more child support money, in order to provide their daughter with the lavish lifestyle she had become accustomed to.

Jay Kay
The goofy-hat-wearing lead singer of Jamiroquai was huge in his U.K. homeland before bringing his Dr. Seuss style to the United States with hit single "Virtual Insanity." Kay continued to make headlines in Europe by dating celebs, breaking speed limits, and assaulting paparazzi—three times since 2001.

Flavio Briatore
Briatore tried a few careers (ski instructor, restaurant manager, insurance sales-man, Benetton's head of American operations) before settling on Italian millionaire supermodel-dating playboy.

After quitting as head of the successful Benetton Formula 1 racing team and divorcing his wife of two years, Briatore lived with the twenty-six-years-younger model Heming in his Paris house.

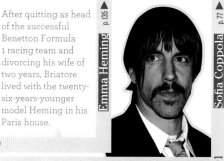

Emma Heming p. 135 ▲

Sofia Coppola p. 77 ▲

1991

1993–1996

Jaime Rishar p. 26 ▶

Rishar and Kiedis started dating when he was thirty and she was only seventeen. They broke up when Kiedis got sober.

Naomi Campbell p. 54 ▶

1998–1999

1998–2003

1990

Kay met Klum on the set of the music video for Jamiroquai's "Love Foolosophy," in which she drove in his car next to a big white afghan dog. But the relationship left something to be desired for Kay. "I'll never do that celebrity thing again," he said, "unless there was someone I really liked."

In the long line of supermodels bedded by Briatore, Klum is unique as the mother of his only child, daughter Helene "Leni" Klum. When they first announced the pregnancy, Briatore said, "I am happier than I have ever been." Then he demanded a paternity test.

Anthony Kiedis
Voted by PETA as 2008's sexiest vegetarian celebrity, Kiedis turned his troubled Los Angeles upbringing into recording gold with Flea, his high school friend and fellow Red Hot Chili Pepper.

Demi Moore p. 135 ▶

2002

1987–1990

Ione Skye NEXT ▶

Seal
Let's dispel some common Seal misconceptions—he was born in London, he's not half Brazilian, and the scars on his face are from discoid lupus erythematosus. Seal hit international stardom with "Kiss from a Rose," which may have been the best part of *Batman Forever*, and won a Grammy in 1996.

Days after announcing her divorce from hair man Ric Pipino, Klum was on tour in Australia with Kiedis. They dated for a while but it was never serious, at least for the Chili Pepper, who said, "We're not getting married anytime soon, I can tell you that."

2005–2008

Kiedis and Christie had their first kid, Everly Bear Kiedis, in 2007 but ended their relationship soon after.

After Seal and Klum spent their first night together, she came clean and told him she was pregnant. "I laughed and said, 'Already? That's amazing!' She said, 'Not with you, stupid.'" Seal proposed in an igloo on a glacier in Whistler, British Columbia, and the couple were married a year after her daughter, Leni, was born.

2002

2003–2004

2002–2003

Heidi Klum
In 1992, eighteen-year-old Klum won a German modeling competition and launched her career (but not before finishing high school). By 1997 she was in the Victoria's Secret fashion show, but it wasn't until 2004 that her true talent was revealed—making "Auf Wiedersehen" the new gesundheit on *Project Runway*.

2004–

Heather Christie
Model

Ric Pipino
Australian hairstylist

🔒 1997–2002

Only months before they separated, Klum revealed that she had bought a dog as a kid substitute for herself and Pipino. "I would love to have a baby soon, and I do get quite broody, which is why we got the dog . . . we would love a baby."

The couple lived together, and in Kiedis's 2004 memoir *Scar Tissue*, he brags about having sex with fifteen-year-old Skye when he was twenty-two. Statute of limitations on statutory rape in California? Three years.

◄ BACK **Anthony Kiedis**

◄ p. 46 **Rachel McAdams**

Ben Lee p. 112

Skye and Lee were married in 2008 in a traditional Hindu ceremony in India, presided over by Lee's spiritual guru, Sakthi Narayani Amma. And with a name like that, you don't need a punch line.

They played out one of the most memorable love stories on film in *The Notebook*, but during the shoot the actors constantly argued. The sparks continued to fly with an on-and-off three-year romance.

2005–2009 💔

Jenny Shimizu p. 104

Just a few months after officially divorcing Adam Horovitz, Skye and Netto got engaged, and then pregnant. Their daughter Kate inspired his line of sleek baby furniture.

David Netto
Interior designer

2001–2004 🐍

1998–2001 💔

2008– 🔒

1987–1990 💔

Ione Skye
Skye, the daughter of hurdy-gurdy rock-and-roller Donovan, is best known as the uptight valedictorian in *Say Anything* who is seduced by John Cusack's (pg. 121) boom-box serenade. Two out of three husbands indicate she's drawn to musicians like dad.

1997– 🔒

Ryan Gosling
At thirteen, Gosling appeared in *The Mickey Mouse Club* alongside Britney Spears (pg. 33) and Justin Timberlake (pg. 98) and was reprimanded by Disney for talking about sexual positions and other lewd acts (possibly making him Britney's first bad influence).

Kathleen Hanna
Lead singer for band Bikini Kill

Ryan Phillippe
Phillippe began his career playing the first gay teenager on a daytime soap opera, Billy Douglas on *One Life to Live*, before breaking out in *I Know What You Did Last Summer*.

It took nearly a decade for Phillippe's cruel intentions to become clear. After revelations of an extramarital affair with his *Stop Loss* costar Abbie Cornish, he split from longtime love Witherspoon.

1997–2007

Jake Gyllenhaal
You may not remember him as Billy Crystal's son in *City Slickers*, but that role was Gyllenhaal's acting debut. His Hollywood parents (his dad's a director, and his mother's a producer) sent mixed messages, letting him audition for parts and then nixing the gigs when he got them.

2008 💔

Immediately after drying out in rehab, Dunst filled the void with Gosling, whom she brought with her to twelve-step meetings. Is that in the rules?

2007– ♥

💔 💔

Matthew McConaughey
McConaughey was not only named *People* magazine's "Sexiest Man Alive" in 2005 but, when hurricane Katrina hit, the big-hearted guy rescued cats, dogs, and hamsters that were stranded after the flooding. Who can resist a guy who rescues hamsters?

Reese Witherspoon
The blonde star of the *Legally Blonde* films often plays honest, loveable girlie girls on screen. Off screen, she's not all that different. Not one for dating around, Witherspoon spends her spare time with her two children, helping out charities, and acting as an ambassador for Avon.

2007–2009 💔 💔 2002–2004

Kirsten Dunst

"Gyllenspoon," an auspicious celebrity-couple's nickname if ever there were one, apparently shouldn't share the silver screen. The pair started dating in 2007 and costarred in the flop *Rendition*.

Gyllenhaal's sister Maggie (pg. 38) introduced him to Dunst in 2002 after starring with her in *Mona Lisa Smile*. When Tobey Maguire (pg. 45) briefly dropped out of *Spider-Man 2* because of back problems (or drinking problems, depending on whom you believe), Gyllenhaal was up for the part, thanks to his girl, Dunst.

Kirsten Dunst p. 71

💔
1998–1999

A few weeks after filing for divorce from her husband of eight years, Ad-Rock, Skye told Howard Stern (pg. 104) that she was bisexual and had fallen for lesbian model Jenny Shimizu (pg. 104), whom she went on to date for three years.

1991–1999 🔓

Adam Horovitz

Horovitz, better known as "Ad-Rock" of the Beastie Boys, shares a birthday, but not much else, with fellow white rapper Vanilla Ice (pg. 103). Horovitz wrote most of the music for their Grammy-winning album *Hello Nasty*.

This couple's romance coincided with a hiatus from the Beastie Boys, after their initial hit record, *Licensed to Ill*, and with Horovitz's ill-fated move into the acting world. Yes, Ad-Rock had gone full Hollywood.

1987–1989

After his character stalked her in *Sixteen Candles* (and scored panties), Hall closed the deal during the production of *The Breakfast Club*, calling it "puppy love." Ringwald remembered things differently, saying, "We were like oil and water. Michael drove me crazy."

1984–1985

Anthony Michael Hall

The quintessential 1980s geek in *Sixteen Candles* and *The Breakfast Club* transformed into a muscular jock in the 1990s, with roles in *Edward Scissorhands* and *Six Degrees of Separation*.

Jesse James
Monster Garage host

💔 **1985–1986**

Molly Ringwald

Although she had a recurring role on *The Facts of Life* (let's face it—she was no Tootie), it would take 1984's *Sixteen Candles* to make her a star. But even the Donger couldn't have predicted she'd be the 1980s' most popular cover girl.

They say relationships based on intense experiences never last (at least that's what Bullock said in 1994's *Speed*), but her marriage to celebrity mechanic James has survived a crazed stalker in 2007 and a high-speed head-on collision in 2008. So far, so good.

> Dweezil Zappa p. 22 ▶
> Dweezil Zappa p. 22 ▶

> 2° to Jennifer Aniston ▶
> 3° to Adam Duritz ▶
> 4° to Robin Givens ▶

> Tate Donovan p. 108 ▶

McConaughey and Alves welcomed a son named Levi Alves McConaughey on July 7, 2008, in Los Angeles. The kid was profitable from day one. His baby pictures fetched $3 million from *OK!* magazine.

2005–2006

Camila Alves
Brazilian model

McConaughey said the language barrier (Cruz's native tongue is Spanish) kept him on his toes. "I can get by in Spanish, but when they get going . . . I'm breaking a sweat staying in conversation . . . it becomes a little bit more like charades."

Bullock met Gosling on the set of *Murder by Numbers,* and she got just a little incensed when reporters pointed out their sixteen-year age difference. She said, "There are so many grandpas dating Barbie dolls in Hollywood. Why is it seen as unacceptable the other way around?"

2002–2003

2003–

1997

1992–1995

Sandra Bullock

Pop quiz—you're on a booby-trapped bus with Keanu Reeves (pg. 141) in 1994's *Speed*. What do you do? If you're Bullock, you launch an A-list acting career and become Hollywood's hot-but-dorky brunette leading lady. And all without a single nude scene, unless you count 1993's *Fire on the Amazon*, in which Bullock reportedly duct taped her breasts for a modest sex scene. Ouch.

1995

In 1997, Judd told *Harper's Bazaar*, "In ten professional outings, [I was involved with] exactly two of my costars, both of which were wonderful love affairs." She named McConaughey, but kept the identity of the other man a secret.

Ashley Judd p. 55 ▼

Penelope Cruz p. 70 ▼

The pair met on the set of *A Time to Kill*. After their breakup in 1999, Bullock, discussing the possibility of future relationships, said, "I can't see finding anyone—in or out of the business." That's why she was *Miss Congeniality*, not Miss Optimistic.

1998–1999 💔

Love Fades; Tattoos Are Permanent

Maybe it's because their relationships seem so fleeting that celebrities emblazon their love on their skin in permanent ink. But what happens when the relationship tanks? Then it's time to get creative and rewrite history. Johnny Depp (pg. 114) is the classic example—he turned his "Winona Forever" tattoo into "Wino Forever" when his engagement to Winona Ryder (pg. 113) ended. He may have been the first, but he's definitely not the last: Angelina Jolie (pg. 105) went the laser route to remove her "Billy Bob" (pg. 142) scroll work. Another way to go is to change the story: Previously, when Jolie had had an H tattooed on her wrist to commemorate boyfriend Timothy Hutton (pg. 151) and later broke up with him, she said that it really referred to her brother James Haven.

Christy Turlington (pg. 158) put a rose over the initials of ill-fated husband Roger Wilson (pg. 158). Denise Richards (pg. 133) filmed the cover-up of her "Charlie" tattoo on her 2008 reality show. Pamela Anderson (pg. 29) turned her "Tommy" tat into "Mommy" when she split from Tommy Lee (pg. 32) the first time. (No comment on any alterations to the "Pamela" tattoo on his penis.) Tom Arnold had a whole collection of disturbing Roseanne Barr body art removed after their divorce. Even young Alaskan dad Levi Johnston told Tyra Banks (pg. 15) in 2009 that "maybe it wasn't the smartest thing" to get Bristol Palin's name tattooed on his ring finger. Celebs, take a word of advice: Commemorate your love with a hickey; the mark will last about the right amount of time.

The Cougars of Hollywood

Jack Nicholson (pg. 59) and Bruce Willis (pg. 138) aren't the only geezers stepping out of the nursing home to find love with younger generations. The women of Hollywood are in on the game as well (and they have an advantage—women live about five years longer than men). Long before Ashton Kutcher (pg. 135), thirty-one, married Demi Moore (pg. 135), forty-six, Barbara Hershey, fifty-seven, had already hooked up with *Lost*'s Iraqi torturer, Naveen Andrews, thirty-six. Andrews said, "I've always been attracted to older women. They look infinitely better to me." Ralph Fiennes (pg. 156) dumped *ER* doc Alex Kingston (pg. 157) for British actress Francesca Annis (pg. 156), who was eighteen years older than he, and Lorraine Bracco rebounded from Edward James Olmos with the almost-twenty-years-younger basketball star Jason Cipolla. But despite all the happiness between older women and youngish boys, Cameron Diaz (pg. 98) still got lambasted for being a mere nine years older than Justin Timberlake (pg. 98). Where is the love?!

Rick Fox p.14 ▲ 2006–2008 ❣

Christy Turlington p.158 ▲

Stone met Ferguson on his late-night show when they sang "Ye Cannae Shove Yer Granny Aff a Bus." A mutual friend later remarked, "It isn't everyone who can get Sharon singing on TV . . . never mind singing a daft Scottish song about someone's grandma."

❣ 2005–2007

Craig Ferguson
Ferguson, host of *The Late Late Show*, flipped the format on its ear with no cohost, no band, no notes—just rants, puppets, and the nightly exclamation, "It's a great day for America!"

During a break from longtime girlfriend Nina Huang, Slater dated Turlington in New York. When he and Huang got back together, Huang made him sell the Manhattan duplex where the fling took place. Couldn't he have just changed the sheets?

❣ 1994

❣ 1990–1995

Christian Slater
Dubbed the new Jack Nicholson (pg. 59) for his uncanny channeling of Jack when he appeared in *Heathers*, Slater made a name for himself as the bad boy of the 1990s with roles in *Young Guns* and *True Romance* and a string of arrests for drunk driving, taking a gun on a plane, and biting a man on the stomach.

Sharon Stone
Stone had acted in *Irreconcilable Differences* (playing the role inspired by Cybill Shepherd and *Total Recall*, but it was her performance as bisexual serial killer Catherine Tramell in 1992's *Basic Instinct* that spread her name far and wide and set the standard for appropriate interrogation attire.

❣ 2006–2007

Slater and Stone met up on the set of *Bobby*. They weren't together long, but they didn't intend to be, at least according to one friend who said, "It's a fun fling for the holidays . . ."

❣ 1996

Stone and Zappa, twelve years her junior, first appeared in public at the *Mission: Impossible* screening, and their relationship may have been just that— Stone called it off a few days later, apparently suddenly realizing he was very young.

After splitting up, Huang sued Slater for a "verbal agreement" they made that she would receive half his earnings if they ever broke up. Things must've gotten pretty heated, because during their period of legal wrangling, the two narrowly escaped from a fire that broke out in Slater's home.

Nina Huang
Model

◀ p.19 Sandra Bullock

Zappa and Bullock really liked each other for a moment in 1997. He said she was "sweet, funny, down-to-earth, and beautiful." She limited herself to two adjectives to describe him—"handsome and hilarious."

1996

2005–

1997 ❣

Lauren Knudsen
Fashion stylist

Zappa met Ringwald on the set of *Pretty in Pink*, his acting debut. And, although she initially praised the young rocker, saying, "He's not the type who wears tight jeans; I think I'm in love," they allegedly broke up because she demanded that he dress up.

Katie Wagner
Daughter of actors Marion Marshall and Robert Wagner, Katie was living with stepmother Natalie Wood (pg. 140) when the older actress drowned in 1981. Katie went on to interview celebrities as a Hollywood reporter for HBO, E!, and the TV Guide Channel.

Wagner, twenty-two at the time, was briefly her seventeen-year-old boyfriend Zappa's legal guardian because he needed an adult to sign for him while he was filming a small part in *The Running Man* with Arnold Schwarzenegger.

1987 ❣

1985–1986

Dweezil Zappa
Originally named Ian Donald Calvin Euclid Zappa because the hospital nurse refused to put "Dweezil" on the form, this second child of Frank Zappa was an early MTV VJ and rock musician who composed and performed the theme for Ben Stiller's (pg. 122) *The Ben Stiller Show*.

❣ 1998–2004

Melanie Brown
English pop singer known as Scary Spice of the Spice Girls

Brown and Murphy got tattooed with each other's names three days into the relationship. But things got messy when Brown got pregnant and Murphy questioned whether he was the father. A DNA test proved he was.

Nicole Mitchell
Fashion model

1988–2005 🔓

Duchovny was introduced to Loeb by an *X-Files* director in a Vancouver bar (the show filmed in Canada) just days after getting dumped by Winona Ryder (pg. 113). Apparently Loeb was a big fan of his sci-fi series and ready to get abducted (and probed?) by its star.

Lisa Loeb
Cat-eyed crooner Loeb was discovered by her NYC neighbor Ethan Hawke (pg. 159), who heard her perform and passed a tape to his director on *Reality Bites*, Ben Stiller (pg. 122). The song, "Stay," went on to become the first number one single ever from an unsigned artist.

This couple specialized in the incongruous, from her performance with Zappa on the Ozzy Osbourne tribute album *Bat Head Soup* to their 2004 Food Network cooking show.

2006 💔 | **1980** | 📂 **2008**

Robin Givens p.104 ▲

Eddie Murphy
Murphy is known for playing multiple characters—there's the stand-up comedian Murphy, the Murphy who's a box office star, the Murphy who's a box office flop, the married Murphy who got caught with a transsexual prostitute, and the man-about-town Murphy finding out that he has fathered yet another child (eight at last count).

1997 💔 | 📂 **1997–**

David Duchovny
Duchovny gave up a career as a doctor of English literature when he abandoned his Ph.D. program at Yale to pursue acting. He made it big on *The X-Files*. Lately, he's been known for his sex addiction and related travails, which mirror those of his character in *Californication*. Publicity ploy? Only time will tell.

Tracey Edmonds
Film and television producer

Reports suggested that Murphy may have divorced Edmonds two weeks after their "symbolic" wedding in Bora Bora because her brother had secretly brokered a product placement deal to get Jimmy Choo shoes on the bride and bridesmaids and then in a photo in *People* magazine.

💔 **1989**

Though still married, Duchovny and Leoni went through a separation in 2008, and the truth of what happened is pretty out there. Duchovny became addicted to pornography and checked himself into rehab, but they appear to have reconciled.

💔 **1996**

In a classic example of crossed signals between the genders, Duchovny said, "I'm happy, and I'm in love," while Ryder was telling gossip columnist Liz Smith that they were "casually dating" and that she was "completely single."

💗 **2008–** | 🔓 1992–2005

Edmonds hooked up with the famous TV chef soon after her relationship with Eddie Murphy ended.

Rocco DiSpirito
Celebrity chef

Edmonds and Babyface met through music (she auditioned for the video for his song "Whip Appeal" in 1990), but they spent their married time together producing films including *Soul Food*, *Josie and the Pussycats*, and *Good Luck Chuck*. When they split, she reportedly walked away with $70 million.

Kenneth "Babyface" Edmonds
R&B artist

Whitney Houston NEXT ▶

Téa Leoni
Leoni's first name isn't pronounced like the favorite British beverage, thanks to the accent aigu and her Italian heritage (her full last name is Pantaleoni). She got her start in the television series *Angels 89*, a remake of *Charlie's Angels* that never aired.

Winona Ryder p.113 ▼

24

◄ BACK **Eddie Murphy**

Jay-Z p. 82 ▲

Karrine Steffans

Steffans, known by her self-given moniker "Superhead," was a music video dancer and porn star who wrote the best-selling *Confessions of a Video Vixen* in 2005.

2000 💔

While they were dating, Steffans helped Brown get a meeting for a book deal, but Bobby got wasted and missed the meeting. Who could've seen that coming? The botched book deal was a dealbreaker for Steffans, who felt Brown had made her "look like an idiot."

💔 2007

Bobby Brown

Despite being arrested for assault, repeated drug problems, and sexual harassment claims, Brown once enjoyed massive musical success. He also starred in his own reality TV show and had a cameo in *Ghostbusters 2*.

🔒 1989–2006

This couple will always be known for the scene in *Being Bobby Brown* when Brown, referring to their colon cleansing rituals, said, "I've had to dig a dookie bubble out of your butt . . . that turd was too big . . . I had to help her with these hands . . ." To which Whitney responded "That's love . . . black love!"

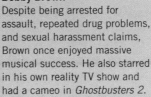

1989 💔
Whitney Houston

Once upon a time, the superstar singer sold 12 million records worldwide. But what goes up must come down, and from 2000 onward Houston's popularity has waned as she slacked off and got involved with drugs—but not crack, though. She made it very clear that "crack is whack."

They dated briefly in 2006, but Cannon called things off when news of Kardashian's infamous sex tape surfaced. It's unclear what really upset Cannon—the fact that there was a tape or that he wasn't in it.

Reggie Bush NFL player for the New Orleans Saints

Bush hated the constant media attention focused on their relationship, but Kardashian explained that they get along because her work is just as important to her as football is important to him. There's just one flaw in that argument: What work?

♥ 2007–

Early in their on-and-off relationship, Ray J wrote a song bagging on Bobby Brown with the lyrics "Is that your wife . . . well I'm her boyfriend . . . Making love is cool, just pull her hair sometimes."

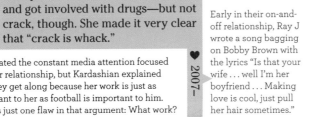

Damon Thomas Songwriter and music producer

Ray J

William Raymond "Ray J" Norwood started out as Brandy's little brother but he quickly stepped out of her shadow via a classy little home movie featuring Kim Kardashian. He has his own reality show, *For the Love of Ray J*. Oh, and he may have recorded some songs too.

Their sex tape effectively vaulted Kardashian into the upper echelons of reality fame, right up there with Paris Hilton (pg. 89) and just under Ray J (get it?).

2006 💔

Kim Kardashian

Socialite Kardashian is famous for being infamous. She's had a string of well-publicized relationships. (You can watch one of them unfold online in all its gory detail.)

◄ p.109 **Nick Lachey**

2004–2006 💔
2007– ♥
2000–2004 🔒
2006 💔

2006 💔

Vin Diesel

Mark Sinclair Vincent, who never met his biological father, went Diesel when he needed a stage name for his job as a bouncer at New York City's club Tunnel. Diesel found exposure in the short film *Multi-Facial* (about issues faced by the multiracial lead). Steven Spielberg saw the film and cast Diesel in *Saving Private Ryan*.

Diesel and Carey spent a biracial (both of their fathers are black, both mothers white) holiday together in Aspen where, according to one reporter, Carey brought her Jack Russell terrier out on a date and hand-fed the pup an entire steak.

2002–2003

Paloma Jimenez
Mexican model

Diesel and Jimenez had their first child, a daughter, in April 2008. It was a big surprise for the gossip press. "I'm not gonna put it out there on a magazine cover like some other actors. I come from the Harrison Ford (pg. 121), Marlon Brando (pg. 146), Robert De Niro (pg. 55), Al Pacino (pg. 10) code of silence."

1997–1998

Mariah Carey

Only The Beatles beat this superstar diva in number one hits, but life isn't easy at the top. In 2001 she suffered an emotional breakdown and was dropped by her record label, but she later bounced back with a new album and sold-out worldwide tour.

2001

They hooked up while filming *The Fast and the Furious* in 2001 (which probably explains the heat in their on-screen sex scene). It didn't last very long, but that didn't stop Rodriguez from telling the press that she would always be open to "being his friend."

Michelle Rodriguez

Rodriguez is known for playing tough, street-wise women in action films like *The Fast and the Furious* and *S.W.A.T.* Not one to miss out on a good thing, she has stated she is not gay but has experimented with both sexes.

Although Rodriguez refuses to confirm that anything happened on the set of the vampire flick *Bloodrayne*, Loken hinted about the lesbian fling in an interview for *Advocate* magazine.

2006

2007–

Kristanna Loken

The sexy action-movie actress is best known for her role as the hot Terminatrix battling Arnie and company in *Terminator 3*. She caused quite a stir by stating that she is a bisexual who has had more satisfying relationships with women than she has with men.

— Derek Jeter NEXT ▶

Tommy Mottola

When he's not marrying the talent, you can thank music mogul Mottola for mentoring the likes of Carly Simon, Diana Ross (pg. 57), Jennifer Lopez (pg. 81), and, err, Ricky Martin.

1988–1997

1998–2001

Luis Miguel
Latin music star

It should have been a dream union: The top-selling Latin American artist dated one of the most successful American solo artists of all time. But it ended shortly before Mariah suffered an emotional breakdown.

Carey and Mottola got together when the superstar was recording her first album. Mariah has explained that Tommy was like a "strict father." He has never confirmed that she was like a spoiled brat, but you have to wonder.

2008–

Carey and Cannon waited one whole month after meeting to get married (officially welcoming Carey to the land of the cougars—she's eleven years older than him).

Nick Cannon

The rapper-comedian-actor-director-dancer-host appears to be an all-rounder in both life and love—the women he's been with include singers, dancers, socialites, and lingerie models.

2007

The two got engaged when Cannon proposed to her via a JumboTron in New York City's Times Square. That kind of gesture is unforgettable—unlike their relationship, which ended five months later.

Selita Ebanks

Ebanks has posed for Victoria's Secret, but she hasn't dated the requisite thirty dudes that go along with a lingerie model's career. Maybe the fact that she has seven brothers has something to do with that.

A lack of trust ended their two-and-a-half-year relationship. Cannon couldn't trust Milian because she hacked into his e-mail. Milian couldn't trust Cannon because she caught him cheating—by hacking into his e-mail.

2003–2005

Christina Milian
American pop singer and actress

Jaime Rishar
Model

Anthony Kiedis   1993–1996

Andrew Form
Horror film producer

Brewster married her *Texas Chainsaw Massacre* producer after the two started dating in 2006.

🔒 2007–

In 2000, a year into his relationship with Brewster, Wahlberg told reporters, "I really have this idea in my head of getting married and having children and spending the rest of my life with one woman." He even introduced her to his *Planet of the Apes* cast mates as his wife. Maybe he was just monkeying around.

Just a few months after the birth of his daughter, Ella Rae, with model (and fiancée) Rhea Durham, Wahlberg allegedly canceled wedding plans and stepped out with Alba, spending the 2004 New Year's holiday with her.

Alba sparked controversy when she started dating her *Dark Angel* costar Weatherly, twelve years her senior. "People always have to make it sound so titillating. 'She's a minor!' No? It's like people think my interest in Jessica could only be of a sexual nature," said luckiest-man-alive Weatherly.

Michael Weatherly Jr.
American actor

💔 1999–2001

1999–2001 💔

Jordana Brewster

A man, a plan, a hot actress. Brewster was born in Panama, the daughter of a Brazilian *Sports Illustrated* model and an investment banker who apparently spent his money well. She got her start in Robert Rodriguez's high school horror flick *The Faculty* in 1998.

Cash Warren
Director's assistant

Jessica met Cash on the set of *The Fantastic Four*, where he was the director's assistant and she was the movie star. The relationship led to a marriage and the birth of daughter Honor Marie Warren.

Brewster was a senior at Yale when she brought Jeter out for a night at the local college bar Toad's Place. The spot was mobbed with undergrads seeking photos and buying drinks for the couple.

The two started dating shortly after Carey's divorce from Tommy Mottola (pg. 25), but her hookup with Jeter ended before it ever really began, a lot like her film career.

2002–2003

2003–2002

2002–2003

🔒 2004–

1999–2003 💔

2003–2004 💔

Jessica Alba

Alba had a series of big roles in 2005—*Sin City*, *The Fantastic Four*, and *Into the Blue*, in which she repeatedly dove into the Caribbean in a little bikini to find, um—why was she swimming again? She has said that her ideal man would be much older than she is, referencing Morgan Freeman, Sean Connery (pg. 55), Robert Redford, and Michael Caine (pg. 49).

◀ BACK **Mariah Carey**   1997–1998

Amid rumors that she had hooked up with Tom Brady (pg. 63) and Orlando Bloom (pg. 71), and that he had gotten together with Jessica Alba, Minnillo dated Jeter on and off for almost three years.

◀ p. 70 **Vanessa Minnillo**   2003–2006 💔

Derek Jeter
Ever since shortstop Jeter became a regular for the Yankees, he's had his bases loaded with beautiful ladies.

2004

2004 💔

In the midst of his hot-and-cold relationship with Vanessa Minnillo (pg. 70), Jeter briefly dated Alba and, according to seriously unreliable sources, gave the starlet herpes. Big deal—roughly 70 percent of American adults have it, so the odds are that she had it already.

Rachel Hunter

Kiwi *Sports Illustrated* model Hunter began an acting career that didn't take off until a string of reality TV gigs beginning in 2003, including *Dancing with the Stars* and *Make Me a Supermodel*. She's best known for marrying up (in age, anyway), when she said "I do" to Rod Stewart in 1990.

Wahlberg and Hunter met on the set of 2001's *Rock Star* and carried on a super double-top-secret relationship that included Hunter sneaking out of a London club at 3:45 AM in cap and sunglasses to avoid being seen together.

🔒 2001–

The couple separated in 1999 with Stewart saying at the time, "I'm not having to answer to anybody for the first time in nine years, so I can play the field." But he didn't sound as happy a few years later: "When Rachel left, that was a bolt of lightning. Fuck me, it was terrible. But I don't blame Rachel. I married her too young."

🔒 1990–2006

Britt Ekland p.140 ▲
Carole Mallory p.55 ▲

Rod Stewart

He may have sung "Forever Young," but Rod Stewart was not destined to be young forever. But age is just a number, and one that's not nearly as important as the number of fans who still pack stadiums to hear him sing.

💔 1975–1977
💔 1978

Mallory dated Stewart near the height of his fame. Her best friend at the time (and Stewart's future wife), Alana Hamilton, said, "At one point, [Mallory] was complaining that Rod was calling her for late-night sex. He'd call at 11:30 PM and say 'Come on over.' I told her, 'No man will respect you if they can treat you that way.'"

Mark Wahlberg

Wahlberg dropped out of brother Donnie Wahlberg's band, New Kids on the Block, to launch his own career as Marky Mark and the Funky Bunch. His bad-boy image, backed up by a charge of attempted murder fueled by PCP (he served forty-five days) when he was sixteen, buoyed an underwear modeling career and later a film career.

2003–2004 💔
1998 💔
2000 💔

Rhea Durham NEXT ▶

Jackie Titone
Actress

1999– 🔒

When Sandler decided to settle down with *Big Daddy* costar Titone, people thought the perpetual man-child would finally grow up, but a wedding featuring his bulldog, Meatball, dressed in tuxedo and yarmulke, proved otherwise.

Adam Sandler

Sandler got his start playing Malcolm-Jamal Warner's friend on *The Cosby Show* and "Stud Boy" on MTV's *Remote Control* before landing a spot on *Saturday Night Live*, thanks to Dennis Miller. Since then, he's made a living playing some of the dumbest characters on film.

Silverstone and her reps did their best to cover up this relationship, but then she was spotted in Los Angeles wearing a *Happy Gilmore* t-shirt and baseball cap. Seriously, what other reason could there possibly be for that fashion faux pas?

1998 💔
Wahlberg started dating Chow after they shot *The Big Hit*, a film in which he and Lou Diamond Phillips kidnap her and get more than they bargained for.

This unlikely couple was spotted swimming topless in the French Riviera while she was supposedly dating Steve Coogan. What does it mean? You be the judge.

💔 2008

China Chow

Daughter of actor-turned-restaurateur Michael Chow (of Mr. Chow's fame), China started modeling for Tommy Hilfiger and Calvin Klein before making her acting debut in *The Big Hit* with Mark Wahlberg. Even cooler, she voiced Katie Zhan in *Grand Theft Auto: San Andreas*.

Keanu Reeves p.141 ▼

Alicia Silverstone

From her first role in *The Crush* (*Fatal Attraction* for teenyboppers) to her ass-kicking turns in Aerosmith videos, Silverstone made a name for herself playing girls who go after what they want.

1996 💔

Silverstone and Jarecki married in 2005 in Lake Tahoe—but don't be fooled by the rock-and-roll cred. This vegan pair live in an ecofriendly L.A. abode, rescue lost dogs, and drive hybrid cars. At their wedding guests noshed on vegan burgers, cashew cheese, and soy lattes!

🔒 1997–
💔 1995

Christopher Jarecki
Singer in the band Underdogs

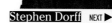
Stephen Dorff NEXT ▶

Beyoncé

Houston girl Beyoncé came up as the lead singer of Destiny's Child and starred as the Diana Ross (pg. 57) character in *Dreamgirls*, but we loved her best as Foxxy Cleopatra in *Goldmember*.

Beyoncé had the potential to create the most gorgeous children on Earth until she married brilliant but homely rapper-cum-mogul Jay-Z. At least they'll be rich and talented.

2002–

2002

Carmen Bryan

Bryan found fame as rapper Nas's baby mama and was the focal point of the feud between Nas and Jay-Z. Her best-selling book *It's No Secret* revealed that Jay-Z flossed his backside with a washcloth in the shower.

Bryan snuck off with Jay-Z while dating Nas, sparking an epic battle of lyrics between the two rap artists, with Jay-Z telling Nas, "I came in ya Bentley backseat. Left condoms in tha baby seat," in the track *Supa Ugly*.

2001–2002

1992–2001

1996–2001

Former music biz receptionist Bryan met Nas early in his career and got pregnant several times before she gave birth to his daughter, Destiny, in 1994.

◄ p. 24   **Karrine Steffans**   2000

◄ BACK   **Mark Wahlberg**

In 2002, during a period in which they were broken up and Wahlberg was dating around, he had to contend with Durham's friend Tara Reid (pg. 63), who punched him at a Los Angles club. Friends had to pry the two apart after Wahlberg had enough and put Reid in a headlock.

Jay-Z

Shawn Corey Carter turned childhood nickname "Jazzy" into "Jay-Z" as a tribute to the J and Z lines of the Brooklyn subway that ran by the Marcy Projects, where he grew up. His first big-label album for Def Jam in 1997 was inspired by the death of childhood friend, The Notorious B.I.G.

Nas

Born Nasir bin Olu Dara Jones, the former Nasty Nas released his highly praised debut album, *Illmatic*, in 1994.

Bryan described Iverson as a "lean and muscled" sexual "warrior" and said he was so strong he "thought nothing of picking me up and creating the most erotic of poses," which, according to her, included doggy style on a hotel table.

This pair met while filming Aerosmith's "Cryin'" video, which was named the number one "All-Time Favorite Video" by MTV viewers in 1994. The classic video ended with a fake suicide bungee-jump with blurred bird flip kicker.

2001–

Allan Iverson
Basketball player

Rhea Durham
Fashion model

After Durham dumped him for Mark Wahlberg (pg. 27), Dorff was so steamed that, when the model later cracked her head at a club (a bloody wound that required stapling), he sat in his seat and didn't even get up to see if she was okay.

1999–2001

Courtney Wagner
Daughter of Natalie Wood and Robert Wagner

◄ BACK   **Alicia Silverstone**

◄ p. 60   **May Andersen**

After getting chucked by long-time dude Justin Timberlake (pg. 98), Diaz combined a love of surfing and boys to hook up with da kine champion surfer Slater for a surfing safari that took them from Hawaii to Australia.

◄ p. 98   **Cameron Diaz**

2004

Max LeRoy   p. 145 ▼

Rachel Stevens
Singer for British group S Club (7)

1991–1993
2006
1995
2003–2004

2004–2005

Stephen Dorff

Dorff transcended his last name to star as the hunk, first in numerous 1990s music videos and then in films (*Backbeat*, *I Shot Andy Warhol*, *Blade*, *World Trade Center*).

Gisele Bündchen p. 72 ▲

2002 ❤ 2003 ❤

Blu Cantrell

Soul singer Cantrell posed in *Black Tail* magazine, but she turned down the cover of *Playboy* in 2003, saying, "I felt it was going to make me more of a sex symbol."

2005–2006 ❤

At the start of this five-month romance, Anderson said she had to ask Dorff a personal question—had they ever slept together before? When you've been around the block so many times, you sometimes forget where you live.

2003 ❤

Kelly Slater

The greatest surfer since King Kamehameha, Slater has won nine APS World Championships, making him the youngest and oldest to ever win the title.

2007 2007

Bar Refaeli p. 73 ▼

Slater hooked up with Refaeli (his second DiCaprio, pg. 73, castaway) in Tel Aviv while on a promotional trip with Surfing for Peace. He apparently ignored that organization's mission when he brawled with paparazzi trying to take the couple's picture outside their hotel.

Rick Salomon p. 88 ▲

🔒 2007–2008 ❤ 2001

Pamela Anderson

Canadian Anderson was a brunette before she moved to L.A. and got the part as the first "Tool Time" girl on *Home Improvement*. She played C. J. Parker on *Baywatch*, but she's probably best known for a more improvisational video with Tommy Lee (pg. 32) of Mötley Crüe.

1994–1998 ❤

Slater has described Anderson as "the tear that hangs inside my soul forever," and it isn't hard to understand why. She broke up with him in 1994 and married Tommy Lee (pg. 32) a week later. Then dumped Slater a second time during a break from Lee.

They dated for a short while, but King said in 2009 that she still listens to Kid's music. "He's got a beautiful voice and he's a great country musician, which not a lot of people realize."

❤ 2000

Jaime King
Model and actress ❤ 1995–1996

2001–2006 🔓

Kid Rock

Kid Rock may come off as a trailer-bred redneck, but he was raised in an affluent family in the suburbs of Detroit. An early deal with Jive Records went bust after Vanilla Ice (pg. 103) fizzled and brought down all white rappers, but Rock made a comeback to become a working-class arena rocker.

Photographer Sorrenti dated King (who was then called James) when she started modeling, and the two rode heroin chic to full-blown addiction, ending in his death from an overdose and her trip to rehab.

Anderson started dating Swedish underwear model Schenkenberg (which means "porkville" in German) after witnessing him rescuing a bird from a toilet in Monaco.

Marcus Schenkenberg
Swedish model

This relationship was the typical "boy meets girl, boy marries girl a few days later, boy and girl star in private porn tape, boy goes to jail for kicking girl, boy gets back together with girl, boy and girl break up, boy and girl get back together and star in reality show" romance.

🔒 1995
❤ 1995
❤ 1990–1993

Tommy Lee p. 32 ▶
Tommy Lee p. 32 ▶
Jon Peters p. 118 ▶
Scott Baio p. 131 ▶

Anderson wore a white bikini for their yacht-borne wedding, but things went south when Kid Rock accused her of faking a miscarriage. He was also upset by her role in *Borat*, in which Sacha Baron-Cohen masturbates to her magazine spreads and tries to kidnap her in a sack.

Baio said his relationship with Anderson ended when she decided to get her breasts augmented. "I was surprised. My initial response [was], 'Reduced?' She already had large, beautiful, natural breasts."

❤ 2001

Sheryl Crow p. 100 ▶

Crow's relationship with Rock ended when he hooked up with Pamela Anderson at a New York party. That didn't stop Anderson from promoting Crow and Rock's country duet "Picture" by personally handing it to radio host Rick Dees and making it a hit.

Davide Sorrenti
Fashion photographer

Celebrity Pet Names

Love makes you stupid. It's a proven fact. If you have any doubt, the following sweet and sick nicknames celebrities have for each other will convince you:

Jennifer Aniston (pg. 108) called John Mayer (pg. 109) "Mayo," based on his love for the creamy condiment, while he dubbed her "Tushie," in reference to her sweet assets.

"T-Bone Steak" was Pamela Anderson's (pg. 29) pet name for Tommy Lee (pg. 32), and we don't really want any information about its origins.

When Britney Spears (pg. 33) dated Justin Timberlake (pg. 98), she called him "Stinky"—a term she might have augmented once they split.

Jessica Simpson (pg. 109) used the moniker "FBD" for Tony Romo (pg. 109)—the acronym stood for "Future Baby Daddy." But nicknames can communicate other feelings besides just mushy romance. Guy Ritchie (pg. 103) took to calling Madonna (pg. 103) "It" toward the end of their marriage, as in "It's in a bad mood today" and "We can't make It angry."

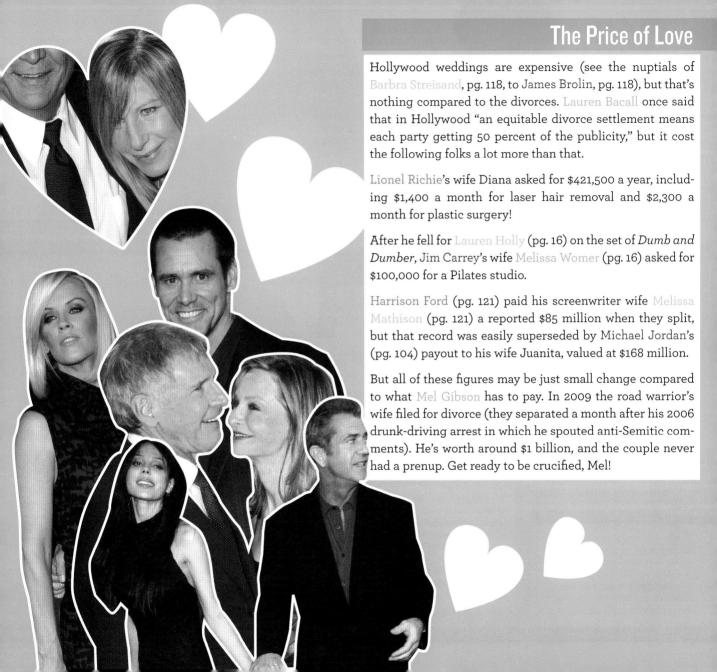

The Price of Love

Hollywood weddings are expensive (see the nuptials of Barbra Streisand, pg. 118, to James Brolin, pg. 118), but that's nothing compared to the divorces. Lauren Bacall once said that in Hollywood "an equitable divorce settlement means each party getting 50 percent of the publicity," but it cost the following folks a lot more than that.

Lionel Richie's wife Diana asked for $421,500 a year, including $1,400 a month for laser hair removal and $2,300 a month for plastic surgery!

After he fell for Lauren Holly (pg. 16) on the set of *Dumb and Dumber*, Jim Carrey's wife Melissa Womer (pg. 16) asked for $100,000 for a Pilates studio.

Harrison Ford (pg. 121) paid his screenwriter wife Melissa Mathison (pg. 121) a reported $85 million when they split, but that record was easily superseded by Michael Jordan's (pg. 104) payout to his wife Juanita, valued at $168 million.

But all of these figures may be just small change compared to what Mel Gibson has to pay. In 2009 the road warrior's wife filed for divorce (they separated a month after his 2006 drunk-driving arrest in which he spouted anti-Semitic comments). He's worth around $1 billion, and the couple never had a prenup. Get ready to be crucified, Mel!

1985–1993 🔒
2003 💔

1985

Kitaen revealed that, during a coke-fueled night with Lee, he spent the evening teaching her how to throw a knife into a bedroom wall.

1985

Robbin Crosby
Crosby played lead guitar for 1980s glam metal band Ratt of "Round and Round" fame before falling into a heroin addiction, gaining close to 400 pounds due to AIDS complications, and dying of a heroin overdose in 2002.

Kitaen and Crosby started dating in high school and moved to Los Angeles together to pursue their dreams.

💔 1978–1984
💔 1984–1985
💔 1991

2003

Tawny Kitaen
You may recall Kitaen doing the splits on a Jaguar in the video for Whitesnake's "Here I Go Again," but she's more than a rock-and-roll hood ornament. She starred in *Bachelor Party* opposite Tom Hanks. But, instead of following his path to the Oscars, ended up on *The Surreal Life* and *Celebrity Rehab*.

Tommy Lee
Bad boy Mötley Crüe drummer Lee went to prison for kicking wife Anderson while she was holding his baby and bared a swastika tattoo while beating up a Jewish paparazzo in 1996.

1995

Stewart dated Kitaen after she made a guest appearance on his original talk show.

1995

Jon Stewart
Jonathan Stuart Leibowitz got his start playing the most comedic of all instruments, the French horn, in his high school band. The syndicated *Jon Stewart Show* replaced *The Arsenio Hall Show* on Fox but was quickly canceled. It wasn't until he took over *The Daily Show* that the comedy mastermind took over the world.

Everhart and Hamilton's biggest fight started when her ex, Sylvester Stallone (pg. 138), bought her a Porsche. The marriage lasted fifty-five days, during which time Everhart quashed rumors she was pregnant, saying, "These days, if I got pregnant, it would have to be by immaculate conception."

1996–1997

2000 💔 🔒

1995 👶

"He tells me what to eat, what to drink, how to think," she said of Stallone after breaking off their engagement. After Stallone banned her from eating candy or pasta, she moved out of his $24 million Miami mansion, leaving a $23,000 engagement ring behind.

Angie Everhart
The first redhead to ever grace the cover of *Glamour* magazine (but not the first one to be featured on a *Playboy* cover), Everhart began her career on a lark when her mom sent snapshots to a local modeling agency. She debuted in Arnold Schwarzenegger's *Last Action Hero* in 1993.

Everhart dated an even shorter Italian than 5'7" Sylvester Stallone (pg. 138) when she started seeing 5'4" Pesci. But the breakup was a difficult one, with Pesci dumping her nine months after proposing. The split hit her hard, and Everhart was arrested for drunk driving a few days later.

2007–2008

Everhart seemed poised to succeed in pinning down royal bachelor Prince Albert once and for all. There was even talk of petitioning the Vatican to annul her marriage to Ashley Hamilton (pg. 46) so the royal could wed with the church's blessing.

1997–2001 💔

Joe Pesci
American actor

Kitaen dated Simpson while she was with Robbin Crosby (pg. 32). Simpson wasn't interested in sharing and ultimately chased Crosby down at a hotel where Crosby and Kitaen were staying together. Crosby broke it off with Kitaen saying, "I didn't want him to break my neck."

O. J. Simpson

If there is anything worse than murder, it may be Simpson's attempt to capitalize on it with his 2006 book *If I Did It*. Does anyone remember when he was just a football player and a bad actor (*Towering Inferno, Naked Gun*)?

Jessica Sklar
Public relations executive

Weeks after returning to New York from her honeymoon in Italy with husband Eric Nederlander, Sklar met Seinfeld at the Reebok Sports Club, and the two started dating. They got married in 1999 and have three children.

Carol Leifer

Leifer is a successful comedy writer and producer who created Ellen DeGeneres's (pg. 152) *The Ellen Show*.

Seinfeld's TV buddy Elaine Benes, played by Julia Louis-Dreyfus, was modeled on his relationship with comedienne Leifer.

Kitaen worked on *The New WKRP in Cincinnati* near Seinfeld's sitcom set. The two dated until she got pregnant with concurrent boyfriend Chuck Finley's child.

Jerry Seinfeld

Seinfeld was the highest earning entertainer in 1998 (oh, just $267 million), the year his top-rated sitcom ended. He created the "no hugging, no learning" show about nothing with Larry David based on their own twisted relationships and petty friends.

🔒 1998–

💋 1982

💋 1993–1997

Seinfeld met Lonstein in Central Park. Her parents were fine with their seventeen-year-old daughter dating the thirty-nine-year-old TV star. Rumors of proposals drifted throughout their relationship, but the couple split in 1997.

Shoshanna Lonstein

Lonstein hit the big time dating Jerry Seinfeld at seventeen, but she wasn't in it for his money—the young socialite had her dad's Infocrossing fortune and went on to start her own successful clothing line after dating Jerry.

2001　Scott Wolf　p. 95 ▶

Tracy McShane
Veterinary nurse

2000–

Stewart was set up on a blind date with McShane by a random crew member on a shoot in 1996. He almost blew it after spending the dollar bill he had written her number on, but, when they finally connected, it was love. They both officially changed their name to "Stewart" in 2001.

In 2000 Spears declared that she would remain a virgin until she got married, but after they split due to rumors of her cheating with her choreographer Wade Robson, Timberlake said, "She lost her virginity a while ago—and I should know."

1998–2002 💋

Britney Spears

Like future beau Justin Timberlake (pg. 98), Spears appeared on *Star Search* and went on to star in *The New Mickey Mouse Club* in 1993. However, she demolished him on the billboard charts, with more than 85 million records sold.

Spears married childhood friend Alexander at The Little White Wedding Chapel in Las Vegas after they decided to do something "wild, crazy." Perhaps the "craziest" thing about the fiasco was that they did it sober! The marriage was annulled fifty-five hours later.

🔒 2004

💋 2003

K-Fed ditched his family for Spears, and after a whirlwind few months the pair got married in 2004. Two years and two kids later, Spears filed for divorce and went into an emotional nosedive. She locked herself in a room with son Jayden while under the influence, and K-Fed was given sole custody of their children.

🔒 2004–2006

Jason Alexander
Britney Spears's childhood friend

Though Britney would vehemently deny ever sleeping with him, Durst claims that not only did they do it, but they did it without protection. The classy Durst allegedly wrote the song "Just Drop Dead" about Britney, calling her a "whore" and a "bitch."

Fred Durst　NEXT ▶

Kevin Federline
Backup dancer

Danny Wood
New Kids on the Block singer

Long before we ever heard of her (and before her nose job), Berry dated rattailed New Kid on the Block Danny Wood, but he broke up with her because the band thought she was a groupie.

Kimberly McCullough
Emmy-winning McCullough began playing *General Hospital*'s Robin Drake when she was only seven, and the character has grown up in real time ever since.

Wesley Snipes
He's been a half-blooded vampire, a drag queen, and a fugitive from the law, and sometimes not exclusively on film. Snipes cut the government a $5 million check toward back taxes after fleeing the country.

In an interview, R&B singer Christopher Williams identified Snipes as the man whose physical abuse resulted in severe hearing loss in Berry's right ear.

Berry was so distraught over her divorce from Justice that she almost killed herself. She later said that she had taken her two dogs into the garage to end it together. "I was going to sit in the car, asphyxiate myself," she said, but something told her, "Girl, don't do it." Was it the ASPCA?

David Justice
Baseball player

Eric Benet
R&B singer

While they dated, Prinze and McCullough exchanged Irish Claddagh rings to symbolize that they were really serious but not serious enough to get engaged. The rings were all the rage in 1998: Jennifer Aniston (pg. 108) got one from Tate Donovan (pg. 108), and the character Buffy (played by Prinze's future wife) got one from Angel before they consummated their necrophiliac relationship on *Buffy the Vampire Slayer*.

Freddie Prinze Jr.
🔒 2002–

At age twenty, Prinze Jr. played a high school senior whose girlfriend gets pregnant in the *Afterschool Special* "Too Soon for Jeff." Only a year later, he broke out in the feature *I Know What You Did Last Summer*.

💔 1996–2000

Fred Durst always had a thing for *Playboy* Playmates like Bergman, and for a while they seemed to have a thing for him ... then the '90s were over. Durst still likes his Playmates, but now he has to love them in the pages of *Playboy* like everybody else.

After splitting with her cheating husband Eric Benet, Berry went out with Durst, who was working on the *Gothika* soundtrack. Take all the time you need to process that, but remember: If you wanted to piss off your ex, who better to date than Fred Durst?

1990 💔
1989–1990 💔
1993–1997 🔒
2001–2005 🔒

2003 💔

Halle Berry
Berry was the first runner-up in the Miss USA pageant in 1986. Spike Lee harnessed that beauty for her breakout role as a drug addict in *Jungle Fever*, which ultimately brought us the open-mouthed kiss from Adrien Brody (pg. 134) when Berry won an Oscar for *Monsters Ball*.

Fred Durst
The Limp Bizkit front man is best known for being a real dick. Besides calling Slipknot fans "fat ugly kids," Durst was given a suspended 120-day jail sentence after hitting two people while driving drunk.

💔 1999
💔 2003
💔 2001

Michelle Dupont
Dupont, the modern-day version of legendary groupie Pamela Des Barres (pg. 120), goes by the moniker "Rock Chik" and claims to have bedded Fred Durst, Perry Farrell, and Dave Navarro (pg. 40), though not at the same time. "To me, a groupie really goes all the way and tries for it," she said.

Brody was so smitten with music-industry assistant and world-class groupie Dupont that when he found out that the head of his management company had been mean to her, he threatened to sack his manager.

David Boreanaz

Before brooding vampires became all the rage, Boreanaz held his own as the vampire Angel on *Buffy the Vampire Slayer*. These days he still spends time around the dead, but now it's on the TV series *Bones*.

🔒 2001–

Gellar and Prinze tied the knot in 2002 and starred as cartoon lovers Fred and Daphne in two *Scooby Doo* films before Gellar went old-fashioned and ditched her maiden name.

Gellar was quick to shout down criticism when her character had sex with Boreanaz's Angel without protection on *Buffy The Vampire Slayer*. "This is a sixteen-year-old girl having sex with a 240-year-old vampire. He shoots blanks!"

🔒 2002–

2000

Jaime Bergman
Playboy Playmate

💔

1999

Durst isn't usually modest, but he had a hard time fessing up to dating Spice Girl Geri Halliwell, exclaiming, "I am not dating anyone … you've seen me in a picture with lately!" He later admitted to going out on some dates after the fact.

2003 💔

Geri Halliwell

As Ginger Spice, Halliwell's job was to, in her own words, "[dress] like a drag queen." And she nailed it with iconic outfits like the skimpy Union Jack dress that sold for £36,000 at a charity auction in 1998. That same year, she quit the band, sending the Spices into a girl-group tailspin from which they never recovered.

2000–2001 💔

Music lovers Halliwell and Williams never committed. Williams said, "We are just good friends … who have the occasional shag." Williams even introduced her to Sacha Gervasi, who ended up having a daughter, Bluebell Madonna, with Halliwell after a six-week fling (she tried to keep the identity of the father secret).

Robbie Williams
British singer and songwriter

Sarah Michelle Gellar

Gellar replaced actress Kristy Swanson when *Buffy the Vampire Slayer* went from film to TV (Swanson didn't want to do TV—maybe not the best career choice). Just before she fired him, her William Morris agent said in a *New Yorker* article, "[*The Grudge*] takes our client Sarah Michelle Gellar, who now is nothing at all, and … makes her a star, potentially."

💔 2003

💔 2005–2006

💔 1999

Chris Evans

Evans's career ignited when he took on the role of Johnny Storm in 2005's *Fantastic Four*, opposite Jessica Alba (pg. 26) and Michael Chiklis. He even got a trophy for the part—a Teen Choice Award for "Hottest Man on Screen."

2003

Jerry O'Connell   NEXT ▶

After meeting on the set of British flick *Fat Slags* (which roughly translates to "ho bag" or "douche bag"), Halliwell and O'Connell dated for a few weeks. She broke it off because "his sense of humour was immature"—exactly the humor that his future wife Rebecca Romijn has cited as her favorite.

💔 1999   **Jerry O'Connell**   NEXT ▶

Sacha Gervasi
British journalist

Halliwell broke up with Gervasi while she was pregnant, and after giving birth, she refused to let him see her daughter. As a United Nations ambassador, you'd expect her to work harder to foster peaceful relations.

💔 2006   **Gisele Bündchen**   p. 72 ▶

💔 2004–2006   **Jessica Biel**   p. 98 ▶

    Craig Logan   p. 68 ▶

Warren and O'Connell bounced in the sack in *Kangaroo Jack* (although Warren claims they never sullied their art by dating while filming). Warren seduced her leading man with the oldest trick in the book—games of Boggle.

2002

◀ BACK **Geri Halliwell** 2003 💔

Bruce Willis p. 180 ▲

At the same time he was telling boys of all sorts to back off from his young daughter Rumer ("I think I'll just kill the first one that turns up and hope the word gets around"), forty-seven-year-old Willis was dating twenty-three-year-old Warren.

2001–2002
💔

Estella Warren

2002 💔 As one of the only humans in 2001's *Planet of the Apes*, Warren barely had to use her *Maxim* "Hottest Woman of 2000" charms to win over Mark Wahlberg (pg. 27). *The Sports Illustrated* model was always comfortable in a swimsuit, having represented Canada in synchronized swimming at the World Aquatic Championships.

💔 2002–2006

💔 2000

💔 2006

Bill Rancic

Rancic is one of the few who managed to turn a reality TV win (his on the first *Apprentice*) into a successful career (his in motivational speaking) and a kick-ass marriage to a gorgeous lady (his to Giuliana Rancic).

Jerry O'Connell

O'Connell played chubby, bumbling Vern "Cherry-flavored Pez" Tessio in *Stand by Me*. By the time he played super teen Andrew Clements in the series *My Secret Identity* and Quinn Mallory in *Sliders* he'd hit his hunk phase—and, karmically, become the hottest of the *Stand by Me* alums. Sorry, Wil Wheaton.

Donald Trump's first *Apprentice* Bill Rancic got more than a job when he won the reality television show. He met Giuliana DePandi, Ryan Seacrest's (pg. 128) coanchor on *E! News*. The two wed in 2007.

🔒 2006–

💔 2003–2004 💔 1999 🔒 2005–

Romijn was working on her documentary *Wet Dreams* (about creating an original water show for the fancy fountain at the Bellagio in Vegas) when she met O'Connell poolside. He offered to help and "spent a week operating the microphone, but later he told me he would have done anything." A year and a half later they were engaged.

The two Canadians joined forces after she starred in an INXS music video for the song "Afterglow" (Fortune won the TV competition for the lead singer spot, after the death of Michael Hutchence, pg. 73).

Giuliana Rancic

Giuliana DePandi (pre-Rancic) was the host of *E! News* on the E! Network!! With a master's degree in journalism, she's probably the most overqualified red-carpet reporter in history. But she put those writing skills to use penning a book: *Think Like a Guy: How to Get a Guy by Thinking Like One*.

They dated briefly and split up, for which O'Connell blamed his "goofball" behavior and inability to commit. Afterward, he pined for the heart slayer, saying, "She's the cutest, and she knows it. [But] she's much too smart for me."

◀ BACK **Sarah Michelle Gellar**

2005– 🔒

Rebecca Romijn

Romijn was studying singing at U.C. Santa Cruz when the siren song of modeling called her away after her freshman year. Never afraid of playing the freak, the superhot supermodel had her screen debut in *Friends* as David Schwimmer's (pg. 66) appallingly messy girlfriend. In the *X-Men* series she plays Mystique, whose scaly blue skin is no deterrent to xenophilia.

Rose McGowan   NEXT ▶

Michael Pitt

Pouty Jersey boy Pitt has had some of the best roles imaginable: He started off as Michelle Williams's (pg. 77) love interest on *Dawson's Creek*, got it on with gorgeous Eva Green and her brother in *The Dreamers*, was married to Keira Knightley (pg. 84) in *Silk*, fell for Alison Lohman in *Delirious*, and murdered Naomi Watts (pg. 76) in *Funny Games*. Okay, that last role wasn't so fun.

Vincent Gallo

Actor-director Gallo has talked about his compulsive teenage masturbation, and this may have had some influence on his masturbatory feature *The Brown Bunny*—which caused critics to laugh at the 2003 Cannes Film Festival.

Kevin Ian "Kip" Pardue

Kevin Ian Pardue ("Kip") played football at Yale before launching a modeling career for Armani and Polo. His first feature was gay-makeover comedy *But I'm a Cheerleader*, and he harnessed his gridiron skills in *Remember the Titans*. ❞

2001   2003

Pitt and Argento hooked up on the set of her *The Heart Is Deceitful Above All Things* and continued the romance on Gus Van Sant's *Last Days*. She played the Courtney Love–like (pg. 61) character to his Kurt Cobain–type (pg. 61) role. But the romance ended at "cut."

2004 1998 ❞ ❞

Argento claimed that Gallo broke her heart twice, but he topped her in the sensitivity department, threatening to drop out of her father's film *Giallo* when Asia was also cast. "I'd rather not be in a movie with her," Gallo said. "I'm not a fan."

Peter Berg
Film director

Actor-turned-director Berg had an enviable relationship with model-turned-actress Warren. In 2004 they were kicked out of Scores, after she mounted him for a free topless lap dance.

Asia Argento

Italian actress Asia is the daughter of horror-film director Dario Argento. The two aren't close—she starred in his films just to get his attention before moving on to English-language gigs like *New Rose Hotel*, *xXx*, and *Marie Antoinette* in 2006.

Argento met Meyers on the set of heist movie *B. Monkey*, and while his on-screen performance got mixed reviews, Meyers was panned off-screen when Argento later reported, "Actors are very dull lovers."

J. D. Fortune
Rock singer

Jeremy Northam

Northam had the honor of replacing Daniel Day-Lewis (pg. 16) in the role of *Hamlet* at the Royal National Theatre in 1989. Specializing in historical dramas, he has starred in *Wuthering Heights*, followed by *Emma*, in which he played Gwyneth Paltrow's (pg. 79) love interest, Mr. Knightley.

Toni Collette
Australian actress

Collette dated Meyers for a year after they met on *Velvet Goldmine* and said she had panic attacks for eight months after they broke up. Meyers said, "I was only nineteen and not mature enough. I'm a selfish boyfriend."

1998–1999 ❞

Jonathan Rhys Meyers

2000 ❞   1997 2003
             ❞   ❞

Born with the kitchen-sink Irish name Jonathan Michael Francis O'Keeffe, Meyers was introduced to audiences in *Velvet Goldmine*. The star has battled alcohol addiction and checked himself into rehab in 2005, 2007, and 2009. No word on 2011 yet.

Lisa Butcher
British model and television host

❞

The short fling between Butcher and Meyers was not without its casualties. Years later, Butcher admitted, "When we split up, it was probably the most pain I've ever been in."

2001 1999–2000

Northam was the second of her love interests to end up on the Showtime series *The Tudors* (the other is Jonathan Rhys Meyers). Butcher didn't want to talk about Northam while they were dating, saying, "I am fed up with people going on and on about the men in my life. It's boring." Not to us.

Maggie Gyllenhaal

Gyllenhaal played the sister to her real brother, Jake Gyllenhaal (pg. 18), in the freak hit *Donnie Darko* but really got noticed as a naughty S&M assistant to James Spader (pg. 56) in *Secretary*, a role that she says "[spilled] over into [her] life." Tell us more.

Shalom Harlow
Canadian model

Sarsgaard's ex-girlfriend Dita Von Teese said he cheated on her with Shalom Harlow, who also claimed that Sarsgaard slept around. But the next relationship stuck. Gyllenhaal and Sarsgaard got married in 2009 after having their last-name-challenged daughter, Ramona, in 2006.

Von Teese dated Sarsgaard (who played Dr. Alfred Kinsey's sexual research assistant in the film *Kinsey*) until she discovered that he was cheating on her with model Shalom Harlow. But she admitted the cheating allowed her to hook up with later love Marilyn Manson—who then cheated on her too.

2000–2002

2001

Dita Von Teese
The Queen of Burlesque started out as stripper, but, disappointed at the other dancers' lack of originality, she embraced the world of fetishism to make her act distinctive. It worked! These days she can be seen sitting in the front row of fashion shows or appearing in *Vogue*.

2001–2006

Peter Sarsgaard

Actor Sarsgaard got to showcase his lighter side on *Saturday Night Live*, where he promoted a line of face masks called Peter Sarsgaard's SARS Guards.

This match must have been made in—someplace other than heaven. The two bonded over burlesque, absinthe, and vintage fashion, and their relationship seemed like it would last forever (in true vampire style). But things didn't work out that way. Von Teese divorced him, saying, "I wasn't supportive of his partying or his relationship with another girl," who turned out to be nineteen-year-old Evan Rachel Wood.

2002–

Their relationship bloomed at the height of Lillard's career, but, when Taylor was cast as Marcia in *The Brady Bunch Movie* and her career took off, they split up.

Robert Rodriguez
Film director

While shooting *Grindhouse*, Rodriguez and McGowan got it on, which would have been fine and good, except Rodriguez was married. He quickly divorced his wife and cast McGowan in his follow-up *Machete*, but they split in 2009 with Rodriguez explaining that he is "very difficult to live with."

2007–2009

◀ p. 122 Christine Taylor

◀ p. 122 Neve Campbell

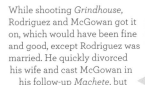

After he tied up her father with duct tape and tried to kill her with a kitchen knife in *Scream*, Lillard's next logical step was a brief on-set romance with Campbell.

1997–1998

1995

Pardue and McGowan costarred in the indie films *Vacuums* and *Rat in the Can* in 2001. Working together and sleeping together doesn't sound too bad, does it?

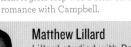

Matthew Lillard
Lillard studied with Paul Rudd at California's American Academy of Dramatic Arts and then with Philip Seymour Hoffman at Circle in the Square in New York. But he ultimately found fame as Shaggy, sidekick to a CGI dog, in *Scooby Doo*.

1996

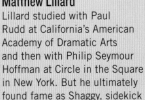

Rose McGowan

McGowan spent her childhood in the Children of God cult, a controversial group that encouraged its young female members to sleep around in a recruitment practice called "flirty fishing." At fifteen she became emancipated from her parents and focused on her film career, which would soon take off.

◀ BACK Kip Pardue

2001

Jameson revealed this affair in her autobiography, *How to Make Love Like a Porn Star: A Cautionary Tale*, claiming she had to kiss and tell because Manson had been going around bragging about it. It wasn't all bad—she said he was "smart and interesting" and enormously endowed.

Porn star met ultimate fighter on MySpace in 2006, and Ortiz later canceled an appearance as guest of honor at a Marine Corps ball because Jenna wasn't invited.

Tito Ortiz
Ultimate Fighting champion

1997

1997

Marilyn Manson

When it comes to scary-meets-weird, the rock prince of darkness is your go-to guy. But take a look at Manson's gorgeous roster of relationships and you might start to think that wearing cataract contacts and pretending to be the anti-Christ is just the ticket.

2007–

Jenna Jameson

Starting out as an underage Las Vegas stripper, Jameson moved into porn to get back at her ex-boyfriend (that showed him!) and rode the industry to the top, eventually setting up her own multimillion-dollar Web site and landing roles in regular (not porn) TV programs and films. She admits to sleeping with "only" one hundred women and thirty men off screen.

Jameson married her porn flick costar Armstrong (real name Rodney Hopkins) in 1996, but they split only ten weeks later and divorced in 2001 after Armstrong discovered she was having an affair with Jorge Araya Montoya, whom she met in Costa Rica. However, they continued to screw on camera—hey, it's a job.

2006–

🔒 1996–2001

Brad Armstrong
Canadian porn star

💔 2006   Dave Navarro NEXT ▶

1997–2001

Manson met McGowan at a screening of the cult film *Gummo*. The ensuing four-year relationship played out in public—she appeared beside him at the 1998 MTV Video Music Awards wearing a transparent fishnet dress. Their engagement was later called off due to "lifestyle differences." Who could have expected that?

1997–2001

Wood's not-quite-secret relationship with Manson caused his divorce from then-wife Dita Von Teese. Wood and Manson split in 2009 amid rumors that she was dating her *The Wrestler* costar Mickey Rourke, but rekindled the romance and got engaged in 2009.

Jamie Bell

The young British actor first graced the silver screen playing the lead in the ballet-dancing film with balls, *Billy Elliot*. After taking time out to enjoy puberty, he returned to the movies starring in *King Kong*, *Jumpers*, and as Tintin in Steven Spielberg's adaptation of the comic.

Evan Rachel Wood

Wood made a name for herself in a series of precocious sexual teen roles, but she describes her real-life persona as "laid back"—as laid back as you can be with a Tae Kwon Do black belt and a reputation as one of the best actresses in a generation.

2005–2006

After Wood left Bell to marry Marilyn Manson, she admitted that the "J" tattooed on her ankle was dedicated to her first love, Jamie. "We had matching tattoos because we knew our love would last forever. Trouble is, it didn't." Bell took it a wee bit harder saying, "I'm still utterly in love with her."

💔 2005–2006

2001–2002

Zappa and McGowan met on the set of 2000's *Ready to Rumble*. "I have a rad boyfriend that makes me laugh hysterically, funniest person I've ever met," she said, but by 2002 Zappa's marriage dreams with McGowan were over.

Ahmet Zappa

His full name is Ahmet Emuukha Rodan Zappa, and he's dated a hot brunette for each weird syllable. The son of Frank Zappa is an accomplished writer with two children's books and the film version of *Fraggle Rock* in the works.

🔓 2003–2006

Selma Blair   p. 153 ▶

Navarro and Goddard were married in a nonlegal pagan hand-fasting ceremony in 1990. During the ritual they cut their palms and mingled their blood, then got matching tattoos on the scars before splitting up a short time later.

1990–1993

Monet Mazur p.134

Fred Durst p.34

1999

1996–1997

Tania Goddard
Makeup artist

1994–1997

Rob Patterson
Guitarist
for band Korn

Carmen Electra

The actress and all-around sex symbol shot to fame as the subject of a *Playboy* centerfold and, at 36C, more than filled the bikini deficit left by Pamela Anderson (pg. 29, 34C) when she departed *Baywatch*. But you won't find Electra chatting up surfer dudes—when it comes to men she prefers guys with tattoos who apparently avoid all forms of water.

2008–

The couple started dating in early 2008, and a few months later Patterson popped the question at a nightclub in Las Vegas. Electra said they don't have a wedding date: "We're taking it slow."

Dave Navarro

The former Jane's Addiction and Red Hot Chili Peppers lead guitarist has been married and divorced three times. Whether with music or women, he clearly has a problem with commitment.

During a drunken night in Vegas, "Dennis the Menace" and then-girlfriend Electra made a rash decision: They went to the Little Chapel of the Flowers and tied the knot. Ten days later the marriage was annulled.

Michelle Moyer

The current Mrs. Dennis Rodman did pretty well for herself when she appeared on *Dr. Phil* to dish on Rodman's alcohol issues. The good doc reportedly lavished her with a scholarship for hair-training school and a new car for her appearance.

2006

2000–2006

They met on a blind date in 2000 and married three years later. Like all loving couples, they let MTV make a reality TV show about their relationship, *Till Death Do Us Part: Carmen and Dave.* By 2006 they weren't dead, but they were divorced.

◄ BACK 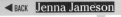 Jenna Jameson

In 2006, a few weeks after Navarro had split up with his wife of six years, Carmen Electra, he started dating Jameson, finally proving the emotional healing powers of porn.

◄ p.103 Madonna

In 1994, Chicago Bulls crazy-man Rodman was at the height of his fame (the result of reinventing himself as a badboy after a 1993 failed suicide attempt). He and Madonna had a fling, during which Rodman claims that she begged to have his child.

1994

1998–1999

Though they are now estranged, Rodman and wife Moyer lived miles apart from the moment they said their vows. She lived with their kids and would visit Rodman on weekends.

After Rodman announced his engagement to busty model Douvall, one of her breast implants exploded, prompting her to sue her plastic surgeon. Was the wedding called off because Alicia was suddenly half the girl she used to be?

Dennis Rodman

Former basketball star Rodman likes to explore all of the options available to him. He was known to take his teammates to gay bars and once wore a wedding dress to promote his book. He has since claimed to be bisexual.

2003

2004

Alicia Douvall
Model

◄ p.134 Adrien Brody

The couple bonded over a mutual love of hip-hop and all things reckless and dangerous. For his twenty-eighth birthday, Nellor kidnapped the star for an impromptu sky-diving session—she jumped first.

Sky Nellor
Australian model

2000–2002

2003

B-Real

B-Real relied on his real-life experiences in a gang to launch the top-selling Latin rap group Cypress Hill. Apparently gangbangers smoke a ton of weed.

Before Electra became an international sex symbol she dated B-Real, who can take a lot of credit for helping her become the star she is today; it was he who paid for her talented implants.

Common

Lonnie Rashid Lynn Jr. took the nom de rap Common Sense but shortened it to the populist Common after getting sued by a similarly named reggae group. He courted controversy in the 2008 presidential election by saying, "Obviously, the media has an agenda," regarding coverage of his (and Barack Obama's) pastor, Rev. Jeremiah Wright.

While rumors of an impending engagement began to swirl around this couple in 2008, Williams checked expectations in 2009, saying, "Right now, I'm dating my tennis racket." Is that a cute pet name?

♥ 2007–

💔 2004–2005

Despite their shared Grammy for "Love of My Life" in 2003, Badu was blamed for Common's descent into psychedelic experimentation on his album *Electric Circus* (which didn't sell) and bad fashion, which he referred to in later lyrics: "They say 'The crochet pants and the sweater was wack.' Now they say, 'That nigga's back.'"

💔 2005

Serena Williams

Serena took the World Number One title from her sister, tennis player Venus Williams, in 2002 after crushing her at the French Open. She shocked the prudish tennis world with a faux-leather-finish body suit at the 2002 US Open and a denim skirt two years later (outrageous!).

Tracy "The D.O.C." Curry

Dallas rapper The D.O.C. wrote for N.W.A and Eazy-E in the golden age of gansta rap, but his career (and vocal cords) were cut short by an accident after the release of his debut album in 1989. He continued to write for Dr. Dre, and in 2009 he learned that his vocal cords could be reconstructed.

Fellow Dallas artists Badu and The D.O.C. made more than beautiful music together when they released daughter Puma Rose Sabti in 2004.

2003–2004

Brett Ratner p. 44 ▶

Taraji Henson

Henson triumphed over troubles growing up (her parents were divorced, her father was homeless, and she became a single mom in her junior year in college). As an adult, she has played shocking, real characters like the prostitute Shug in *Hustle and Flow* and Queenie in *The Curious Case of Benjamin Button*, for which she received an Oscar nomination.

2000–2003

Andre "3000" Benjamin

Andre "3000" Benjamin met Antwan "Big Boi" Patton in high school, and a few years later Outkast was hitting the charts with their single "Player's Ball." Since then Andre 3000 has done it all—acting, producing his cartoon series, promoting his vegan lifestyle, and Erykah Badu, with whom he has a son.

1995–1998

Badu and Benjamin had son Seven early in their relationship and split about a year later, inspiring some of their most personal and successful tracks ("Green Eyes" from Badu and "Ms. Jackson" from Outkast).

💔 💔

Erykah Badu

Badu remixed her name (originally Erica Abi Wright) and added a "kah" meaning "inner self" and "ba-du" for jazz vocalist scat singing. She's a Grammy-winning hip-hop artist whose only real competition for the spotlight in the new soul genre may be her own big hair.

Jay Electronica
Rapper and producer

♥ 2005–

Badu and longtime boyfriend rapper-producer Electronica brought their audience closer than ever before by Twittering live updates from the birth of their daughter Mars Merkaba, born in 2009. Updates included: "Morning! I'm in labour!" "doing foot rubs when the contractions hit," "dilated to 8½ cm!" and "I see the head! It's covered in hair!"

Celebrity Sex Tapes

Rob Lowe (pg. 13) had no idea he was launching a decades-long trend when the tape he had shot of himself and two girls (one only sixteen) getting it on surfaced in 1988 and torpedoed his career. It was one of the first commercially available celebrity sex tapes (earlier stag films of Marilyn Monroe and others were hand-copied and traded). Twenty years later, it might have boosted his career as similar homemade porn tapes did for Pamela Anderson (pg. 29), Paris Hilton (pg. 89), and Kim Kardashian (pg. 24). They sued but eventually accepted cuts of the proceeds from the tape distributors. Colin Farell (pg. 135), however, managed to stop the distribution of a tape he'd shot with his former girlfriend, *Playboy*'s Miss January 2002, Nicole Narain—despite the fact that she, as its "cocreator," claimed she had the right to sell the tape. *Gossip Girl* star Leighton Meester's sex tape surfaced in 2009 and featured a quirky foot job. But the prize for creepiest celebrity sex act has to go to Dustin Diamond, "Screech" on *Saved by the Bell*, who tried to boost his career with a sex tape that featured the aptly named "Dirty Sanchez" as its big set piece.

Bromosexuals

Over the years, Hollywood has had its fair share of gay men playing straight, from Rock Hudson to (allegedly gay) Marlon Brando (pg. 146) and James Dean (pg. 146). But in recent years, the straights have gotten in on the "gaym," with regular guys buddying up and spending way too much time together. Ben Affleck (pg. 80) and Matt Damon (pg. 113) started the trend and were even awarded an Oscar for their film collaboration, but subsequent steady-seeming marriages quashed the rumors. Matthew McConaughey (pg. 18) joked, "We tried it. Wasn't for us," when rumors of his extra-close relationship with Lance Armstrong (pg. 100) swirled in 2006. They even had nicknames for each other: "Livestrong" and the "Redneck Buddha." Best buddies like these do lots of things together: party in Cabo (Brody Jenner, pg. 90, and Frankie Delgado, pg. 93), promote world-dominating sci-fi cults (Will Smith and Tom Cruise, pg. 70), and skinny dip (Owen Wilson, pg. 101, and Woody Harrelson, pg. 9, in the Atlantic Ocean in 2008).

Their breakup was documented on camera when the sisters were shooting their reality series, *Venus and Serena: For Real*. Serena dumped Ratner, saying, "I've been home for three weeks. You come on Saturday, and you leave on Sunday, and I'm sorry but that's just not good enough for me."

2004–2005

Brett Ratner

Critically panned but commercially successful, Ratner directed the *Rush Hour* series of films as well as *X-Men: The Last Stand*. In 2007 he gave the *Advocate* a couple of interesting biographical details: "There's no hair on my ass. I have no hair on my balls," and "My first blow job was from a man, but I didn't know it was a man."

1988–1999

Rebecca Gayheart p. 94

Ratner's short relationship with Meyer busted up his engagement with long-term love Rebecca Gayheart (pg. 94). When Gayheart heard rumors about herself saying that she was ready to jump out the window because she was distraught with grief, she said, "That would be pretty amazing, since I live on the ground floor."

◄ p. 41 Serena Williams

Mark Ronson
DJ and brother of Samantha Ronson (pg. 93)

Though they later broke off their engagement, Ronson proposed to Jones by creating a crossword puzzle with the phrase "Will You Marry Me" contained therein. Apparently Rashida is a romantic and a cruciverbalist.

Jones dumped Maguire for his incessant flirting, but things got worse when he started dating her best friend, Jennifer Meyer, and then married her. "He broke Rashida's heart, and Jen knew it," said a source at the time.

The chemistry between *The Office* costars Krasinki and Jones spilled over into real life, and the two began dating. Neither the real nor fictional relationship was meant to be.

John Krasinski
The goofy-faced Bostonian perfected the art of the sarcastic grin playing Jim on the American version of *The Office*. Krasinski appeared in *Kinsey* as the world's wrongest man, a husband who's convinced oral sex will make his wife infertile.

2005–2006 2001–2002 2002–2004

Rashida Jones
Jones is the daughter of Quincy Jones and an accomplished singer in her own right. You can hear her voice on Maroon 5's record *Songs About Jane* and on Tupac's album *The Rose That Grew from Concrete*.

Jordan Bratman
Music marketer

Aguilera married Jordan Bratman in 2005 after a three-year courtship and later told Ellen DeGeneres (pg. 152) that she and the hubby like to be nude on Sundays to "keep marriage alive, spice it up." The spices must have worked, since they delivered son Max Liron Bratman in 2008, booking $1.5 million from *People* magazine for the photos.

2002– 2002–

2008–

When asked about Krasinski's proposal, Blunt joked, ". . . there were flutes playing in the background, butterflies, there were angels showering us with rainbow drops." Krasinski remembered it differently saying, "I cried, and we cried, and then everyone around us was crying."

Emily Blunt
British actress

Aguilera was ordered to ditch Iglesias when music bosses began to worry that she'd lose her male audience. They were also worried that her hookups were creating too sharp a contrast with the clean-cut image of Britney Spears (pg. 33), who at the time was known for her virginity. How things change.

Christina Aguilera
Rumors about the pop princess suggest promiscuity and naughtiness—Eminem linked her to three guys in just one song, and Kelly Osbourne called her "one of the most disgusting human beings in the world." Yet the former Disney Club kid has kept it legit and outlived her detractors on the charts.

Singer-songwriter-cagefighter Aguilera literally sang Santos's praises in the song "Infatuation," but later said, "The breakup was actually with my first love . . . but it's cool. I'm thinking about my little breakup song now!"

2000   2000

Jennifer Meyer

Meyer is the daughter of Ron Meyer, head of Universal Entertainment. She learned jewelry making from her grand-mother at age six; her signature gold leaf charm made its debut on the neck of Jennifer Aniston (pg. 108), who wore it in the film *The Break-Up*.

1999

Maguire met Meyer when he was shooting *Seabiscuit* for her father's company, Universal Entertainment. They had a long-term, low-profile relationship, had a daughter, and bucked tradition by getting married nine months later.

2003–

2002

Tobey Maguire

The *Spider-Man* star spent his childhood career competing for roles with friend Leonardo DiCaprio (pg. 73). He dropped out of 1995's *Empire Records* to tackle an alcohol problem, and it wasn't the last time—he was almost fired from *Spider-Man 2* for drinking.

2001–2002

Aguilera reportedly sang a sultry Marilyn Monroe–style rendition of "Happy Birthday" to Maguire at his twenty-seventh birthday party (thrown by best bud Leonardo DiCaprio, pg. 73) but the singing star's fling with the web slinger was short.

2002

Heather Graham NEXT ▶

2001

Kirsten Dunst p. 71 ▶

Rick Salomon p. 88 ▶

Judd Nelson

In 1985's *The Breakfast Club*, Nelson played "the criminal" John Bender and will forever be known for earning extra detention by saying "Eat . . . my . . . shorts."

These star-crossed psychos met on the set of their film *Blindfold* and had an affair while Doherty was engaged to Dean Factor. When Factor found out, he jumped the sneaky couple in a Hollywood club, forcing them to flee to Dallas, where Nelson kicked a heckler in the head and ended up serving two years of probation for the assault.

Jorge Santos

Backup dancer

1993

2002

Shannen Doherty

Doherty starred in *Heathers* with Winona Ryder (pg. 113) and was perfectly cast as bitchy bad girl Brenda Walsh in *Beverly Hills, 90210*. She was known for flipping out, on set and off, and famously screamed at her neighbor, Molly Ringwald, "You don't live here, bitch! You only rent!"

1993–1994

2001–2002

She-devil Doherty brings out the best in people—her *Charmed* costar McMahon left his wife, Brooke Burns, and their one-year-old baby to get with Doherty. They split soon after she was sentenced to three years of probation for drunk driving.

Salomon and Doherty were married for nine months (perhaps a record for both), and Salomon's sex tape sparked a hair-pulling cat fight between Doherty and his costar, Paris Hilton (pg. 89). When Doherty saw the tape, she said, "I look at what he did with Paris and think, 'God, that is disgusting.'"

Ashley Hamilton NEXT ▶

1992–1993

Dannii Minogue p. 68 ▶

Julian McMahon

Aussie McMahon (the son of for-mer Australian prime minister Sir William McMahon) plays the face of face-lifts as Dr. Christian Troy on the hit show *Nip/Tuck*, which featured an explicit sex-on-a-fur-rug scene with Rosie O'Donnell.

1999–2001 Brooke Burns p. 138 ▼

Well-mannered McMahon "offered me his arm and opened all the doors for me," when they started dating, said Burns. The chivalry continued when she got pregnant and he asked to make it legal, but his manners started to slip when he dated his *Charmed* costar Shannen Doherty while still married to Burns.

Salma Hayek p.60 ▲

2003

Christopher Guest

Who knew that the comic genius behind the mockumentaries *Best In Show*, *Waiting for Guffman*, and *This Is Spinal Tap* is of noble blood? His formal title in the United Kingdom is Christopher Haden-Guest, 5th Baron Haden-Guest. (Barons don't go up to 11.)

Jamie Lee Curtis

Curtis launched her career by screaming and running away from the camera in such classic horror flicks as *The Fog*, *Prom Night*, and *Halloween* (and some of its sequels).

1984– ♥

She may have been only sixteen when they met, but Ant insists Donohoe had "a perfectly formed woman's body." More than just eye candy, Donohoe protected her man by punching an obsessed fan who tried to knife him.

1978–1981

1983–1984

After splitting from Lucas, McAdams was asked on the red carpet how best to cope with breakups. "It's different for everyone," she said, "Do what you love."

"Our meeting was like a first date where you're both ultra-polite, touching each other surreptitiously and starting conversations just so you can look into each other's eyes," said Mr. Ant. "We snogged in the back row of a cinema ..."

💔 2009

💔 2008

Josh Lucas

Lucas says he tells people who confuse him with Matthew McConaughey (pg. 18), "Once the naked bongo incident happened, I changed my name." He debuted in the "tastes like chicken" survival film *Alive*.

Graham picked up Lucas's scent at a NYC Cares coat drive in December '04 while he was dating model Liliana Dominguez. There's something about the spirit of giving that makes people want to share more than just used winter wear.

◀ BACK Tobey Maguire

◀ p.123 Matthew Perry

Heather Graham was just one of many "friends" with benefits that Perry had in 2002.

Raffaello Follieri
Italian con artist

2004–2008

Follieri spent four years whisking Hathaway to exotic locations around the world while claiming to sell properties for the Vatican. She dumped him right before he was arrested for allegedly defrauding billionaire Ronald Burkle of $50 million. As part of the investigation, the FBI confiscated Hathaway's (princess) diaries.

Rachel McAdams

Canadian actress McAdams first grabbed attention playing Regina George in the teen hit *Mean Girls*. She allegedly turned down starring roles in *Casino Royale*, *The Devil Wears Prada*, *Iron Man*, and *The Dark Knight*.

💔 2005–2009

Hathaway and Lucas went on a romantic date to the 2008 Democratic National Convention in Denver, proving that Obama truly is a uniting force in America.

Anne Hathaway
American actress

This engagement lasted longer than Hamilton's marriages, but Foster had some issues that may have gotten in the way. "When I was engaged to Ashley Hamilton," she said, "because of his first name I used to hear constantly, 'Have you become a lesbian?'"

♥ 2000–2001

Ryan Gosling p.18

◀ p.32 Angie Everhart

1996–1997

A few days after getting dumped by Judd Nelson (pg. 45), twenty-three-year-old Doherty wedded nineteen-year-old Hamilton for a short, five-month marriage. Hamilton claimed that Doherty had tried to run him over with her car during those five months.

Ashley Hamilton

Son of perma-tanned actor George Hamilton, Ashley had a typical Hollywood childhood, complete with drug overdoses ("I was in a coma and lost the use of the left side of my body, 'cause I was on my side for three days") and doomed celebrity weddings.

◀ BACK Shannen Doherty

1993–1994 🔒

Amanda Donohoe

Donohoe has the honor of partaking in the first girl-on-girl kiss ever broadcast on American television when her *LA Law* character kissed Michelle Greene in 1991. "My first sexual experiences were with women," she said.

1984
1993

Ant said his relationship with Graham saved him from suicide. "Heather seemed like an angel to me ... When I was with her I felt happy." Years later, when he read a letter to the editor of *Time Out* that treated her negatively, he went to a pub wielding a dummy pistol and had to be arrested at gunpoint.

Denise "Vanity" Matthews
Lead singer for Vanity 6

In the '80s, Vanity was Prince's protégé and girlfriend. These days, the born-again Christian claims, "Every song that we sang, everything we did ... was exactly what the Enemy wanted—lust, fornication, death."

1980

Prince   p. 14 ▶

Adam Ant

He don't drink, he don't smoke, but that didn't stop Mr. Ant, born Stuart Leslie Goddard, from winning MTV's "Sexiest Man in America" title in 1983. Was it the white streak of makeup or the now-quaint sexuality of the banned song "Strip" ("If I strip for you, will you strip for me")?

James Woods   p. 130 ▶

Woods met Graham when they were shooting *Diggstown*. He caught her reading *The Brothers Karamazov* and said, "I thought this could genuinely be love." A few years later, Graham said, "I can't believe I ever went out with him. It was more looking for a father figure."

2004–2005

2002
2002

Foster had to settle for number two on the list of the world's top tennis players—the highest rank earned by German player Haas back in 2002. The two were introduced by mutual friend Kate Hudson (pg. 101).

Heather Graham

Best known for her role as Roller Girl ("I never take my skates off") in *Boogie Nights*, Graham has come a long way from her strict Catholic upbringing in Milwaukee, Wisconsin. Some say an early romance with James Woods boosted her career, while others point to her amazing breasts—and drool.

1993
1993

1997–1998   Stephen Hopkins   p. 77 ▶

Graham had this revelation about dating on a movie set a couple of years after getting with Hopkins, her director on *Lost in Space*: "I felt that when I was on a film set pretending to be in love with someone it helped to take an extra step and really do so. But a movie set is fake."

2001–2002   Elijah Blue Allman   p. 89 ▶

Elias Koteas
Greek Canadian actor Koteas studied under Ellen Burstyn before getting a break in John Hughes's *Some Kind of Wonderful* as the world's friendliest skinhead.

2006
2000–2001   Heath Ledger   p. 77 ▼
1998–2000   Ed Burns   p. 157 ▼
2001–2002
1997–1998

Tommy Haas
Tennis player

Scott Speedman
American actor

2007–

Sara Foster

Sara, daughter of David Foster (composer of "Love Theme from *St. Elmo's Fire*"), modeled, then dated celebs, then acted in 2004's *The Big Bounce*, followed by a few TV roles and a cameo as a model who dates a celeb (big stretch) on *Entourage*.

2004–2006
2002

Benicio Del Toro   NEXT ▶
Benicio Del Toro   NEXT ▶
Leonardo DiCaprio   p. 73 ▶

Gooding cheated on Kylie Minogue (pg. 67) with Dahl, later boasting that the two had flown to New York to carry on their affair. But it's all cool—according to him, Minogue had agreed that he could sleep with other people.

James Gooding ▲ p. 66

Mick Jagger

She was younger than his eldest daughter, Jade, but that didn't stop Jagger (who studied accounting and should be able to do the math) from dating Dahl.

💔 2000

Heather Graham

💔 2001–2002

◀ BACK

Benicio Del Toro

Del Toro abandoned the family business (both his parents and godmother were lawyers) when he changed majors, and then quit college, to pursue acting. Mumbling through *The Usual Suspects* ultimately led him to win an Oscar for 2000's *Traffic*. And his dad worried that there was no future in acting!

💔 2002

Although she denied her own "sarcastic quote" that she had had sex with Del Toro in an elevator at the Chateau Marmont before the 2004 Oscars, observers did spy them making out at a party that night, and their rooms were upstairs, and elevators are so convenient. So you decide.

💔 2002   💔 2002

Sophie Dahl

The plus-size model and granddaughter of author Roald Dahl made a splash when her 2000 nude-on-a-fur-rug billboard ad for Opium perfume was banned in Britain. She said, "I'd rather be . . . booked because a client likes the look of me, not because I'm size 16 with big tits."

🔒 2009–

Dahl got engaged to jazz musician Cullum after performing with him at a charity event in 2007. The six-foot-tall model towers over her five-foot, four-inch beau and doesn't understand why that's so freakin' fascinating. "People have treated us like we're a carnival show."

💔 2004   💔 2004

Scarlett Johansson

Johansson made her film debut in *North*, about which Roger Ebert said, "I hated this movie. Hated, hated, hated, hated." Her acting talents are obviously in critical favorites *The Horse Whisperer*, *Ghost World*, and *Lost in Translation*, and she has won the admiration of Woody Allen (pg. 141), who has featured her in numerous films.

Jamie Cullum
British jazz pianist

🔒 2007–

They started dating in 2007 and a year later announced their engagement. Although Reynolds had previously been engaged to Alanis Morissette for almost three years, he didn't let the engagement linger this time. Within four months of proposing, he and Johansson were wedded in Canada, which still counts.

Alanis Morissette

Morissette transcended her modest start on the slimy Nickelodeon series *You Can't Do That on Television* to become one of the biggest-selling female rock artists ever—and that's with one hand in her pocket!

2002–2007 💙

Ryan Reynolds

The Canadian-born actor made a name for himself playing the cool, charming guy in films like *Van Wilder* and *Waiting*. After beefing up to star in *Blade 3*, Reynolds has used his hot new body to score roles in action films.

They met at Drew Barrymore's (pg. 78) twenty-seventh birthday party and quickly started dating, but a mutual love of Canada couldn't keep this engaged couple together. Soon after the split, Morissette put out an angsty album, *Flavors of Entanglement*, and Reynolds put out with Scarlett Johansson.

Robert Torricelli
United States senator

1999–2000

It's refreshing to see folks from opposite sides of the political aisle come together in a bipartisan fashion, and Ingraham and Torricelli did. Even more refreshing: a relationship involving a politician that doesn't involve cigars, instant messages, airport bathrooms, or trips to South America.

Laura Ingraham
With best-selling books and a radio program that falls just under Glenn Beck's in popularity and frequency of Sarah Palin interviews, Ingraham is one of the top female voices in the modern conservative movement.

If only New Jersey senator Torricelli had been the first prominent American lawmaker linked to Jagger, this story would have been new and fresh. But she'd gotten it on with senator Chris Dodd thirteen years earlier.

When Connecticut senator Dodd fell into the arms of Jagger after a divorce, it nearly destroyed his political career. She was a well-known Castro sympathizer and a public relations representative for the Marxists who were fighting for control of Nicaragua. But she was just so hot!

1982–1983

When Chris Dodd ran for president in '08, he may not have seemed as youthful as John Edwards or as cool as Obama, but his track record with the ladies proves otherwise. Dodd's days of carousing with the likes of Fisher are, as he puts it, "A long time ago in a galaxy far, far away."

Chris Dodd
Democratic senator

1983

Carrie Fisher
In 2008 Fisher published *Wishful Drinking*, a memoir, in which she described her drug addiction, alcoholism, and struggles with bipolar disorder. But really, there is nothing she could write that would get the image of her in a bronze bikini as Princess Leia out of teenage boys' heads.

1995

The bride was four months pregnant with a daughter, Jade Jagger, when she married Mick in Saint-Tropez, but the press was more shocked by her white YSL pants suit. Bianca called her wedding "one of the saddest days of her life," partly because Mick surprised her with a prenup hours before the ceremony.

1971–1979 🔒

Bianca Jagger
Bianca was a hard-core party girl before, during, and after her marriage to Mick (Andy Warhol described her as "sex crazed"). She helped hype Studio 54 by riding a white horse into the club for her thirty-second birthday party, but since the late 1970s she's been more focused on human rights than humid nights.

1966

Known then as Bianca Perez Morena de Macias, the future Mrs. Jagger was twenty-one and modeling in Paris when she dated the thirty-three-year-old Caine. He shacked up with her for a year, just like his character in the film *Alfie*, which had just premiered.

Michael Caine
Caine achieved fame as the model womanizer in 1966's *Alfie*, the character who said, "I don't want no bird's respect. I wouldn't know what to do with it." These days, after starring in more than one hundred films, he's more likely to be the wise butler than the dashing rake.

🔒 **1973–**

🔒 **1955–1958**

Paul Simon
Singer-songwriter

Patricia Haines
British actress

🔒 **1983–1984**

Mick Jagger NEXT ▶
Mick Jagger NEXT ▶
Ryan O'Neal p. 56 ▶

1977

Caine fell in love with the former Miss Guyana after seeing her in a coffee commercial in 1971. "I found myself down on my knees in front of the set trying to get a closer look at this vision—only to be confronted with a shot of a Maxwell House coffee jar," he said. He tracked her down (or stalked her, as we would call it today), and they've been happily married ever since.

Caine, who had just finished his service as a Royal Fusilier in the British Army, had only been acting for two years when he married actress Haines. His reason for marrying? He wanted to prove to his father that, unlike most actors (and fusiliers!), he wasn't gay.

Shakira Caine
Fashion model

Jack Nicholson p.59

Mick filed an injunction to keep Shrimpton from publishing the love notes he'd written to her—a bit hypocritical since Jagger allegedly wrote the songs "Under My Thumb," "19th Nervous Breakdown," and "Stupid Girl" about Chrissie.

Chrissie Shrimpton
British model

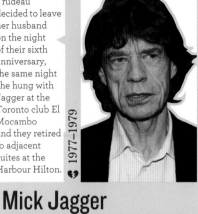

1977–1979

1979

Trudeau decided to leave her husband on the night of their sixth anniversary, the same night she hung with Jagger at the Toronto club El Mocambo and they retired to adjacent suites at the Harbour Hilton.

Hall filed for divorce in 1999, after nine years of marriage, and learned that Jagger saw their relationship in a different, un-married light when he challenged the legality of their 1990 Balinese ceremony. He won in court and Hall walked away with a mere $25 million.

Geraldo Rivera
Best known for his over-hyped *Al Capone's Vault* TV special, or having his nose broken by white supremacists on his talk show, Rivera actually started out as a semi-real journalist.

1980

Classy reporter Rivera revealed in his 1991 tell-all that he'd gotten it on with Trudeau in a rowboat in Central Park. "I rowed us to a secluded spot . . ." he wrote. "Right there, the estranged First Lady of Canada lent new meaning to the term 'head of state.'"

Margaret Trudeau
Canadian prime minister Pierre Trudeau's young wife melted the frigid north with sexual scandals, including a 1979 Britney Spears (pg. 33) style paparazzi crotch shot that was published in porn magazine *High Society*.

1977–1979

1963–1966

Mick Jagger
A rock icon and international ladies man, Jagger made plump lips a fashion acces-sory fifteen years before collagen was invented. He was studying economics when The Rolling Stones got their start in 1960, and those math skills must come in handy when he steps away from his long line of lovers to count his millions.

🔒 1990–1999
💔 1966–1970
💔 1999
💔 1967
💔 1977

◀ BACK Bianca Jagger
◀ p.120 Patti D'Arbanville

1971–1979 🔒

1970 💔

D'Arbanville began dating Jagger when she was nineteen, and dumped Cat Stevens to be with him.

2000 💔

1972 💔

Beatty has said, "Let's be hon-est. That song is about me," but Simon has refused to confirm or deny any-thing. That didn't stop (vain) Beatty from calling her up and thanking her when the song debuted.

Simon's "You're So Vain" had the world guessing whom the song was written about—stud Warren Beatty (pg. 140) or backing vocalist Mick Jagger?

💔

1998

Verity, British TV personality and nanny to the stars, was only on the job for a few hours before Jagger pulled her pants down and screwed her in the kitchen. "I was making coffee when Mick came in. The kitchen was so small we kept bumping into each other."

◀ p.140 Warren Beatty

1970 💔

1971–1972 💔

Cat Stevens p.120

Carly Simon
Singer Simon has remained mum about the man who inspired her song "You're So Vain"; she did, how-ever, auction off the information in 2003 for a charity. The winner paid $50,000 but is bound by contract not to reveal the person's name.

1972

Before this musically and politically active couple divorced, they had two children, Ben and Sarah. Sarah's birth was immortalized in the song, "Sarah Maria," on James Taylor's 1975 album, *Gorilla*.

James Taylor
American singer-songwriter

Claire Verity
Controversial British nanny

Sophie Dahl p.120

◀ BACK

🔓 1972–1983

Jerry Hall
American model

2007–2008

After divorcing Paul McCartney, Heather Mills hopped into the arms of another rich Brit, Marc Sinden. Mills's plan is to take as much money from as many wealthy Britons as she can and put the Queen of England out of business.

Marc Sinden
British theater producer

Marianne Faithfull
British singer

Heather Mills
If Heather Mills isn't the most-hated woman in England, she's certainly the most-hated one-legged woman in England. Her reputation as a part-time model, full-time gold digger has got the better of her.

♥ 2008–

🔓 2002–2008

When Mills married Sir Paul, she may as well have been ascending to the throne. He lost $50 million to Mills in their divorce—a small price to pay to be rid of the wretch!

Paul McCartney
Known as the dreamy, living one from The Beatles (sorry Ringo), McCartney is an outspoken activist for many causes including vegetarianism, ridding the world of land mines, and protecting seals. But his first act of activism may have occurred in 1967 when he added his name to a petition for the legalization of cannabis.

In 1995, a paparazzo snapped a picture of Jagger making out with Thurman at the Viper Room in Los Angeles. Jagger had security tackle the photographer and destroy the film, an incident that cost him $600,000 in court.

In what must be the classic tale of rock, sex, and drugs, twenty police officers stormed Keith Richards's estate in England in 1967 on suspicion of drug possession and claimed they found Jagger eating a Mars bar held by Faithfull in her vagina. A Snickers may have been more satisfying.

Uma Thurman p. 54 ▶
Pamela Des Barres p. 120 ▶
♥ 1998 Marc Anthony p. 81 ▶
♥ 1999–2002 Olivier Martinez p. 67 ▶

Mira Sorvino
Harvard graduate Sorvino won an Oscar for her role in Woody Allen's *Mighty Aphrodite*. In honor of her entomologist role in *Mimic*, a compound excreted by the sunburst diving beetle was named mirasorvone.

♥ 1998

When Sorvino dated Costner, Quentin Tarantino was so upset he told Howard Stern (pg. 104) that he'd never cast Costner in any film of his. Ever.

John Phillips (pg. 58), Mackenzie's father, approved of Jagger sleeping with Mackenzie in his apartment when she turned eighteen. According to Mackenzie, Jagger said, "I have been waiting for this since you were ten years old."

Mackenzie Phillips
Mackenzie Phillips is the daughter of John Phillips (pg. 58) of The Mamas and the Papas. The actress appeared in *American Graffiti* and *One Day at a Time*.

♥
1979–1989 John Phillips

p. 58 ▼

After Costner split from his civilian wife of sixteen years, Cindy Silva, he found solace in the arms of Macpherson. The supermodel left New York to live down the block from Costner in Hollywood. "I feel I have met my equal with this beautiful, talented, funny, and lovely person," said Costner.

1996

Kevin Costner
You can laugh because *Dances with Wolves* is a ridiculous title for a movie, but it won seven Oscars so Costner got something right. He also got some things very wrong—one (compound) word: *Waterworld*.

♥ 1993–1994 Tim Jeffries p. 67 ▶

Elle Macpherson
The Australian beauty came to America intending to spend a gap year between high school and college earning some tuition money as a model. As luck would have it, she became a supermodel and even founded her own modeling agency, Elle Macpherson Inc.

After dating for years and having two kids, Macpherson and Busson broke their engagement with a statement reading "Whilst remaining the greatest of friends, we have decided to spend some time apart." Rumors alleged it was because he was a strict Catholic and she was a divorcée.

👶 1997–2005 Arpad A. Busson p. 54 ▶

Breaking Up Is Easy to Do

It takes a convincing actor to pull off the classic "It's not you; it's me," but when it comes to splitting with a star, some celebrities literally phone it in. Britney Spears (pg. 33) divorced baby daddy Kevin Federline (pg. 33) via text message in an awkward moment captured on film by a crew from Canada's MuchMusic channel. Adam Levine was a man of fewer words when he cut it off with Jessica Simpson (pg. 109) via a telegram-style text message reading "Really busy. Need space." But that kind of brush-off existed long before the T9. Daniel Day-Lewis (pg. 16) reportedly let his seven-months-pregnant girlfriend Isabelle Adjani (pg. 140) know that their relationship was over via fax, way back in 1995.

Married in Spirit (Sort Of)

Celebrities are a passionate breed and like to express that passion by getting married, but the smart ones (or those with a good manager) avoid the pesky legal and financial requirements by getting hitched in a foreign land. Mick Jagger (pg. 50) showed his love for Jerry Hall (pg. 51) in a Hindu ceremony conducted in Bali; when she filed for divorce a few years later, he successfully argued the wedding wasn't legit in the first place. Kate Moss (pg. 60) planned an identical unofficial ceremony in Bali, but the nuptials fell apart when lover Pete Doherty (pg. 60) got nailed for drug possession before the wedding. Even an eighteen-year-old Christy Turlington (pg. 158) had the sense to marry her *Porky*'s-star boyfriend Roger Wilson (pg. 158) in a "symbolic" Thai wedding, instead of tying the knot for real.

1995

1995–1996

1998–2004

1989–1992

Though they were married, neither Oldman nor Uma have spoken publicly about those years or what may have gone wrong. Oldman responded to a question about their breakup by saying, "How do you live with an angel?"

Gary Oldman
After playing Sid Vicious, British-born Oldman's parts got steadily more villainous, with roles as Lee Harvey Oswald, Dracula, a violent pimp, a corrupt DEA agent, a sadistic prison warden, a Russian terrorist, and, yes, even Pontius Pilate.

Flavio Briatore p.17 ▲

Mike Tyson p.104 ▲

Campbell may have honed her fighting ways during a short relationship with Tyson. Years later, in 2005, her former close friend Yvonne Scio said Campbell "first shoved [her] against a wall . . . and finally she let rip with two or three violent punches in my face . . . She was like Mike Tyson."

Toukie Smith
American actress

Four years after they broke up, Smith and De Niro became the proud parents of test-tube twins, born to a surrogate mother. The two decided to stay split while sharing the parenting of this distinctly modern brood.

1999

Uma Thurman
Uma's father, a Buddhist professor, named her in reference to the ancient Indian god Kali's Crone aspect, also called "Mother Death," or "the Black Mother." She certainly leaves broken hearts in her wake.

💬 1993

2004–2007

Possibly the palest of De Niro's girlfriends, Uma Thurman hooked up with him on the set of *Mad Dog and Glory*. In this gangster-themed film, Bill Murray plays a mob boss who trades Thurman to De Niro for saving his life in a convenience-store holdup.

2007–2009

1997–2005

Katherine Ford
Head of Ford Models

Thurman and multimillionaire Busson broke off their engagement in 2009 so Thurman didn't play the part of The Bride in real life, though she may revisit the role in *Kill Bill* 3.

A scandalous hair-pulling squabble between Campbell and *Dynasty* star Troy Berger may have closed the book on her romance with De Niro. A year later De Niro would really piss her off when he didn't cast her in his directing debut, *A Bronx Tale*.

1985–2003

Arpad A. Busson
French financier

1998–2003

1989

1991–1992

Andre Balazs
Balazs is the hotelier to the stars (and wannabes) with posh, hip properties like Chateau Marmont, The Mercer, and The Standard in Hollywood, where semi-nude model-actresses read books in a fish tank behind the lobby desk.

While dating Balazs, Campbell was arrested for kicking a Heathrow police officer in the thigh with her stiletto-heeled boot and smashing another with her cell phone (classic Campbell weaponry).

Naomi Campbell
Known for her wacko temper, supermodel Campbell has been arrested for assaulting several assistants using phones—sometimes with a BlackBerry (2005's beating of assistant Amanda Brack), and sometimes with a classic land line (2000's assault on assistant Georgina Galanis).

Campbell's hair-trigger temper may have suited her Russian beau, Doronin, just fine—soon after they started dating, he slugged a paparazzo in the gut for photographing the couple in Miami.

2008–2009

2007–2008 💬

Vladimir Doronin
Russian billionaire property mogul

1994 💬

1998 💬

Shelley Winters
Oscar-winning
American actress 🎤 1956

Winters slept with Connery when he was an unknown actor. Years later, when he was voted *People* magazine's "Sexiest Man Alive" in 1989, she said, "To be his leading lady, I'd lose fifty pounds and get my face lifted. As a matter of fact, I'd get everything lifted!"

Winters took an interest in a struggling young De Niro, and the relationship paid off for him. She cast him in her stage play *One Night Stands of a Noisy Passenger* (a performance she described as "sexual lightning onstage") and helped him get an early film role playing her son in 1970's *Bloody Mama*.

Sean Connery
Connery's 007 reputation with the ladies was sullied when he told Barbara Walters in 1987 (and *Playboy* decades earlier) that slapping a woman was an okay thing to do, provided "all the other alternatives fail and there's been plenty of warning."

During rehearsals for their film *The Gang That Couldn't Shoot Straight*, Taylor-Young and De Niro walked through New York in character to practice their accents. De Niro, who played a kleptomaniac, took it too far and got caught stealing shirts from Macy's. Both were almost arrested before Leigh was recognized.

Leigh Taylor-Young NEXT ▶

Grace Hightower
Former flight attendant

De Niro and Hightower had a son, Elliot, in 1998. Soon after, De Niro filed for divorce but never actually went through with it. The marriage is still strong (as least on paper).

🔒 1997–

1990–1992 🎤
1993 🎤
1991–1992 🎤

1969–1970 🎤

Robert De Niro

You talking to him? Two-time Oscar winner and committed Method actor De Niro was first noticed in Martin Scorsese's *Mean Streets* in 1973. The next year, he won an Oscar for his Don Vito in *The Godfather Part II*, and the gangster roles haven't stopped since.

🎤 1971
🎤 1975
🎤 1995

Mallory bumped into De Niro, who was married to Diahnne Abbott at the time, while waiting for the elevator at the Chateau Marmont, and they had a two-week fling. Mallory's take on De Niro: "He likes to have sex with women who don't talk. I think he should go to a morgue."

1976 Warren Beatty p.140 ▶
1970–1975 Richard Gere p.154 ▶
🎤 🎤

1976–1988 🔓

Abbott married De Niro in 1976, the same year she rejected him on film in her role as the porn-theater candy-counter clerk in *Taxi Driver*.

Diahnne Abbott
American actress

De Niro vowed never to step foot in France again after getting nabbed for screwing Sinclair, who was part of a high-class international prostitution ring. According to her, De Niro said she had a better butt than Naomi Campbell did.

Charmaine Sinclair
Porn actress and escort

1993–1995 🎤

Judd and De Niro hooked up while shooting 1995's *Heat*, but the odds were against it. Judd said, "In ten professional outings, [I was involved with] exactly two of my costars . . . Just 20 percent. Which, by the way, is well below the national average."

1995 🎤

Ashley Judd

The country music success of Ashley Judd's mother (Naomi Judd) and sister (Wynonna Judd) left Ashley with "feelings of resentment, loneliness and anger that she . . . harbored since childhood."

🎤 1995

Carole Mallory
American actress and model 🎤 1983–1992

Norman Mailer
Writer

After Mailer's death in 2007, Mallory, who was his mistress for ten years, sold seven boxes of photos and documents about their relationship to Harvard University.

🎤 1996–1997

Bolton claims he "fell in love with the entire Judd family" before he fell for Ashley, which is creepy enough without the mullet.

Michael Bolton p.129 ▶
Matthew McConaughey p.18 ▶

Dave Mason
Guitarist for band Traffic

Mason and Taylor-Young had a thing in 1977, right before her marriage to McElwaine. Much later, in 1994, they reignited the rock-and-roll passion when he joined Fleetwood Mac and a friend let him know she was newly available.

1994–1996

Guy McElwaine
Former head of Columbia Pictures

McElwaine wanted Taylor-Young at home and didn't support her career. A ruling by the California Court of Appeals (the Hug Decision) right before their divorce meant she was entitled to his stock options in the divorce—a ruling that motivated McElwaine to settle fast.

1978–1985

Tatum O'Neal recalls Andress saying, "I don't want to sleep with you while your daughter is in the bed. It's weird." And she was right.

Ursula Andress ▲ p.146

Joanna Cook Moore
American actress

After their divorce, Moore slipped into a deep depression made worse when O'Neal instantly married Leigh Taylor-Young. She started taking drugs—lots of drugs. Daughter Tatum (pg. 13) described fending for herself, stealing food from a local liquor store, and sleeping in a maggot-infested bathroom.

Ross would see O'Neal jogging naked along the Malibu beach in front of the house she shared with then-husband Robert Ellis. That, and his fling with her idol, Barbra Streisand (pg. 118), made their dalliance inevitable. The roles in the film *The Bodyguard* were written for this couple to play.

1971

Leigh Taylor-Young
Young was a budding New York stage actress when a quick trip to Los Angeles turned into a seven-year contract on *Peyton Place*; she was hired to replace Mia Farrow (pg. 141), who quit on orders from her man, Frank Sinatra.

O'Neal and Taylor-Young tied the knot when she was already three months pregnant, doubling the scandal of O'Neal's infidelity to previous wife Joanne Moore.

◀ BACK Robert De Niro

James Spader
Spader is one of very few actors who have won consecutive Emmys for playing the same character on more than one series—he played Alan Shore on *The Practice* in 2004 and on *Boston Legal* in 2005.

2005–

Leslie Stefanson
Although some think she's from Fargo, North Dakota, *General's Daughter* star Stefanson actually hails from the lesser-known, but equally icy, twin city of Moorhead, Minnesota.

Beautiful starlet Stefanson dated O'Neal during one of the off periods in his on-and-off affair with Farrah Fawcett.

1967–1973

1967–1973

1971

1963–1967

Ryan O'Neal
O'Neal broke out playing opposite Ali MacGraw in *Love Story*—a romance that Al Gore claimed was based on his with Tipper. An on-again, off-again relationship with Farrah Fawcett continued until her death in 2009, interrupted only by his flings with starlets in the 1970s and 1980s and drunken brawls with addict son Griffin in the 2000s.

1978

1979–2009

1997

1970

1975

1973–1974

1977

1975

◀ p.118 Barbra Streisand
◀ p.154 Diane von Furstenberg
◀ p.119 Melanie Griffith

Anjelica Huston

Bianca Jagger

Jon Voight
American actor from *Midnight Cowboy*

Twenty-six years after presenting him with an Oscar for best actor, Ross and Voight hooked up. The relationship reportedly failed because Voight didn't appreciate Ross's diva lifestyle.

2005–2006

1965–1970

Although Gordy reported that he "couldn't get it up" the first time he slept with Ross, the two were deep into their secret affair when he decided to turn The Supremes into her backing group. When Ross got pregnant in 1970, she covered it up by marrying publicist Robert Ellis.

Berry Gordy Jr.
Gordy discovered The Miracles in 1957 and wrote songs for the group before leader Smokey Robinson encouraged him to start Motown records in 1959. Motown launched the careers of Diana Ross, Marvin Gaye, and the young Michael Jackson (pg. 13), but Gordy only slept with Ross.

Arne Næss Jr.
Norwegian shipping heir and mountaineer

1978

1986–1999

Næss and Ross lived apart (he in London, she in Connecticut) for most of their marriage but still found the time to have two monomaniacally named boys: Ross Arne Næss and actor Evan Ross. She found out she was getting divorced when her husband announced it on a Norwegian interview show. Overraskelse! ("Surprise!")

Diana Ross

Ross (with her Supremes) was discovered by Motown Records' Berry Gordy, with whom she had a five-year illicit affair as he maneuvered to launch her solo career.

When Ross realized she was pregnant with Berry Gordy's child, she quickly married Ellis (the first of her two white husbands) to cover up the infidelity. She only came clean when daughter Rhonda Ross Kendrick was noticeably "blacker" than their other two children.

Robert Ellis
Music manager for Motown

1971–1977

The prime-time superstar couple (he on the *The Six Million Dollar Man*, she on *Charlie's Angels*) claimed they split because of job stress, but the real reason was soon revealed, and his name was Ryan O'Neal. At their divorce hearing in 1982, Fawcett said that Majors had a million-dollar heart as well: He wanted to renew their wedding vows despite her cheating.

Lee Majors
American actor from *The Six Million Dollar Man* and *The Fall Guy*

Fawcett and Orr ended up in court, where she sued him for slamming her head into the ground and choking her. In turn, he accused her of beating him with a bar stool. Orr claimed he was trying to calm Fawcett down after she destroyed his house with a bat, and the judge bought it, sentencing him to three years' probation and no prison time.

James Orr
Film director

1997–1998

1973–1979

O'Neal competed with Jack Nicholson for Huston's love and won, at least some of the time. She spent enough time in the O'Neal home for Tatum (pg. 13) to describe her as "the official joint roller in our household because she was the best at it."

Anjelica Huston NEXT ▶

1979–2009

Farrah Fawcett

From 1979 on, O'Neal and Fawcett were in a scandal-filled relationship that produced one drug-addicted son, Redmond O'Neal, and countless tabloid headlines. She famously called him "overweight and boring" in a 1997 split, but their respective battles with cancer and troubles with their son brought them back together until her death from cancer in 2009.

Fawcett's famous red-bathing-suit poster, shot at her home in front of an Indian blanket the photographer had covering his car seat, sold more than 12 million copies and made her image a fixture in dorm rooms, mechanic shops, and hair salons around the world. She was only on *Charlie's Angels* for one year before quitting and being replaced by Cheryl Ladd.

According to Angela Bowie, O'Neal spent a lot of drunken nights in London trying to bed Bianca Jagger. It must have worked, because his daughter, Tatum (pg. 13), was so inspired by her father's girlfriend that she modeled her Oscar acceptance outfit, a custom tux, on Bianca's wedding suit.

Bianca Jagger p. 49 ▶

Robert Graham
American sculptor

After Huston married monumental sculptor Robert Graham in 1992, she insisted that he build her a massive, windowless fortress if he wanted to continue living in sketchy Venice Beach, California. He complied, and they were happily married until his death in 2008.

Mackenzie's 2009 memoirs included a bombshell: She alleged that her father, John Phillips, raped her before her 1979 wedding and carried on a sexual relationship with her for ten years thereafter. Her mother, Michelle Phillips, refuted the claim, citing Mackenzie's history of mental illness and drug abuse.

◄ p. 51 Mackenzie Phillips

◄ p. 56 Ryan O'Neal

1979–1989

Bob Richardson
Fashion photographer

Huston met rebel photographer Richardson while posing for a *Harper's Bazaar* spread and started dating him when she was eighteen and he was forty-two. His iconic photos of her, particularly a black-and-white portrait showing Anjelica with smoke curling out of her mouth, helped define her on-screen persona.

1992–2008

1969–1972

Nicholson has called Huston the love of his life. Although they both dated other people, it was different when Nicholson told her he'd impregnated actress Rebecca Broussard in 1989. "Anjelica's first response was, 'You have to support this woman.' Her second response was to 'beat the hell out of me,'" reports Nicholson.

1973–1989

1975

Anjelica Huston
The daughter of renowned director John Huston, Anjelica's acting career took off when she costarred with Jack Nicholson in a remake of *The Postman Always Rings Twice*. By then she'd already been living with him for eight years. Their home was the center of the 1970s Hollywood drug scene and the place where Roman Polanski was arrested for drugging and raping a thirteen-year-old model in 1977.

John Phillips
Singer in The Mamas and the Papas

John and Michelle Phillips made beautiful music together literally and figuratively until Michelle's infidelity split them apart and contributed to the fracturing of their band, The Mamas and the Papas.

Denny Doherty
Singer in The Mamas and the Papas

While John Phillips was California Dreamin' that everything was fine with his marriage, his wife Michelle was getting it on with band- and housemate Doherty. The Phillipses moved out, and the band ditched Michelle temporarily.

1965–1966

1962–1970

Michelle Phillips
Michelle married John Phillips in 1962; three years later, they became the lighter half of The Mamas and the Papas. The band ultimately broke up over Michelle Phillips's affair with the other Papa, Denny Doherty—which infuriated John and hurt Mama Cass Elliot, who had a thing for Doherty. Talk about keeping it in the family!

Dennis Hopper
The Kansas native has been nominated for two Oscars, once as an actor in *Hoosiers* and once as a writer of the epic *Easy Rider*, but Gen X-ers may prefer his turn as King Koopa in 1993's *Super Mario Bros.* adaptation.

Despite the brevity of their marriage, Phillips contends, "We were married for eight days and truly . . . they were the happiest days of my life."

1970

1991

◄ p. 140 Warren Beatty

1970–1972

Sandra Knight
Painter

Susan Anspach
American actress from *Five Easy Pieces*

Nicholson met Broussard while she was waitressing at Helena's in Los Angeles and got her some parts in a few of his movies. He also got her pregnant (twice) and broke up his decades-long relationship with Anjelica Huston in the process.

Rebecca Broussard
American actress

Topher Grace

Born Christopher John Grace, Topher settled on the second and third syllables for his name. He grew up in Darien, Connecticut, where his sister played soccer with Kate Bosworth (pg. 70) and his babysitter was Chlöe Sevigny. But nepotism didn't pay off until his boarding school classmate's producer parent cast him as Eric Forman in *That '70s Show* and launched his (well-deserved) career.

Grace and fashion model Trump dated for a brief period, appearing in New York and Vegas hot spots and then disappearing into the night.

2006

Ivanka Marie Trump

Daughter of Ivana and The Donald, Ivanka Trump holds the title of Vice President of Real Estate Development and Acquisitions for the Trump Organizations (and that's just the front side of her business card). But this heiress is no Paris (pg. 89)—"I work thirteen-hour days for my money."

Ivanka and Kushner wed in a decidedly un-Trump ceremony (they registered for a $34 Bundt-cake pan at Williams-Sonoma) after she converted to Judaism for the Orthodox Jewish groom.

🔒 2009–

Jared Kushner
Publisher of *New York Observer*

2° to Adam Brody ▶
3° to Kate Moss ▶
4° to Jude Law ▶

Teresa Palmer p. 147 ▶

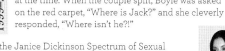

2007–2009

Nicholson's relationship with supermodel Hollman allegedly produced a love child—a claim made by said child, Winnie's daughter, Honey. "We have similar facial features, and my mom says I have the same temper as him. . . . I scream and shout a lot," said Honey, only proving that she could easily be related to Christian Slater (pg. 22).

Winnie Hollman
Danish model

Kate Moss NEXT ▶

Lara Flynn Boyle p. 128 ▶

1980–1982
2004

1999–2001

Boyle was a passenger in her mother's Mercedes when Nicholson drove it head-on into a BMW in the Hollywood Hills in 1999. She fled the scene, possibly because she was also dating David Spade (pg. 129) at the time. When the couple split, Boyle was asked on the red carpet, "Where is Jack?" and she cleverly responded, "Where isn't he?!"

1973–1989
1970–1972
1962–1968 🔒
1968–1970

In 1994, Nicholson had a protracted legal battle with his onetime love, Anspach. He lent the actress $400,000 over the years to pay for her Santa Monica home, but decided to foreclose on the house after she wrote a letter to *Vanity Fair* in 1994, complaining that they hadn't mentioned her baby with Jack in a recent profile.

1990–1993

Jack Nicholson

Nicholson had an unusual childhood. He was raised to believe that his grandparents were his parents and his young mother was his big sister— a mind fuck that may have influenced his acting choices. His first films were *The Cry Baby Killer*, *The Terror*, *The Shooting*, *Back Door to Hell*, and *The St. Valentine's Day Massacre*. And then of course there's *Chinatown*, whose plot line bears a remarkable similarity to his real life.

On the Janice Dickinson Spectrum of Sexual Satisfaction™, the world's first supermodel rated Nicholson as being "OK." For us regular civilians, who haven't banged every star in the Hollywood sky, that translates to "fair to excellent."

1980

Janice Dickinson p. 139

Trudeau met Nicholson while on a book tour to Los Angeles. After sleeping with him in the backseat of a limo, she arranged to run into him to explain her behavior. Instead, she got caught getting it on with Nicholson in the Beverly Wilshire Hotel men's room by a house detective.

1979

Margaret Trudeau p. 50

Moss fell for Brand after being introduced to his stand-up comedy by Sadie Frost (pg. 83), but Brand already had a connection to the model—he had helped her ex Pete Doherty with his heroin addiction by "[holding the spoon] while he cooked up because he didn't have enough hands."

◀ p.147 **Russell Brand**

2006 💔

In 2004, Nicholson was spotted out with Moss and said, "There are two kinds of women. The ones who want to jump into bed with me and the ones who want to slap my face . . . I'm hoping Kate doesn't slap me in the face."

◀ BACK **Jack Nicholson** 2004 💔

◀ p.82 **Daniel Craig** 2004 💔

◀ p.84 **Jamie Dornan** 2006 💔

◀ p.76 **Helena Christensen**

◀ p.143 **Linda Evangelista**

Evangelista's mysterious but beautiful child Augustin James was born in 2006 through an alleged liaison with Gucci billionaire Pinault, who was dating Salma Hayek when the child emerged.

2005–2006

Francois-Henri Pinault
🔒 Gucci heir

Hayek and Pinault's relationship started in 2006 and has had its ups and downs. They broke up, had a daughter, got back together, and eventually wed in 2009.

🔒 2006–

Salma Hayek
Mexican actress (of Lebanese and Spanish descent) Hayek had the title role in the Mexican telenovela *Teresa* but left her homeland to make it in Robert Rodriguez's (pg. 38) *Desperado*. When it comes to love, Hayek has said, "I keep waiting to meet a man who has more balls than I do."

What better candidate to be a "manny" than an ex-boyfriend? That's probably Hayek's philosophy—she still relies on her ex, Lucas, to babysit her daughter, Valentina.

◀ p.46 **Josh Lucas** 2003 💔

◀ p.28 **Stephen Dorff**

Model Moss was wearing a vintage flapper dress from the 1920s when she met Depp for the first time. "I knew from the first moment we talked that we were going to be together," and they were, until they broke off their engagement and he settled down with French singer Vanessa Paradis (pg. 114).

Johnny Depp

💘 1994–1997

Kate Moss

Fourteen-year-old mini-model Moss was discovered at JFK airport and soon personified the "waif" look, which morphed into "heroin chic." Despite her style's nickname, her drug of choice was always cocaine, as uncovered by London's *Daily Mirror* in 1995 when it published snaps of her doing lines (four in forty minutes).

2003 💔

🔒 2005–2007

💔 1999

💔 2005–2006

💔 1998

Edward Norton

The first rule of Ed Norton: You do not talk about Ed Norton. The notoriously closed-lipped anti-celebrity broke out as the crazed killer in 1996's *Primal Fear* and starred in *Fight Club*. When he isn't playing freaks, Norton works with his grandfather's nonprofit, building affordable housing.

1999–2003 💔

Hayek had high hopes for her relationship with Norton, saying "I am thinking about having a child soon." But the couple split, about a month after his ex, Courtney Love (pg. 61), told *Vanity Fair* that Norton would "never marry Hayek—for one, he can barely understand half of what she's saying."

2003–2004 💔

Pete Doherty
Singer for the band The Libertines

Moss met her drug-addled soul mate at her thirty-first birthday and the two snogged, sang, and caroused for a couple of years. The supermodel planned an elaborate Balinese wedding, but the fete was finished when Doherty failed to show after being ordered to rehab following a drug arrest in Britain just two nights before.

Billy Zane

Jamie Burke

Evan Dando

1996–1999

💔 Love credits Norton with saving her life after a descent into despair and drugs following Kurt Cobain's (pg. 61) suicide in 1994. "I was high. And then I met Edward, who came to my rescue. It was an intimidating job to be my boyfriend right then."

May Andersen
Danish Victoria's Secret and *Sports Illustrated* swimsuit model Andersen was involved in an air-rage incident in 2006 in which she reportedly hit a flight attendant and then claimed that she might have been asleep at the time.

Kurt Cobain
Singer and guitarist for band Nirvana

The Sid & Nancy of the 1990s, Cobain and Love were rock incarnate. "I can't believe how much happier I am . . . I'm so blinded by love," said Cobain shortly after getting married. But their romance ended tragically in 1994 with Cobain's suicide.

🔒 1991–1994

Billy Zane
Zane has made a career of playing creeps, both on water (*Dead Calm, Titanic*) and off (*The Case of the Hillside Stranglers, Twin Peaks*). His seafaring oeuvre extends to bad comedies like Adam Sandler's (pg. 27) first feature, *Going Overboard*. Zane claims he shaved his head because he's an avid swimmer—you know, for aquadynamics.

💔 2004–2008

Zane and British babe Brook had planned to tie the knot, until her father's death made her rethink her priorities and call it off.

Kelly Brook
The British glamour model turned actress never shied away from flashing her flesh in the past, but, after filming had finished on the movie *Three*, she requested that the producers cut her nude scenes (they refused).

Johnny Depp p. 114 ▶
Sophie Monk p. 88 ▶

2005–2006

💔 1998–2004

💔

Jason Statham
The English action star is known for doing his own stunts in films like *The Transporter* and *Crank*. And for his bald good looks.

Courtney Love
Rocker Love will always be known as Kurt Cobain's widow and the mother of their daughter, Frances Bean. But, despite the drug addictions, confessions of going down on Ted Nugent at age "twelve and a half," and assorted outbursts and insanities, this girl can rock.

1996–1999

Before she married Kurt Cobain, Love and Corgan were an item. They rekindled their relationship in 2006 when Love was relaunching her music career.

💔 2006–2009

💔 2006

Billy Corgan
Notorious perfectionist Corgan drove the Smashing Pumpkins to stardom but wasn't able to keep the addictions of drummer Jimmy Chamberlin and bassist D'arcy Wretzky from dragging them apart.

Lindsay Lohan p. 93 ▶
Sienna Miller p. 82 ▶

Burke met Moss on Richard Branson's private Caribbean island and then spent a romantic New Year's holiday with her, skiing in Aspen—all to the surprise of his live-in girlfriend, Jessie Leonard. Burke's explanation? "[Moss] swept me off my feet. It was flattering."

Love dated wannabe rocker Burke (he's in the band Bloody Social) and told friends she had found an "Adonis." But she may have found more of a Hermes (Greek mythology, anyone?), since the model flitted back and forth between her and Lindsay Lohan (pg. 93) around the same time.

2005–2006

💔 2006

💔 2006 2007

💔 💔

The couple met at a February 2007 party celebrating Miller's film *Factory Girl*, and they took off for Tulum, Mexico, three weeks later. By June, Burke had dumped Miller over a rumored hookup with Diddy, which the music mogul and Miller both denied.

Steady girlfriend Leonard found out that Burke was cheating on her with Kate Moss (pg. 60) while watching the news over the New Year's holiday. "There was this horrible sick feeling in my stomach. I kept thinking: 'No, no, no,'" she said. She called Burke's mother, who told her, "Unfortunately, you and Jamie need to speak."

Jessie Leonard
Australian model

2004–2005 💔

2007–2008 💔

Jamie Burke
Pasty-complexioned, long-haired Burke modeled for Calvin Klein and hearkened back to the stylish days of grunge and Johnny Depp (pg. 114) during *21 Jump Street*. And the chicks dig him.

Evan Dando NEXT ▶

◄ p.145 **Bijou Phillips**

Orlando Bloom — p.71 ▲

2007–

Whitney Port

Perhaps the most sensible star to emerge from MTV's series of reality soaps, Port appeared on *The Hills* after rooming with Christina Schuller of *Laguna Beach* fame. In 2008 her NYC spin-off *The City* premiered, right around the time she launched her clothing line Eva & A, with the backing of her fashion-businessman father.

Dando was the second Winona Ryder (pg. 113) ex that Moss dated (the first was Johnny Depp, pg. 114). In fact, he was there to help Moss out following that split.

"Real-ationship" or "fauxmance"? In the world of MTV reality, the dividing line is wafer thin. However, according to the DVDs, Lyon met Port while on *The Hills* and things heated up when she moved to New York for her spin-off *The City*.

1995

1998 ❣

Evan Dando

Dando's band, The Lemonheads, scored hits in the 1990s with a cover of "Mrs. Robinson" and "My Drug Buddy," but he spiraled into decline because of crack cocaine, too many celebrity hookups, and a lack of new hits.

◄ BACK **Kate Moss**

Miranda Kerr

When Kerr won an Australian modeling competition at fourteen, conservative Aussies claimed her bathing suit shoot amounted to child pornography (welcome to the modeling biz, Australia). She went on to appear in the Victoria's Secret catalog and was dubbed "the next Macpherson."

These fellow Aussies dated and modeled together, and Kerr even signed with Lyon's sister's PR company. So when Kerr was seen smooching Orlando Bloom (pg. 71) while still supposedly dating Lyon, it was Lyon's sister who fielded the media calls.

This short-lived romance ended when Chasez saw Reid flirting with other dudes in Miami over New Year's. According to friends, he "basically said forget it."

2008–2009 ❣
2004–2007 ❣

Jay Lyon

The Australian model-musician was born Brent Tuhtan but changed his name following a professional "name analysis," starting fresh with his band Tamarama and a starring gig on MTV's *The City*.

2002–2003

2002–2003

2002–2003

2001

◄ p.111 **Nikki DeLoach**   1994–1997 ❣

Josh "J. C." Chasez

J. C., one of the least-gay *NSYNC members, got his start as a Mouseketeer, where he met future bandmate Justin Timberlake (pg. 98).

Further entangling the real-life sexual web between the housewives, Hatcher dated Eva Longoria's ex-boyfriend Stephen Kay, allegedly because she knew it would piss Eva off. No hard feelings, said Longoria's quick-thinking publicist. "Eva and Tony [Parker] have never been happier together, and Eva wishes the same happiness for Teri."

Longoria dated J. C. while also seeing future husband Tony Parker on the side. The split inspired J. C. to write never-released songs that not-so-subtly alluded to their breakup, including "She Wears Me Out," "I Found You Out," and "Fuck with My Mind."

Tony Parker
San Antonio Spurs basketball player

Longoria married Spurs point guard Parker in a lavish Paris wedding in 2007, but her trust was immediately tested when a gossip blog said he'd had an affair with French model Alexandra Paressant. Parker sued for $40 million and the blog recanted.

2004

2004–2005

◄ p.128 **Teri Hatcher**

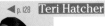

2006–2007

Stephen Kay
New Zealand actor and director

Eva Longoria Parker

When asked about her best sex of the year in 2004, Longoria responded "Probably with my vibrator. I own two." Just two of the reasons she scores *Maxim*'s Hottest Female Star spot twice in 2005 and 2006.

2006–

Dando married English model Moses at the Boathouse in New York's Central Park and vowed to leave his skirt-chasing, drug-taking days behind. So far, so good!

2000–

1993–1995

1993–1994

Elizabeth Moses
Fashion model

This classic of the "are they or aren't they" relationship genre featured Hatfield living with Dando in his Boston grotto, and numerous song collaborations and duets, but no leaked sex tapes or teary confessions on *Oprah* . . . yet.

Juliana Hatfield
The Juliana Hatfield Three album *Become What You Are* was a huge alternative hit in 1993—especially the song "My Sister" and "Spin the Bottle," the latter being featured in the film *Reality Bites.*

Carson Daly
Daly gave up a golf scholarship at Loyola Marymount University (he had caddied for O. J. Simpson, pg. 33) to work as a radio intern for Jimmy Kimmel. His gig as the mellow host of MTV's *TRL* made him the modern-day Casey Kasem.

Daly found out he was single when he "woke up to Howard Stern [pg. 104] telling me my relationship with [Hewitt] was over." She had told her publicist before telling her boyfriend.

💔 1997–1999

♥ 2007–

Kylie Minogue p. 67 ▶

Jennifer Love Hewitt p. 110 ▶

2007 💔

Tara Reid
The *American Pie* beauty was the consummate Hollywood party girl, inspiring Mötley Crüe's Tommy Lee (pg. 32) to say she could drink him under the table. "She's out of her fucking mind." But a photo of her exposed breast (epic nip slip) at Puff Daddy's (pg. 81) thirty-fifth birthday in 2004 led to years of interviews about "doughnut mastopexy."

💔

⛓ 2000–2001

Reid met Daly on an MTV shoot in Cancún in 2000 and he proposed to her three months later, but she called it off mere weeks before the ceremony. "I lost my appetite—I was numb," Reid said. Years later, she said, "If I would have married Carson, I'd probably have kids by now . . . I wouldn't have had all that crazy partying."

💔 2001–2002

Siri Pinter
TV producer

Bridget Moynahan
American model

When QB Brady split with GF Moynahan, he probably expected a clean break with no surprises—it's not like she was pregnant or anything (she was). That would be like having a perfect season and then losing in the Super Bowl (he did).

David Schwimmer p. 66 ▶

💔

2002

Reid stalked Brady (and succeeded!) around the time he won the 2002 Super Bowl. Reports said that he initially didn't call right away when she gave him her number.

After starring in the 2001 *NSYNC-loving feature film *On the Line* with Lance Bass (with whom she was nominated for a Best Lip-Lock Teen Choice Award) and Joey Fatone, Chriqui briefly took up with their hunkier bandmate,

Emmanuelle Chriqui
The *Entourage* star played against type as a Palestinian hair stylist in Adam Sandler's (pg. 27) *You Don't Mess with the Zohan*—the Moroccan actress was raised as an orthodox Jew.

Tom Brady
Brady isn't just a dreamy all-American boy with a cute chin dimple. He can also throw one of those pointy brown balls real good—good enough to lead the New England Patriots to three Super Bowl wins, making him one of the all-time greatest quarterbacks and finally giving the ladies a reason to love football.

2004–2006

💔

🔒 2007–

Gisele Bündchen p. 72 ▶

Claws-Out Catfights

Actors are a high-strung breed, but if you think the starlets can keep the sparks on the set and off the Sunset Strip, you'd be wrong. And, more often than not, the claws come out over a boy. In 2006, Lindsay Lohan (pg. 93), with the help of bad-influence Kate Moss (pg. 60), took Sharpie to tile in the restroom of a New York City bar to scrawl, "Scarlett is a bloody c__t," in reference to Johansson (pg. 48), who dated Lohan's boyfriend Jared Leto (pg. 99). Cameron Diaz (pg. 98) went ballistic for a full forty-minute face-off when Justin Timberlake (pg. 98) showed up at a 2007 Golden Globes party with Jessica Biel (pg. 98), just five days after Diaz and Timberlake had publicly split. And Angelina Jolie (pg. 105) went off on Madonna (pg. 103) over a boy as well—in this case, Madonna's adopted Malawian boy, David. "I would never take a child away from a place where adoption is illegal," Jolie said. She reportedly accused Madonna of adopting for publicity rather than for the child's well-being.

A Match Made in Hollywood

There's no JDate for celebrities, and sometimes even the biggest names need a little Yenta. That's when a good manager, agent, costar, or ex-lover steps in to help two shooting stars form a binary system. After dating briefly in 2003, Lauren Graham (pg. 123) introduced her ex-boyfriend Matthew Perry (pg. 123) to Piper Perabo (pg. 123), whom he dated for a while before going back to Graham in 2008. Brooke Burns (pg. 138) was introduced to superstar Bruce Willis (pg. 138) by her then-boyfriend, super-rich Stephen Bing. Mandy Moore (pg. 111) has her own mom (a tennis fan) to thank for helping her get with Andy Roddick (pg. 111). And Brad Pitt (pg. 105) and Jennifer Aniston (pg. 108) were set up by their managers—who should have been fired immediately.

Carla Alapont
Spanish model

Schwimmer dated model and **American Pie: Band Camp** star Alapont for a couple of years (his second taste of American pie after Tara Reid). According to a friend of hers, he asked for Alapont's hand in marriage. Why she refused is anybody's guess.

Mili Avital
Israeli actress Avital left a successful career in the Holy Land to move to sinful Manhattan in 1994 and a starring role in *Stargate*.

Gina Lee
Punk musician

Blonde Asian model-turned-punk-rocker Gina Lee dumped Schwimmer, apparently blowing his mind and causing him to call her constantly and hit on her friends.

Tina Barrett
British pop singer

The couple met on the set of the aptly titled **Kissing a Fool** in 1997. "A lot of men today don't have the courage to fall in love," Schwimmer said. "The only one I really fell for was Mili." The relationship was doomed when mutual **Friend** Jennifer Aniston (pg. 108) married Brad Pitt (pg. 105) and Avital put pressure on Schwimmer to follow suit with her.

Schwimmer beat out Fred Durst (pg. 34) for the heart of Barrett, who had dated the Limp Bizkit singer only days before she met Schwimmer in London.

▲ p. 48

Sophie Dahl   2002
♥

James Gooding
British model

Minogue was asked if she thought she would marry Gooding, to which she replied, "I think so . . . yes. I always try and not say yes or no, because who knows? But I'm sure it will happen." They split a few months later.

2000–2002

1993–1994

◄ p. 62 Evan Dando

Zoe Buckman
British photographer

Schwimmer met the waitress-turned-photographer while shooting his directorial debut, **Run Fatboy Run**, in London's East End. Things moved fast with the Brit, twenty years his junior, and Schwimmer spent Christmas 2008 with her family in Stoke Newington, in the London borough of Hackney.

Schwimmer met his first **American Pie** starlet at the Lennox Lewis–Hasim Rahman fight in Las Vegas, and they were inseparable for the next few months, although his **Friends** costars reportedly didn't like her.

2007–
2002–2003
2003–2004
1998–2001
2004

David Schwimmer

Best known as Ross Geller by anyone who turned on a television between 1994 and 2004, Schwimmer got his start acting in plays at Beverly Hills High School. Schwimmer has never married, perhaps because his mother was the divorce lawyer to the stars, helping Elizabeth Taylor, Roseanne Barr, and more screw their spouses (in the legal sense).

Claudia Schiffer

Schiffer, the dreamy dame from Deutschland, has graced more than 500 magazine covers and bears a shocking resemblance to beauty Brigitte Bardot.

When Copperfield hooked up with Schiffer, it gave hope to magic geeks everywhere. Unfortunately, the man who made a career of making things disappear couldn't do the same for their work schedules. As Copperfield explained, "We're married to our careers and we basically cheated on our careers by stealing time to be together."

♥ 1993–1999
♥ 1999–2000

When Schiffer broke off her engagement to British lothario Tim Jeffries, rumors swirled it was because he couldn't afford her. Schiffer denied it, claiming, "We separated because of personal reasons," and not because she didn't get the diamond-encrusted Rolls-Royce with mink interior that she wanted for Christmas.

David Copperfield
Despite dating the world's most beautiful women, Copperfield, the most commercially successful magician in history, continues to combat rumors about his sexuality. "I'm not gay . . . I've got 300 women in my little black book." Fine, whatever—just tell us how you made the Statue of Liberty disappear, and we'll drop it.

◄ p. 63 Tara Reid   2001–2002 ♥

Minogue and Martinez held strong for four years, but their relationship broke down during the summer of 2007 when she walked out on him after a public argument at a Saint-Tropez restaurant.

Olivier Martinez
French actor

1999–2002

Mira Sorvino p. 51 ▲

Sorvino's father seemed a little smitten with Martinez himself when he said, "We had a dinner. He has such personal charm . . . a man, a real man."

David Spade p. 129 ▲

David Spade copped to a quick fling but kept mum about the possibility of impregnation until DNA tests confirmed that he was the father of Grace's daughter, born in August 2008. Score one for the little guys!

Grace met Shore at the Playboy mansion and gave him her number. He was "too busy" to go on an official date, so they just went back to his place instead. She told Howard Stern (pg. 104) that the weasel was surprisingly good in the sack.

2007–2008

Pauly Shore

If you have basic cable and have been home on a Saturday afternoon, chances are you've seen a Pauly Shore movie. The MTV personality became a hit with Gen-Xers in the 1990s, but not with critics. Shore won the Razzie award for "Worst New Star of the Decade" in 2000.

💔 2005
💔 1997

Jillian Grace
Playboy Playmate

Lenny Kravitz p. 69 ▶

This early 1990s relationship blossomed inside Kravitz's New York loft, where Minogue was confronted by Kravitz's pet snake, a six-foot python, Rex.

2003–2007

Kylie Minogue

When Aussie Minogue burst onto the 1980s music scene with a poppy remake of "The Loco-Motion," who knew that she would still be belting them out today? She transformed herself from girl-next-door to gay icon and sex symbol, and she survived breast cancer. But she garnered her biggest audience, 13.31 million viewers, with a cameo on a *Dr. Who* episode.

💔 1997
💔 1993
💔 1988–1991
💔 1996–1998
💔 2003
💔 1994

💔 1998

Michael Hutchence p. 73 ▶

Having met by chance in a bar, INXS front man Hutchence and Minogue were all the rage in Australia in the late 1980s. Though the couple broke up in 1991 and Hutchence died in 1997, Minogue says he speaks to her from beyond the grave. "I have had one particularly intense experience that let me know that Michael was still around, like he had come to say 'hello.'"

In the mid-1990s, Kylie's career entered a downward spiral and she credited photographer-filmmaker Sednaoui with helping her get her life back on track. After they split, Kylie told the press that she might never find the right man.

Tim Jeffries
British heir and playboy

Jean Claude Van Damme p. 13 ▼

Jay Kay p. 17 ▼

When Kylie dated Green Shield Stamps heir Jeffries, her style of dress became noticeably more upmarket. However, other than changes to her fashion, the Brit didn't do much for Kylie, and he was promptly ousted.

Stephane Sednaoui
French photographer

Natalie Imbruglia NEXT ▶

1993–1994

1996–1997

British heir Jeffries got together with Macpherson just a month after his grandfather, tycoon Richard Tompkins, died, leaving his grandson a $231 million fortune. Good timing, Elle!

Elle Macpherson p. 51 ▶

Jason Momoa

Momoa starred in *Stargate Atlantis*, where his signature dreads became so painful that he had to petition the executive producers to write an episode in which his character has them cut. The nice producers allowed him to replace the five pounds of nap with a custom $10,000 wig.

2006– ♥

Momoa broke fiancée Simmone Jade Mackinnon's heart when he began seeing Bonet. He and Bonet have two kids, including son Nakoa-Wolf Manakauapo Namakaeha Momoa—a name you rarely find on those gift store souvenir license plates.

Lisa Bonet

Bonet is the daughter of unusual parents—not because her father is black and her mother is Jewish, but because her father was an opera singer. Freakish! She became a star in 1984 as Denise Huxtable, hottest daughter on *The Cosby Show*. Her popularity led to the spin-off *A Different World*, but a graphic sex scene with Mickey Rourke in 1987's *Angel Heart* tainted that stardom.

When Bonet married Kravitz (known as "Romeo Blue" at the time) at the height of her *Cosby Show* fame, his corrupting influence was obvious to all—from Bonet's personality conflicts with coworkers to her even more shocking pierced nose. The couple lasted for a few happy years before Kravitz split for a bachelor pad in the Bahamas, saying, "Maybe I just don't care that much about sex. It's great, but I believe music's better."

1993

The twenty-three-year-old Imbruglia had a lasting influence on thirty-three-year-old Kravitz: She persuaded the rocker to snip his signature dreads. Rumor has it that Imbruglia was in cahoots with his ex-wife, Lisa Bonet, who is said to have wielded the shears.

1998

Kylie Minogue

◄ BACK

Minogue was engaged to racing champ Villeneuve until '01, when the singer called it off so that she could focus on her acting career which, so far, is stuck in a pit stop.

1999–2001 ♘

Jacques Villeneuve
Canadian race car driver

Dannii Minogue

Pop sensation Kylie Minogue (pg. 67) and her younger sister, Dannii, both got started as child actors in Australian soaps. Danii joined the successful but cloyingly named *Young Talent Time*, and her solos on that show carried her to sold-out nationwide tours.

Craig Logan
British boy-band member

2002 ♥♥
2003

1992–1993

When Imbruglia reentered the world of casual dating in 2008, she stuck to the familiar territory of rock stars at first, enjoying a brief romance in London with Followill.

William "will.i.am" Adams Jr.

When he's not hanging with Fergie (pg. 98) or creating an Emmy-winning song to support Barack Obama, will.i.am is busy working on his film career.

Nathan Followill
Drummer for band Kings of Leon

2008

will.i.am couldn't keep his hands off Imbruglia's lovely lady lumps during a makeout session at the end of 2008 while partying in a nightclub in London.

2008 ♥♥

Daniel Paul Johns

The front man of rock band Silverchair is something of a comeback king. After battling anorexia in 1997, Johns was later diagnosed with reactive arthritis and it was thought he might never play guitar again. However, within a year he was back on tour and in 2007 was number eighteen on *Rolling Stone*'s list of the twenty-five most-underrated guitarists.

1997

1998

Natalie Imbruglia

If you're Australian and want a music career, get a role on the soap opera *Neighbours*. It worked for Kylie Minogue (pg. 67) and years later for Imbruglia. Her first single, a cover of "Torn," was a huge hit, but songwriter Anne Preven called it a "lobotomized" rendition.

Two years into his *Friends* roller-coaster ride, Schwimmer dumped un-famous girlfriend Sarah Trimble and started seeing Imbruglia. It was a passionate affair—Schwimmer threatened to quit *Friends* to accompany homesick Imbruglia Down Under.

1996–1997 ♥♥ 🔒 2003–2008

Vanessa Paradis p. 114 ▶

Lima (five feet, ten inches) is a cool three inches taller than Kravitz (five feet, seven inches), but he was (and remains) seventeen years older, so perhaps this cancels it out. They dated for a while, and possibly even got engaged, after she appeared in his video for "Yesterday Is Gone."

Adriana Lima

The Victoria's Secret model is a devout Catholic and attends church weekly. "Sex is for after marriage," said Spike TV's "Hottest Girl on the Planet" for 2007.

1987–1993 🔒
1992–1995 💔

2001–2003
💔 2007 ♂

2001–2003 ♂
2005–2007 💔
2009– 🔒

On the verge of an official breakup from Josh Hartnett (pg. 72) in May 2007, Cruz postponed a trip to Europe multiple times so she could spend time with Kravitz while he was on tour and celebrate her thirty-third birthday together.

Penelope Cruz NEXT ▶

Lenny Kravitz

One of the few possessors of a true Jewfro, Kravitz was born to Jewish producer Sy Kravitz and Bahamian actress Roxie Roker, known for playing Helen Willis on *The Jeffersons*. Record labels were initially concerned that his sound wasn't black enough for R&B or white enough for rock-and-roll.

💔 2003–2004 ♂

Lima was the world's hottest virgin until she married Jaric in early 2009, and they were expecting their baby by the end of the year. Jaric uttered the understatement of the decade when he said, "We wanted this. We were ready."

In a 2007 *Vanity Fair* article, Kidman dropped the bomb that she had been secretly engaged to a mysterious partner between her marriages to Tom Cruise (pg. 70) and Keith Urban. Kravitz was the only person seen entering or leaving her apartment building during that time, so it was either him or the doorman.

Marco Jaric
Basketball player

Prince Wenzeslaus of Liechtenstein
Prince of Liechtenstein

Keith Urban
New Zealand–born country singer

2003–2004
2003–2004 ♂

2005– 🔒

Nicole Kidman

Kidman was born in Honolulu, Hawaii (her father was a fellow at the U.S. National Institute of Mental Health), but moved back to Australia at age four. It was a role in *Days of Thunder* that brought her Tom Cruise (pg. 70) and a romance that her psychologist father should have warned her about!

Kidman and Q-Tip were introduced by Kidman's hairstylist friend. They went to the premiere of her film *The Hours* together, and Q-Tip was almost kicked out by a publicist who thought he shouldn't be there.

Q-Tip
Hip-hop artist

2003 💔

🔒 1990–2000
💔 1991

Tom Cruise NEXT ▶

Russell Crowe p. 143 ▶

Despite her denials, there is ample evidence that Kidman dated Crowe back in their early Aussie acting days. At a Hollywood awards ceremony in 2003, Crowe introduced her saying, "You used to be my secret, my dirty little secret." Then there are the lyrics to his band's song, "Somebody Else's Princess," that start with "Red hair, blue eyes, my baby gets me so good" and end with "So deeply imbedded in somebody else's princess."

Melissa Gilbert p.131

Katie Holmes p.150

Javier Bardem

Bardem (who is sometimes mistaken for Jeffrey Dean Morgan, pg. 153, of *Grey's Anatomy*) won an Academy Award for best supporting actor for his chilling portrayal of a sociopath in *No Country for Old Men*.

From *Jamón, Jamón* to *Vicky Christina Barcelona*, Cruz and Bardem's fictional on-screen affairs provide a mere glimpse into how mind-blowing their real sex life might be.

2007–
1999

2007
2005–2006
2001–2004

Penelope Cruz

Cruz studied classical ballet before hanging up her tutu for an acting career at age fifteen. The film *Jamón, Jamón* ("Ham! Ham!") made Cruz a star in the Spanish-speaking world, but her appearance in *Vanilla Sky* opposite Tom Cruise introduced her to the American audience.

◄ BACK Lenny Kravitz

◄ p.18 Matthew McConaughey

"Tom was seriously thinking of becoming a monk. And he thought he had to be celibate to maintain the purity of his instrument . . ." Rogers said, explaining their split. But first, she introduced him to Scientology.

1981
2005

Mimi Rogers
American actress

1987–1990

Cruise and Kidman were the ultimate celebrity couple after they met on *Days of Thunder*. They separated just before their tenth anniversary, and three months into Kidman's pregnancy; she later miscarried.

◄ BACK Nicole Kidman
1990–2000

Tom Cruise

Tom Cruise "the actor" has long been overshadowed by Tom Cruise "the overexuberant Scientologist" (it cured his dyslexia!). But there was a time when the talented star did his entertaining in movies like *Risky Business*, *The Color of Money*, and *Rain Man*, instead of in the tabloids.

2001–2004

On the set of *Vanilla Sky*, freshly single Cruise successfully caught Hollywood newcomer Cruz, maybe with a line something like, "If we marry, you won't even need to change the pronunciation of your last name."

Kate Bosworth

Bosworth got her break thanks to her girl-crush on ponies (actually, she was a champion equestrian), which earned her a part in 1998's *The Horse Whisperer*. She went from riding horses to riding waves in *Blue Crush*, and, next thing you know, she thinks she's Mrs. Superman.

Bosworth and Czuchry didn't just land their first TV series with the WB's *Young Americans*—they also got their first celebrity romance, which lasted a year longer than the show. The part, along with a role in *Remember the Titans*, convinced Bosworth to defer an acceptance to Princeton. The school eventually rescinded the offer.

James Rousseau
British model

2006–2008
2000–2002

Matt Czuchry
American actor

Lachey and Minnillo met when he made a guest appearance on her show *TRL*. They moved in together in 2007, the same year they were photographed having sex in a hotel hot tub by Mexican paparazzi.

Vanessa Minnillo

Minnillo is half Filipina and all fine, coming in at number fifteen on *Maxim*'s 2006 hot list (just above Christina Aguilera, pg. 44). She won the Miss Teen USA pageant in 1998, representing South Carolina, and went on to host MTV's *TRL* for four years.

◄ p.109 Nick Lachey

◄ p.26 Derek Jeter

◄ p.82 Sienna Miller

2006– ♥
2003–2006

In the midst of shooting ***All The Pretty Horses***, Damon broke up with Winona Ryder (pg. 113) and started seeing Cruz. Although both of them denied it, the horses weren't the only things running wild on set.

Matt Damon p. 113 ▲

Ben Foster
Foster isn't a murderous, bisexual psychopath, but you wouldn't know it from the characters he's played in films like *Hostage*, *3:10 to Yuma*, and the HBO series *Six Feet Under*.

Andy Samberg
American actor and comedian

This supposedly exclusive, supposedly secret relationship came to be because Dunst found Samberg funny—see, personality is important!

71

2007

Bloom and Dunst got "close" on the set of ***Elizabethtown*** in 2004, but the timing was off (they were both dating other people). Not so a year later, when Bloom was on a break from Bosworth and ambiguously declared, "If you want to screw around, it's your choice and you accept it when you're caught."

2000–2001

2005

2006

Josh Hartnett NEXT ▶

2008–2009   **Josh Hartnett** NEXT ▶

Dunst has a tendency to deny every relationship vehemently, but this time she was outed by ***Spider-Man*** director Sam Raimi: "I'm so dumb, because I met with them for dinner one night during the shooting . . . . And then I ask Kirsten, 'Can I drive you home?' And they look at each other and she goes, 'No, no, I'm going to play a game of Touch Ten with Toby.'"

2006

Cruz literally fell into Bloom's lap at L.A. hot spot Hyde. The pair danced the night away to "Runaround Sue," but after a few weeks of public hand-holding, the relationship seemingly evaporated.

2002–2006

Though Bloom declared, "It's heavenly when you're falling for someone and can't stop thinking about her," Bosworth ultimately wasn't that person.

Bloom went on at least one hot date with Minnillo only hours after she interviewed him on ***TRL***; she admitted she was nervous just standing near him.

2005 💕

Kirsten Dunst
She was a ten-year-old bloodsucking brat when she kissed Brad Pitt (pg. 105) in *Interview with the Vampire*, earning a Golden Globe nomination. Her Mary Jane turn in the *Spider-Man* films has been her biggest role to date, and also the closest she's gotten to drug addiction, despite rumors that she went to rehab in 2008. She says she was recovering from depression.

💕 2001	**Toby Maguire**	p. 45 ▶
💕 2002–2004	**Jake Gyllenhaal**	p. 18 ▶
💕 2005	**Zach Braff**	p. 111 ▶
💕 2007	**Fabrizio Moretti**	p. 78 ▶
💕 2008	**Justin Long**	p. 78 ▶

2007

	Helena Christensen	p. 76 ▶
	Adam Brody	p. 147 ▶

When Dunst moved on to Johnny Borrell, Brody was so broken up that he couldn't even see ***Spider-Man 3***, saying, "I don't want to weep on my popcorn all through the thing."

Orlando Bloom
For a practicing Buddhist, Bloom is strangely drawn to violence, having battled with a sword in eight of fifteen movie roles. He's said (jokingly, perhaps) that he got into acting for the women, and apparently the plan worked.

2006

2005

💕 2003

Weeks before a date with Edward Norton (pg. 60), Christensen outed her split with baby daddy Norman Reedus (pg. 73) by hanging with Bloom at his ***Pirates of the Caribbean*** premiere party.

2001 💕   💕 **2007–**

Bloom and Kerr started dating quietly in 2007 while she was still seeing model Jay Lyon (pg. 62), but elves are a patient folk. The couple's 2009 visit to her Catholic school's chapel calls into question their denials of any wedding plans.

According to Borrell, his messy ways doomed the relationship: "[Dunst] couldn't stand the smell of stale fags, beer, and kebabs in her nice living room. Can't say I blame her, really."

Johnny Borrell
Singer for British band Razorlight

Miranda Kerr p. 62 ▶

Guys will do anything to get with Bündchen. Brady famously dumped his girlfriend of three years, Bridget Moynahan (pg. 63), when she was three months pregnant for a chance with the apparently even more super model. But karma may be kicking in—since he dumped Moynahan, his Super Bowl success has suffered.

◀ p. 63 **Tom Brady**

Joao-Paulo Diniz
Brazilian supermarket heir

Brazilian supermarket billionaire Diniz pulled some strings to move an *Elle* photo shoot to his estate in Rio and in the process moved half-his-age supermodel Bündchen into his arms for a quick fling.

Playing Wonder Bread to Leonardo DiCaprio's bologna, Hartnett dated Bündchen both before and after she hooked up with the *Titanic* tsunami.

◀ BACK **Penelope Cruz** ❤ 2007

Dunst said Hartnett's on-camera kisses were the best she's had (topping kisses from Tobey Maguire, pg. 45, and Orlando Bloom, pg. 71). She met him on the set of 1999's *The Virgin Suicides*. "Sofia Coppola made me surprise him [in the scene] where I jump on him and start making out with him. It was pretty wonderful."

◀ BACK **Kirsten Dunst**

Johansson and Hartnett met on the set of *The Black Dahlia* and dated for a year. He broke up awith her over the phone after flirting with a New Zealand townie while shooting *Thirty Days of Night*.

◀ p. 35 **Chris Evans**

Kelly Slater p. 29 ▲ **Kelly Slater** p. 29 ▲

Slater supposedly started this relationship using the oldest tricks in the beach-bum book—giving Bündchen surf lessons and rubbing sunblock on her hard-to-reach places. Slater was so upset when they split that he skipped the premiere of his bio film *Letting Go*.

2005–2006 ❤

❍ 2007– 2000–2004 2000

Josh Hartnett
Hartnett took strong and silent to a new level and captured the hearts, and other organs, of girls across America in movies like *The Virgin Suicides* and *Pearl Harbor*— not bad for a squinty guy raised in the frozen tundra of Minnesota.

2007 2000–2004 ❤ ❤

Gisele Bündchen
The most famous of six Brazilian sisters (including Raquel, Graziela, Gabriela, Rafaela, and fraternal twin Patrícia), Gisele isn't just remarkably thin and busty; she's also the richest model on the planet. The girl known as "The Boobs from Brazil" has defended her cleavage, stating, "Some people say my boobs are fake. But all I can say is, go look at my family and you'll see mine are the smallest."

❤ 2000–2004

Christensen denied this relationship, saying they were just "super close friends," but that "super" says it all. The couple got together when Christensen tried to set Hartnett up with Rosario Dawson, and he said that, actually, he'd rather date Christensen.

2008–2009 ❤
2005–2006 ❤

2008 ❤ ❤ ❤
2007–2008

1996–2004

❤ 2007–2008

2006

Scarlett Johansson p. 48 ▼ Rihanna p. 132 ▼ Sienna Miller p. 82 ▼

Ellen Fenster
Childhood sweetheart of Josh Hartnett

Hartnett dated high school sweetheart Fenster in a storybook romance that ended in classic Hollywood style—he dumped her for a starlet named Scarlett. But he did buy her a $3.2 million mansion in their native Minneapolis, Minnesota, first.

2005 Katie Holmes p. 150 ▼

Helena Christensen

Kristen Zang
Fashion model

Nicolas Cage p. 12 ▼ 1992–1994 ❍

Sixteen and already wise to the ways of the world, Elite model Zang sent a photo of herself to INXS before a Detroit show. As a result, she got a backstage pass that she said led to her "first serious relationship," with lead singer Hutchence.

Bar Refaeli

Cover model Refaeli got her start in campaigns for the Israeli brands Pilpel (clothing) and Milki (chocolate pudding) before she became the new face of DiCaprio. In 2007 it was revealed that she had bailed on mandatory military service by faking a marriage to a family friend. "Why is it good to die for our country?" said the media-savvy swimsuit model. "What, isn't it better to live in New York?"

Amber Valletta
Model and actress

Sara Foster p. 47 ▶

2007

2006– ❤

This couple's relationship status is as malleable as a Middle East peace plan and as fraught with danger. Split number two, in 2007, was reportedly caused by DiCaprio's pining for ex-girlfriend Gisele Bündchen, so Refaeli hooked up with Bündchen's ex-boyfriend Kelly Slater (pg. 29) in Tel Aviv as a proportional retaliatory strike.

1998 2002 1995

Leonardo DiCaprio

Things got off to a "slow" start for the *Titanic* star, who began his career playing the adopted homeless boy on the last season of *Growing Pains*, followed by Johnny Depp's (pg. 114) developmentally delayed brother in *What's Eating Gilbert Grape* ("Gilbeeeeeeeert!").

Three years after they broke up, Hall allegedly leaked, then denied, rumors that she had lost her virginity to DiCaprio and found the experience disappointing.

1997 ❤

Bridget Hall

Texan Bridget Hall posed for her first swimsuit calendar at sixteen and reached the top of the swimsuit food chain, posing for the *Sports Illustrated* Swimsuit Issue in 2002.

2000–2004 ❤

Although the 2001 engagement rumors were debunked ("I'm only twenty years old," said Gisele), the couple's up-and-down relationship had its romantic moments, including long vacations spent in hotel rooms and "enviro" trips to rainy Machu Picchu. After they split Gisele put the jewelry DiCaprio had given her up for auction at Christie's.

1996-2000

DiCaprio and Zang split because of her understandable dislike of his obnoxious friends (known then as the "Pussy Posse") and their habit of inviting harems of girls over to party. Even a wedding proposal from DiCaprio didn't persuade her that he could grow up.

Norman Reedus

Reedus starred as Murphy McManus in 1999's *Boondock Saints*, and as Scud in 2002's *Blade II*, but his biggest role may have been as The Boyfriend in 1998's Life of Helena Christensen (pg. 76).

1998–2002

1997

Helena Christensen p. 76 ▶
Helena Christensen p. 76 ▶
Helena Christensen p. 76 ▶
Helena Christensen p. 76 ▶

2° to Heath Ledger ▶
3° to Courtney Love ▶
4° to Sean Combs ▶

Paula Yates

Born to a showgirl-erotic novelist and a popular British television presenter, saucy peroxide blonde rock journalist Yates married Boomtown Rats lead singer Bob Geldof in 1986, with Simon Le Bon as his best man. She died of a heroin overdose in 2000.

1995–1997 ❤

Yates ditched husband Bob Geldof for Hutchence and gave birth to their daughter, Heavenly Hiraani Tiger Lily. When Hutchence was found dead a year later, she battled his mother and sister for custody of Tiger and the rock star's estate. The battle continued until her death, when Geldof got custody of Tiger so she could grow up with her half-siblings.

1991 ❤

Michael Hutchence

The Australian INXS front man had a series of much-publicized relationships with models and singers as his band dominated the charts in the late 1980s. Sadly, however, he's best known for the relationship with himself that ended his life in 1997—a relationship called autoerotic asphyxiation.

1992–1995

1988–1991 ❤

Kylie Minogue p. 67

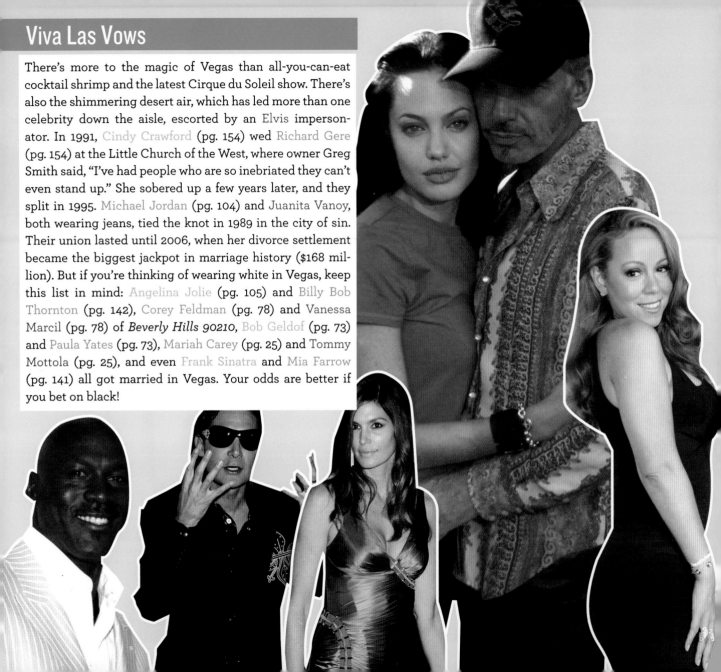

Viva Las Vows

There's more to the magic of Vegas than all-you-can-eat cocktail shrimp and the latest Cirque du Soleil show. There's also the shimmering desert air, which has led more than one celebrity down the aisle, escorted by an Elvis impersonator. In 1991, Cindy Crawford (pg. 154) wed Richard Gere (pg. 154) at the Little Church of the West, where owner Greg Smith said, "I've had people who are so inebriated they can't even stand up." She sobered up a few years later, and they split in 1995. Michael Jordan (pg. 104) and Juanita Vanoy, both wearing jeans, tied the knot in 1989 in the city of sin. Their union lasted until 2006, when her divorce settlement became the biggest jackpot in marriage history ($168 million). But if you're thinking of wearing white in Vegas, keep this list in mind: Angelina Jolie (pg. 105) and Billy Bob Thornton (pg. 142), Corey Feldman (pg. 78) and Vanessa Marcil (pg. 78) of *Beverly Hills 90210*, Bob Geldof (pg. 73) and Paula Yates (pg. 73), Mariah Carey (pg. 25) and Tommy Mottola (pg. 25), and even Frank Sinatra and Mia Farrow (pg. 141) all got married in Vegas. Your odds are better if you bet on black!

It's pretty obvious that celebrities intermingle, but sometimes the lines get more than crossed and what should have been a good old-fashioned love triangle turns into a square. Geena Davis (pg. 143) married her *The Fly* costar, Jeff Goldblum (pg. 142), in 1987, around the time that Renny Harlin (pg. 142) was producing girlfriend Laura Dern (pg. 142) in her Oscar-nominated *Rambling Rose*. In 1993 the couples swapped and Geena Davis started dating *Cliffhanger* director Harlin, while Dern got with Goldblum.

But wait, it gets weirder. Teri Hatcher (pg. 128) and Nicollette Sheridan (pg. 130) must have had interesting conversations on the set of their series *Desperate Housewives*, having both dated Michael Bolton (pg. 129) and David Spade (pg. 129).

Texan Owen Wilson (pg. 101) dated Sheryl Crow (pg. 100) for four years after they costarred in *The Minus Man*, and they split in 2002. She got engaged to Texan cyclist Lance Armstrong (pg. 100) but called it off in 2006, right around the time Wilson was dating Kate Hudson (pg. 101). And just a little while later, Hudson was traveling in Europe with boyfriend Armstrong.

After dating for four years and creating a beautiful child named Mingus Lucien Reedus, Christensen began denying rumors that she was seeing other guys. "I can't go anywhere with someone else who is famous without being linked with him," she said, a few months before coming clean about her split from Reedus.

p. 73 **Norman Reedus**

p. 60 **Ed Norton**

This couple was seen smooching at the *GQ* awards, where Norton was dubbed International Man of the Year, without any hint of Austin Powers irony.

Paul Banks
Lead singer of band Interpol

Banks was latest in a line of rockers to date Christensen, and their relationship continued her trend of dating younger dudes (he's ten years her junior).

2008

2003
1996–2002

p. 73 **Leonardo DiCaprio** 1997

p. 71 **Orlando Bloom** 2003

Helena Christensen

This Victoria's Secret Angel may also be the angel of death—two of her lovers, Michael Hutchence (pg. 73) and Heath Ledger (pg. 77), died untimely deaths. But a string of other famous hunks have survived—so far.

2005–

◀ 2° to Kylie Minogue
◀ 3° to Nicolas Cage
◀ 4° to Sarah Jessica Parker

p. 73 **Michael Hutchence**

Christensen and Hutchence started their affair when he cheated on Kylie Minogue (pg. 67) with her. They ended it when he cheated on her with British TV host, Paula Yates (pg. 73). The infidelity led to one of the most famous *GQ* covers ever, a picture of Christensen with the caption "Would you trade her in for Paula Yates?"

1992–1995
2007–2008
2004–2006

Christensen said that she and Danish rocker Walter-Hansen (of the band Grand Avenue) enjoyed ogling girls at parties. "I sometimes say, 'Look at her, she's got fantastic breasts.' We can sit all night talking about girls."

Rasmus Walter-Hansen
Danish rock star

Naomi Watts

Watts's father was Pink Floyd's road manager (her mother's voice can be heard on "Money" from *The Dark Side of the Moon*). When he passed, her mother moved the family from England to Australia, where Watts went to high school with Nicole Kidman (pg. 69).

1999–2001

Watts and Schreiber met at the Met museum gala in 2005, and the Aussie beauty quickly got aggressive. "I said, in a cheeky way, 'Don't you want my digits?'" He did (duh) and by 2009 they had two children. It turns out that Schreiber is such a devoted dad that he explored the possibility of wearing artificial breasts to improve bonding.

Liev Schreiber

Schreiber was raised by his eccentric mother, who had LSD flashbacks and would only allow him to see black-and-white movies. "You can imagine the resentment that I felt when I saw my first color movie, which was *Star Wars*, in 1977," Schreiber says.

2007–2008

Mary-Kate Olsen

With sister Ashley, Mary-Kate runs Dualstar Entertainment Group, a company that made them millionaires before their tenth birthday. Mary-Kate has taken on several acting roles without her sister after the embarrassment that was *New York Minute*, including a Jesus-loving pothead on *Weeds*.

Romantically linked to Ledger in the final days of his life, Olsen was the first person his masseuse called when she found Ledger's dead or near-dead body. She called Olsen three times before finally calling 911. We may never know what Olsen and the masseuse discussed, because the twin stonewalled a subpoena until the case was closed by New York investigators.

Although she has insisted they were just "close friends," Christensen was on her way to Ledger's apartment when she learned of his death by overdose in 2008. "I had just left him a message and heard his voice on the machine."

p. 72 **Josh Hartnett**

Okay, so like, Mary-Kate was going out with Niarchos back when Paris (pg. 89) and Mary-Kate were, like, totally BFFs. But then Stavros was like, "Whatever," and left Mary-Kate to get with Paris. As if!

p. 92 **Stavros Niarchos III** 2005

2007–2008

Graham bounced back from her breakup with longtime boyfriend Ed Burns (pg. 157) by spending time with the hot young Ledger. He introduced her to his folks on a trip Down Under for his twenty-second birthday, but they split up when he was caught kissing another girl.

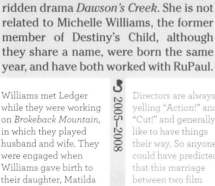

Heather Graham p.47
Heather Graham p.47
Conor Oberst p.113

Only a few months after her coparent Heath Ledger's death in 2008, Williams started dating Jonze after working on his production *Synecdoche, NY*, and auditioning for his version of *Where the Wild Things Are*.

Barrymore may have a hair fetish, because one of her favorite pastimes was tracing her finger along Jonze's moustache when they dated. Rumors swirled that she got with 'stache-less Zach Braff (pg. 111) at the same time—maybe he has some hair we don't know about.

Stephen Hopkins
Film and television director ❧ 1997–1998

Watts was ten years older when she started dating Ledger, her *Ned Kelly* costar, and had to explain to Barbara Walters that "love is love. You fall for the person, not an age." But age was an issue when Watts said, "We all know that fertility slows down at this point . . . I really do want to experience a baby," and Ledger vaguely responded, "I've always dreamed of having children."

1999–2001
2008–2009

2008–2009
2006–2007

Drew Barrymore NEXT ▶

2° to Jane Pratt ▶
2° to Ed Westwick ▶
4° to Brad Pitt ▶

Michelle Williams

Williams played Jen on the teen-angst-ridden drama *Dawson's Creek*. She is not related to Michelle Williams, the former member of Destiny's Child, although they share a name, were born the same year, and have both worked with RuPaul.

Spike Jonze

Born Adam Spiegel (distantly related to the catalog Spiegels), the director-producer-actor-skateboarder started the magazine *Dirt* and acted in *The Game*, before directing freakish *Being John Malkovich* and creating *Jackass!* for MTV.

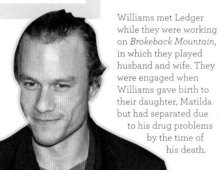

Williams met Ledger while they were working on *Brokeback Mountain*, in which they played husband and wife. They were engaged when Williams gave birth to their daughter, Matilda but had separated due to his drug problems by the time of his death.

2005–2008

2005–2008

Directors are always yelling "Action!" and "Cut!" and generally like to have things their way. So anyone could have predicted that this marriage between two film directors wouldn't last. The career-obsessed photographer character in Coppola's *Lost in Translation* was based on Jonze, so you could say that Bill Murray split them apart.

1999–2003

Sofia Coppola
Francis Ford Coppola cast his young daughter Sofia in all three of the *Godfather* films, and she eventually got pulled into the family business, winning an Oscar and three Golden Globes for *Lost in Translation* in 2004.

2000–2001

2002–2004 ❧

Heath Ledger

Ledger was nominated for an Oscar for his role in *Brokeback Mountain* but didn't win one until after his untimely death in 2008. Authorities labeled it an accidental overdose, but his life insurance company initially refused to pay out on his $15 million policy.

2007–2008 ❧
2007–2008 ❧

This couple met while working on Coppola's first feature, *The Virgin Suicides*, when Mars helped with the music. However, it would be years before they reconnected and had a baby, Romy, in 2006.

♥ ❧
1991
2005–

Anthony Kiedis p.17

Thomas Mars
French musician

Jessica Szohr
Model and actress

2008– ♥

Ed Westwick
Westwick plays the conniving Chuck Bass on *Gossip Girl*. The badass mentality must have worn off, because Westwick got a tattoo that reads "I Heart Romance," after seeing the quote written on a bathroom stall in Brooklyn.

◀ p.154 Cindy Crawford p.156 Ellen Barkin ▲

1984

1996

◀ p.III Zach Braff

◀ p.71 Kirsten Dunst 2007 ♥

Fabrizio Moretti
Drummer for band The Strokes

◀ p.71 Kirsten Dunst

2007 2008

Strokes drummer Moretti and Drew Barrymore broke up only a short while before he started hanging out with Dunst—but the brutal cycle continued when Dunst traded him for Razorlight front man Johnny Borrell (pg. 71).

After breaking up with Drew Barrymore, Mac Daddy Long was seen on the scene with Dunst, kissing more than friends should, despite her denials to the press.

Though they dated for five years, Moretti never tied the knot with Barrymore, saying "marriage is not anything that will secure the future of your relationship," and thus that he plans to "never get married."

2002–2007 ♥

2006–2007 ♥

Drew Barrymore
Barrymore's performance at age seven in *E.T.* made her the Abigail Breslin of the 1980s (or is it the other way around?) but early success led to early drug abuse, and Drew became a preteen rehab alumna. But she's all good now.

♥ 1995

◀ BACK Spike Jonze

2007–2008

1999–2001

1989

1993–1994

Tom Green
Late-night comic

When Barrymore and Green got engaged in 2000, dorks worldwide suddenly had reason to hope that they too could find a hot actress for a wife. The pair survived a massive house fire at their Beverly Hills home in 2001, only to file for divorce ten months later.

Girl-on-girl loving in the pre-LiLo (pg. 93) era wasn't so open. But Pratt spilled the beans on Howard Stern's (pg. 104) radio show when she said, "I did have sex with Drew Barrymore," who just happened to be the first person to grace the cover of *Jane* magazine.

Long was spotted with Tequila engaging in the classic straddle-me-and-eat-my-face pose, proving that a user-friendly interface is a good sales pitch.

After falling victim to drugs and spending time in rehab, fourteen-year-old Barrymore fell into the skinny arms of Feldman, which may have reminded her of why she did drugs in the first place.

Vanessa Marcil 1999–2003 ♥
Actress

♥ Not one to look too far outside of the *90210* cast, Green started dating costar Marcil in 1999. They had a son, Kassius Lijah Marcil-Green, in 2002.

1989–1993

2008 ♥

Tila Tequila
Model and TV personality

2008 2008

2007–2008

2002

Justin Long
Despite a long career performing in *Ed*, *Galaxy Quest*, and more, Long seems destined to be remembered for his portrayal of the Mac opposite John Hodgman's PC in the Apple commercials.

Gimmifer Goodwin p.150 ▼

Corey Feldman
Feldman made six films with his best friend Corey Haim, and in 2007 they teamed up for a reality show, which ended in disaster when Feldman refused to work with Haim until he was drug free.

Brody Jenner p.90 ▼

Val Kilmer

Kilmer's career had a funny start with films like *Top Secret!* and the geek classic *Real Genius*. He soon moved on to action flicks but his *Batman Forever* role had *Variety* questioning "the logic behind adding nipples to the hard-rubber batsuit."

Kilmer and Barrymore started dating when they costarred in *Batman Forever*. The only catch for the man in black was his woman in white— Kilmer was still married to actress Joanne Whalley at the time. Holy vow breaking, Batman!

1996–1999

Luke Wilson and Drew Barrymore dated for three years in the late 1990s and, in a rare Hollywood twist, they remained good friends after their breakup.

Jane Pratt
Magazine editor

Brian Austin Green

Green tried to launch a rap career with the album *One Stop Carnival*. It turned out to be a fitting title, and he has largely dropped out of sight since *Beverly Hills, 90210* ended in 2000.

1993–1995

 2004–

The two started dating in 2004 and got engaged in 2006—right before Fox hit the big time. Will wedding bells ring?

Megan Fox

FHM's "Sexiest Woman in the World" in 2008 was wise beyond her years when she fell for a female stripper at eighteen and learned that "all humans are born with the ability to be attracted to both sexes."

Luke Wilson

The slightly less blond, less famous, and less troubled of the Wilson brothers, Luke has played the befuddled love interest in more than one romantic comedy. In real life, Luke admits he has not yet found "The One."

Although her publicist denied it, no lesser authority than the king and queen of Spain confirmed their son's affair with Paltrow. They hinted that they would have no problem with her nesting with chronic bachelor Prince Felipe and becoming their daughter-in-law.

Prince Felipe of Spain
Real live prince

2002

Life imitated art when *Beverly Hills, 90210* stars Green and Thiessen dated in the mid-1990s.

The incestuous relationship of their characters in *The Royal Tenenbaums* must have rubbed off on them, because Wilson and Paltrow quietly started dating during the shoot.

2001–2002

Gwyneth Paltrow

Paltrow is the daughter of actress Blythe Danner and producer Bruce Paltrow. She is also the goddaughter of Steven Spielberg, who gave her one of her first roles, as the young Wendy Darling in 1991's *Hook*.

2001–2002 **2002**

After meeting backstage at a concert, the pair secretly held a shotgun wedding in California before Paltrow gave birth to their daughter, Apple Blythe Alison Martin in 2004, and son, Moses Bruce Anthony Martin in 2006.

2003–

James Purefoy

The accomplished British stage actor defended his full frontal nudity in *Rome* from rumors of digital enhancement, saying, "There was a penis in the series that may have been slightly enhanced. But it wasn't mine. Mine's all mine, I'm afraid."

Paltrow once commented that "British people don't seem to ask each other out. If someone asks you out they're really going out on a limb." Despite this, she briefly dated Brit Purefoy, who apparently went out on that limb.

1995–1997 **Brad Pitt** p. 105

What's romantic about a movie set full of emaciated corpses and severed heads? Whatever it was, it did the trick in bringing *Se7en* costars Pitt and Paltrow together in a highly publicized but short-lived engagement.

1997–1999 **Ben Affleck** NEXT ▶

Chris Martin

As the front man for Coldplay, Martin is an international celebrity. But despite the band's success, many rock fans stand by the assertion in Paul Rudd's character in *The 40 Year Old Virgin*, "You know how I know you're gay? You like Coldplay."

Affleck dated Rothman on and off after high school, but they parted ways when his career took off and Gwyneth Paltrow came a-calling.

Cheyenne Rothman
Ben Affleck's high school sweetheart

When asked how he reacted to Paltrow's love scenes with Joseph Fiennes (pg. 156) in *Shakespeare in Love*, Affleck said, "With fury and rage, like a man should." After they split, Paltrow revealingly said that Affleck's perfect woman would be "a stripper with a Budweiser in each hand."

◄ BACK **Gwyneth Paltrow**   1997–1999 💔

◄ p.128 **Krista Allen**   2004 💔

Tammy Morris
Canadian stripper   2003 💔

Vancouver stripper Morris sold her story of an oral-sex-filled night with Affleck and three other lap dancers at Brandi's strip club and later at the home of Christian Slater (pg. 22). It also led to a lawsuit, not by Affleck but by one of the strippers, who insisted that she, at least, didn't have sex with the star.

Foley and Garner met on the set of *Felicity* in 1998 and got married two years later. With so much intra-cast dating on the sets of his TV series, J. J. Abrams should add the title of matchmaker to his résumé.

Scott Foley
American actor

Garner went out with *Alias* costar Vartan while they worked on the show. It didn't last, which goes to show that coworkers shouldn't date—especially when one plays a character who's a different person every minute of the day.

Michael Vartan
American actor
2003 💔

1990–1997

Ben Affleck
Affleck got childhood friend Matt Damon (pg. 113) interested in acting, and they both appeared in 1992's *School Ties* before winning the Oscar for *Good Will Hunting*.

Affleck and Garner met on the set of *Daredevil* in 2003 and began a quiet romance (apparently striving not to repeat the media frenzy that surrounded the original Bennifer) that only went public when they were spotted at a Red Sox game in 2004. The *Alias*-style intrigue continued with a secret shotgun wedding four months into her pregnancy.

1998–2003

Janssen starred with Matt Damon (pg. 113) in *Rounders* and he introduced her to buddy Affleck. After they broke up, Janssen said, "I got bored with him," but they got back together when she helped him through rehab later that year.

2001

Famke Janssen
The Dutch former-model-turned-actress made everyone sit up and listen when she used her telekinetic powers to whip off Hugh Jackman's belt in *X-Men*. Then she pushed the boundaries on TV by playing Ava Moore, a transgender woman who seduces pretty much the entire cast on *Nip/Tuck*.

1995–2000   **Tod Williams**
2004–   Director

Gretchen Mol
American actress

💔 2002–2004

💔 2004

One of the original celebrity name mashups, "Bennifer" were inseparable. But, after revelations of Affleck's hot night with four lap dancers (and Christian Slater, pg. 22) at a strip club in Vancouver, Lopez called off their megawedding and blamed it on the media scrutiny.

Vanessa Kerry
John Kerry's daughter

Affleck did his best to support the John Kerry presidential campaign by hooking up with Kerry's daughter Vanessa. He told *Harper's Bazaar* she was "absurdly beautiful" and compared her to a "Nordic milkman's daughter," not a strong endorsement of her candidate father.

2004–

Jennifer Garner
Garner switched from chemistry to drama in college, and she was soon pursuing acting in New York. She landed a recurring role in *Felicity*, which led to her Golden Globe win for *Alias* and subsequent movie roles.

Ojani Noa
Cuban chef

How could Noa have expected Jenny from the block to stick with him after she became a celebrity? At least she let the former waiter manage one of her restaurants for a while in the aftermath of their divorce.

🔒 1995–1998

J.Lo and M.Ant dated briefly in the late 1990s, before his first marriage and her second. They recorded a duet in early 2004, and they were married soon thereafter in a surprise at-home ceremony less than a week after his divorce from Dayanara Torres was finalized.

2004–
🔒

1998
💔

Mira Sorvino p. 51 ▶

Marc Anthony
The New York–born Puerto Rican recording artist and current Mr. Jennifer Lopez began his career as a song-writer and backup singer before gaining fame for his own Spanish-language hits. Anthony had his first Top 5 English-language hit "I Need to Know" in 1999.

Jennifer Lopez

Jenny from the block made the phenomenal transition from *In Living Color* "Fly Girl" to big-screen star in 1995's *Money Train* to Grammy-nominated singer with a number one album her second time out. Soon she was the most influential Hispanic entertainer in the United States, according to *People* (back off, Ricardo Montalban!).

2002–2004 🎵

1984–1995 🎵

Lopez got engaged to her high school boyfriend at fifteen, and he followed her to California when she moved to be a "Fly Girl" on *In Living Color*.

David Cruz
J.Lo's high school sweetheart

Cris Judd
Backup dancer

Combs and Kim Porter endured a roller-coaster relationship for over a decade. Combs once said, "I know she deserves to get married, but I'm just not ready." Their most recent breakup took place in 2007 when it was confirmed Diddy had a love child with Sarah Chapman.

Kimberly Porter
Model

1997–2007 💔

1993–2006 💔

Sarah Chapman
Mother of Sean Combs's love child

💔 1998–2001

1998–2001

2001–2002 🔓

Sean "Diddy" Combs

First he was Puff Daddy, then P. Diddy, and now simply Diddy (except in the United Kingdom where DJ Richard "Diddy" Dearlove is suing Combs for stealing his name). He's been a headliner for years, but in 2002 he opened for *NSYNC on their Celebrity Tour.

In 2007, DNA tests proved that Chapman's fifteen-month-old daughter Chance was Diddy's. Commenting on their relationship, Chapman said, "He and I are friends, we've always been friends." Just two friends who make babies together.

Puffy and J.Lo's ill-fated romance ended for the same reason so many relationships end: They were arrested for having concealed weapons in a nightclub. While Combs was on trial for said incident, Lopez dumped him on Valentine's Day in 2001.

💔 2008

Sienna Miller NEXT ▶

Are they engaged or aren't they? While rumors continue to swirl, one rumor can be put to rest: Combs is dating the singer Cassie Ventura (no relation to big bald former Minnesota governor Jesse Ventura).

♥ 2008–

Cassie Ventura
Ventura is a singer with a budding career whom Diddy first took under his wing and later his bedsheets after signing her to his record label. Ms. Ventura turned some heads after shaving the hair off hers to cultivate an "I don't give a fuck" persona.

Hayden Christensen

Before earning two consecutive Razzies for his wooden portrayal of Anakin Skywalker, Christensen was nominated for a Golden Globe for his performance in *Life as a House*.

There's a fine line between publicity ploy and passion in Hollywood, but when asked about Miller and Christensen's onset romance their *Factory Girl* director said, "I don't know if they had sex on set. You'll have to ask Sienna."

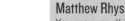
Rachel Bilson 2008 p. 146

Matthew Rhys

You may recall Welsh actor Matthew Rhys hanging naked in a butcher shop, about to be made into mincemeat, in Julie Taymor's *Titus*. If not, rent it! The sets are quite lavish.

Rhys met Miller on the set of *The Edge of Love*, in which they shared a threesome with Keira Knightley (pg. 84). The two (Rhys and Miller) began dating, only to split when Miller hooked up with another Rhys, Rhys Ifans (pg. 83). But wait—it gets worse: Matthew Rhys introduced Miller to his *Brothers & Sisters* costar Balthazar Getty (pg. 101), and when they hooked up neither Rhys was pleased.

With Diddy's hectic schedule in the recording studio, onstage, and promoting his various product lines, it's anyone's guess how he found time for extramarital affairs. But he made time for Miller, including one instance when they were seen out until 9 A.M.

After her final fight with Jude Law, Miller went after her costar Franco on the set of the film *Camille*. Some speculated that Miller became a Francophile to make Law jealous.

◄ BACK Sean "Diddy" Combs 2008 2007

Sienna Miller

Miller's on-screen performances are oft overshadowed by her in-public performances. She's been accused of stealing husbands (Jude Law and Balthazar Getty, pg. 101) and fashion styles (Kate Moss, pg. 60) but that hasn't stopped Miller from building a following, particularly among her male costars.

2006
2004–2006
2005
2007–2008

Miller and Getty started dating in May 2008, just days after Balthazar's wife had the couple's fourth child. It was only after romantic photos with Miller turned up in the press that he announced his separation from his wife.

◄ p. 101 Balthazar Getty 2008– ♥

◄ p. 72 Josh Hartnett 2007–2008

This relationship supposedly severed the love between Miller and Balthazar Getty. Hartnett hooked up with Miller while in London playing the less-autistic role in the stage version of *Rain Man*, and the two bonded over his vegetarian cooking skills. Mmmm lentils!

2001 2007

Despite Miller's tumultuous breakup from a cheating Jude Law (pg. 83), the pair got back together. Then it was Miller's turn to have an affair of her own, and she chose Law's close pal Craig for the part, prompting Jude to kick Miller out of his house.

Mitchell met Craig while producing *The Jacket*, which starred Craig and Adrien Brody (pg. 134) in an implausible time-travel scenario powered not by a DeLorean but by a jacket.

Satsuki Mitchell
Film producer

2005– ♥

Orlando Bloom p. 71

Jamie Burke p. 61

When they dated, Craig said he hated the media attention. "I don't enjoy having [reporters] go to my mother's door." However, he said that, despite having a child, Moss was still "wild" and "independent," which sounds worth the hassle.

◄ p. 60 Kate Moss

2004

Daniel Craig

Best known for his reinvigoration of the James Bond character in 2006's *Casino Royale*, Craig is the sixth actor to portray the spy and is set to star in at least five new Bond movies. This despite losing a fingertip while shooting *Quantum of Solace*.

2005

Ifans proposed to Miller multiple times before she finally accepted after he texted her, "Marry the misfit." But when he searched through her other texts looking for "incriminating evidence" that she had reconnected with her ex, Matthew Rhys, Miller couldn't handle his jealousy and called the whole thing off. Because if you're gonna trust anyone, it should be Sienna Miller, right?

Rhys Ifans
The Wales native delivered a breakout performance as Hugh Grant's character's slovenly roommate in *Notting Hill*. Ifans's surname is pronounced "Evans," but he decided to change to the Welsh spelling to be more difficult. We'd say mission accomplished.

Talan Torriero
One of the "stars" of MTV's *Laguna Beach*, Torriero has attempted to branch out his "career" by pursuing acting and announcing, in 2005, that he would release an album. As of this writing, the world still waits for that load to drop.

Stewart and Torriero announced their engagement after only a few weeks of dating but soon called it off because "it was just too soon to enter into a lifelong commitment."

♻ 2005

♻ 2004–2005

Kimberly Stewart
Rod Stewart's daughter Kimberly had her breasts enlarged at age eighteen but later got the implants removed and said, "Jack Osbourne wanted them, so I framed them and he put them on his bathroom wall."

Cisco Adler

NEXT ▶

James Franco
Franco starred in the old-school Judd Apatow series *Freaks and Geeks* before landing the no-pressure role of *James Dean* (pg. 146) in a 2001 television biopic and winning a Golden Globe.

Miller's engagement to Law ended when he admitted to cheating on her with his children's nanny. Eventually Miller took him back, only to break up with him again in 2006.

2004–2006 ♻

Jude Law
Law has been nominated for Academy Awards and named a Chevalier des Arts et des Lettres. But he may be better known for his gold medal betrayal of Sienna Miller with his nanny.

2008 💔

💔 2008

These two serial daters hooked up in 2008 and were spotted rolling around a front yard in the early hours of the morning, kissing like teenagers. It's a grown-up relationship though: Law has met Stewart's rocker dad for drinks.

💔 2005

The pair split when Francis allegedly invited Stewart's best friend, Paris Hilton (pg. 89), and her then-boyfriend, Stavros Niarchos (pg. 92), to join him on his private island and then tipped off the paparazzi. Hee hee.

Joe Francis
After graduating from USC, Francis stumbled upon a great money-making idea: Videotape drunk college girls flashing their boobies. The million-dollar franchise, *Girls Gone Wild*, was born, much to the consternation of parents of coeds everywhere.

Fiona Loudon
Scottish actress

Wright, the nanny who broke up Law and Sienna Miller, was hired while Law was off filming a movie but stuck around when he returned. They were allegedly caught in the act by one of the children—the psychologically traumatized one.

💔 2005

🔒 1994–2003

Because of his multiple affairs, Frost and Law had an epic divorce battle over their kids and their cash, during which Frost was prescribed beta blockers to control her panic attacks.

Sadie Frost
British actress Frost's mother was only sixteen when she had her with painter and LSD aficionado David Vaughan—who once insisted that the family only wear orange and not eat anything red.

🔒 1992–1994

Daisy Wright
Nanny

💔 2006

Russell Brand p. 147 ▶

Stewart said Adler was her "best friend, her lover and soul mate," and to celebrate their impending union she got a tattoo that read, "Daddy's Little Girl Loves Cisco." A few months after their breakup, she had the tattoo changed so that the "Cisco" became "Disco."

2004–2005

◀ BACK **Kimberly Stewart**

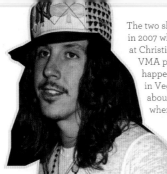

The two shared a brief encounter in 2007 when they made out at Christina Aguilera's (pg. 44) pre-VMA party in Las Vegas. What happened in Vegas did not stay in Vegas and instead was written about in all the celebrity blogs, where it will stay forever.

Kyra Sedgwick
She is the first cousin, once removed, of Andy Warhol's starlet Edie Sedgwick, but Kyra is probably better known for her role in *Phenomenon* opposite John Travolta (pg. 114) and for her latest hit, *The Closer*.

2007

Keira Knightley
Knightley, star of *Bend It Like Beckham* and *Pirates of the Caribbean*, is proud of her many nude scenes, saying, "I always bare my breasts," though she admits to using breast-enhancing makeup in Pirates. "They painted my tits on me for the films, which is extraordinary because it's kind of a dying art form . . . they used to have whole sections of the studios devoted to bosom makeup."

Cisco Adler
The former front man of band Whitestarr (who gained exposure participating in the VH1 series *The Rock Life*) is perhaps better known for his various relationships with famous models and actresses—which, when you think about it, is really what being a rock star is all about.

2007 | Paris Hilton

2005–2007
Adler and Barton split after two years together when a collection of items stolen from Paris Hilton (pg. 89) was posted online, one of the items being a naked picture of Adler.

This longtime Hollywood couple met on the set of the TV teleplay *Lemon Sky*, at a time when Bacon says he was "hitting what [he] considered to be bottom" in his career. They most recently performed together in *The Woodsman*, in which Bacon played a convicted pedophile and Sedgwick played his love interest—how romantic!

2005–2007

Mischa Barton
Barton was born in England and raised in America, but stated that she feels more English than American. Her drama continues offscreen, where she received a DUI and got into a war of words with Paris Hilton (pg. 89).

Not only did Dornan get to date the British starlet for over a year, but after Knightley recommended him to her agent he also launched an acting career!

Jamie Dornan
Model, musician, and actor Dornan was cast in punk period-piece *Marie Antoinette* when girlfriend Knightley dumped him, tainting his reputation. "People knew me in the fashion world before I started going out with Keira because I've done some good work but . . . I can't shake off the title of Keira Knightley's ex-boyfriend."

In a classic "you can't fire me, I quit!" scenario, Reinhardt and Bynes each claimed that they dumped the other. Bynes blamed his celebrity whoring, and Reinhardt said she wouldn't even let him have a "guys' night out."

2007

Barton and Dornan hooked up briefly the week she arrived in London to promote Keds shoes (she became their spokesperson in 2005). But when he flaked on a date, the romance was over. "I think I'm too busy for men. I'm a single girl right now," said Barton.

Amanda Bynes
American actress

2003–2005

2006

Kate Moss

p. 60 ▶

After getting dumped by Keira Knightley, model-rocker Dornan found the ultimate revenge by dating hottest-model-ever Moss (pg. 60) when they appeared together in topless ads for Calvin Klein.

Scott Sartiano p. 99 ▲

Ryan Cabrera
American pop musician

After her breakup with Josh Henderson, Simpson began her streak of dating musicians, starting with the actual boy next door, Cabrera. Simpson and Cabrera shared not only their eyeliner but also their manager—Simpson's father, Joe.

2003–2005 💔

Ashlee Simpson
The youngest daughter of the Simpson dynasty, Ashlee struggled for years to crawl out from under older sis Jessica Simpson's (pg. 109) massive shadow. She wasn't an immediate success—fans will recall her *Saturday Night Live* lip-syncing screwup and subsequent freak-out.

2005 💔

Simpson and Henderson dated for two years before she began filming her eponymous reality show. Simpson was dumped on camera in the second episode. Ouch.

💔 2007

2002–2003 💔

Paris and Henderson dated for a short time in March and April 2007 after her DUI arrest. It was a relationship of convenience for Paris, who needed someone who could help her steer.

Josh Henderson
American actor

💔 2007

💔

Lauren Conrad
Parlaying her fifteen minutes into spin-offs and sequels, L.C. (she hates that) is on track to have her entire life documented by MTV. The reality starlet is set to launch her own fashion line, cleverly titled the "Lauren Conrad Collection."

💔 2008

Conrad and Reinhardt had some history before he showed up on *The Hills*—according to classmates, they first hooked up in high school when the burrito heir threw lavish shindigs in Laguna Beach.

Doug Reinhardt
Reinhardt comes from burrito money (his step-father, Duane Roberts, invented the frozen burrito) and parlayed that status into a spot with the Baltimore Orioles and a guest appearance on *The Hills*.

2008–2009 💔

💔 2009

Paris Hilton p. 89 ▶
Paris Hilton p. 89 ▶
Paris Hilton p. 89 ▶

💔 💔

Stephen Colletti p. 91 ▼
2004–2008

Brody Jenner p. 90 ▼
2006

Jenner dated Conrad after having dated her *Laguna Beach* nemesis Kristin Cavallari. Surely Jenner's only intention was to be a peacemaker between the two.

1988– 🔒

A few years before starring on *Family Ties*, where she met her future husband, Michael J. Fox (pg. 88), Pollan was dating young Bacon, who said, "we spend all of our time together." She married Fox two years after splitting with Bacon, the same year Bacon married Kyra Sedgwick (1988).

1981–1986 💔

Tracy Pollan
Pollan was born on Long Island (along with *Omnivore's Dilemma*-writing brother, Michael) and acted in an *ABC Afterschool Special* in which she played the ugly duckling who gets transformed and enticed into romance. Soon afterward, she appeared in a life-changing-husband-finding role in *Family Ties*.

Kevin Bacon
The initial subject of the "six degrees of separation" theory debuted as an uptight fraternity brother in *Animal House* but really shook things up (and by "things" we mean his ass) in 1984's *Footloose*. He also rocks on guitar with his brother in the cleverly named band *The Bacon Brothers*.

Pollan married Fox after test driving the relationship on *Family Ties* (she played his older girlfriend). Fox was diagnosed with early-onset Parkinson's in 1991. But "there ain't no nothing they can't love each other through," and the relationship remains one of Hollywood's enduring love stories.

1988– 🔒

Michael J. Fox p. 88 ▶

Sex Scene and Be Seen

Actual mad-genius director Lars Von Trier said that the best way to prepare actors for sex scenes is to direct in the nude. And while plenty of directors have guided their actors in getting it on without taking it off, it doesn't sound half as fun: Daniel Radcliffe said of his explicit scenes with the lovely Teresa Palmer (pg. 147), "When you're doing it and you've got people watching you . . . it is not in the least bit exciting." Kate Winslet, who won an Oscar for her full-frontal Nazi in *The Reader* and has appeared nude in a dozen other films, said, "You feel awful. You feel sick. And you remind yourself, you must never agree to do this again." Vampire Robert Pattinson had his first sex scene playing the allegedly homosexual Salvador Dalí, and he said, "I haven't even done a sex scene with a girl in my career and here I am doing a hard-core gay sex scene . . . All the Spanish technicians were giggling." But Michael Caine (pg. 49) nailed the lighter side, saying, "The only time a director ever demonstrates things to you is in the love scenes! Suddenly he feels the need to show you exactly how to hold the actress."

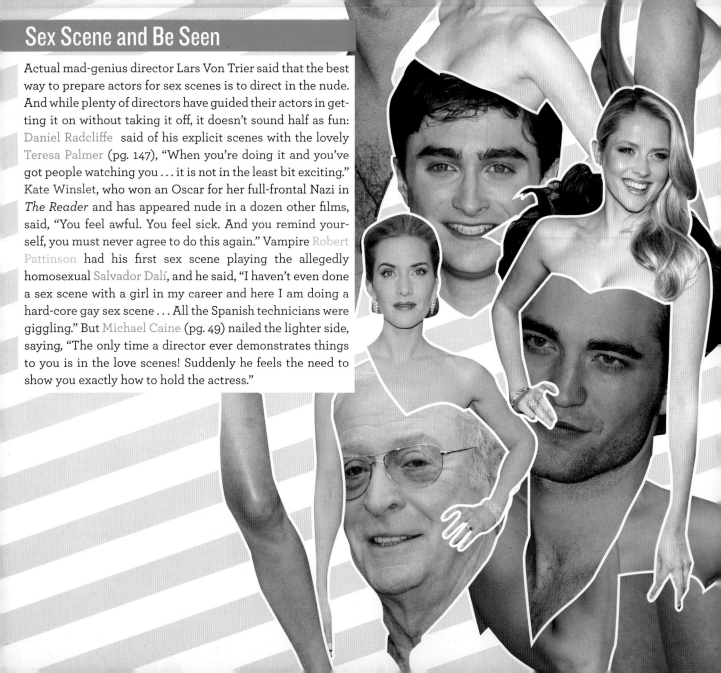

The Love Chateau

If celebrity relationships develop like butterflies do, then Hollywood's Chateau Marmont is their twisted, grubby pupa. It's a swank no-man's-land where the regular rules don't apply and any member of the rich and famous is practically expected to trash a room, cheat on her husband, or at least charge a massive bill to his account. That's what Christian Slater (pg. 22)'s ex Nina Huang (pg. 22) did in 1995 when she dumped him after his fling with Christy Turlington (pg. 158). Following the $1,864 bill at the Chateau, she slapped him with a $100,000 palimony suit. Jessica Simpson (pg. 109) was seen slipping into Adam Levine (pg. 109)'s hotel room while she was still officially with hubby Nick Lachey (pg. 109). Kate Bosworth (pg. 70) got "really close" to Leonardo DiCaprio (pg. 73) at a hotel party in 2008, while he was in the middle of an on-and-off relationship with Bar Refaeli (pg. 73). But Benicio del Toro (pg. 48) topped them all when he hinted he'd gotten it on with Scarlett Johansson (pg. 48) in the hotel elevator (a rumor she's repeatedly denied). He said, "Did I ever have sex in an elevator with Scarlett Johansson after an awards show? . . . Let's leave that to somebody's imagination . . . . I'm sure it has happened before."

Elizabeth Daily

Daily played Paul Reuben's love interest, Dottie, in *Pee-Wee's Big Adventure* and voices Buttercup in *Powerpuff Girls* and a baby penguin in *Happy Feet*.

Shannen Doherty p.45

Pamela Anderson p.29

They had so much in common when they met—okay, maybe just the sex tapes—but it was poker that brought them together. Anderson had a $250,000 gambling debt and Salomon had money. As she told Ellen DeGeneres (pg. 152), "I paid off a poker debt with sexual favors and fell in love. It's so romantic."

2007–2008 🔒
2002 🔒
1995–2000 🔒

Daily reports that her marriage to Salomon ended when she said, "If you don't get some help with your drug problem, I'm going to divorce you," and he charmingly replied, "I'm outta here."

Jason Statham p.61

2005–2006 💔

Sophie Monk
Australian singer

The world collectively experienced TMI when their sex tape hit the Internet a suspicious few weeks before Paris's TV show, *The Simple Life*, debuted on television. Was that blurry image the face that launched a thousand paparazzi?

Rick Salomon

Rich Jersey boy Salomon produced a couple of B movies (including 2007's *Who's Your Caddy*), but his most successful film project will always be a little home movie he made with Paris Hilton called *One Night in Paris*.

💔 2001

While allegedly smoking pot and drinking, the pair made out in an L.A. nightclub, and Hilton even treated Adler to a lap dance. Then Hilton ruined the mood by getting on stage and singing her "hit" song, "The Stars Are Blind."

⟵ p.84 Cisco Adler — 2007
⟵ p.85 Josh Henderson — 2007
⟵ p.85 Doug Reinhardt — 2009

Reinhardt plied Paris with gifts, including an Andy Warhol print of Marilyn Monroe (because her grandmother thought she resembled Marilyn) and a $10,000 teacup Pomeranian—because what Paris really needed was another tiny dog.

Nancy McKeon
American actress

James Lafferty
American actor

1982–1985 💔

Fox dated McKeon when both were sitcom stars—they even attended a White House dinner together. Years later police arrested a stalker named Tina Ledbetter, who had sent Fox thousands of threatening letters because she wanted him to get back together with McKeon.

It's a small world after all on the set of *One Tree Hill* where, after divorcing costar Chad Michael Murray (pg. 89), Bush got together with costar Lafferty—who plays Murray's brother on the show. Infidelity, incest—it's all on a family network.

1988– 🔒

Michael J. Fox

Fox built an impressive comedy career on roles he almost missed out on—first, Matthew Broderick (pg. 11) turned down the role of Alex P. Keaton on *Family Ties*, leaving it open for Fox. Then Eric Stoltz lost the role of Marty McFly in the first weeks of shooting *Back to the Future*.

⟵ p.85 Tracy Pollan

Somewhere in between Carrie Underwood (pg. 153), Jessica Simpson (pg. 109), and a reported lap dance from hot mama Britney Spears (pg. 33) at an L.A. club, Romo fit in a little Bush.

⟵ p.109 Tony Romo

2008– ♥

Sophia Bush

Bush (no relation to the former president—in fact, she stumped for Obama in 2008) broke out on the series *One Tree Hill* as cheerleading captain Brooke Davis. Her pom-pom skills helped her rank number twenty-four in *Maxim*'s 2007 hot list, just beating number twenty-five, Elisha Cuthbert.

2007 💔

Madden and Monk met on the set of a Good Charlotte music video and announced their engagement in early 2007. He gave her an expensive diamond ring and declared his love to the world. A year later, the pair split up. Those are the lifestyles of the rich and famous.

2006–2008
💔

Benji Madden
Guitarist for band Good Charlotte

2001
💔

💔
💔

Paris Hilton

Like her self-made great-grandfather, Conrad Hilton, Paris has made her own fame through modeling, red-carpet antics, and sex tapes (yes, plural). Since then, what hasn't she done? Whether it's writing, recording, or Greek shipping heirs, Paris is on top of it all.

Murray hooked up with Hilton, his costar in the horror film *House of Wax*, while engaged to Sophia Bush. When Bush confronted him with the rumors after they had wed, he came clean and was soon served with divorce papers citing fraud.

2005–2006

Murray and Bush met while working on *One Tree Hill* and dated for two years before getting married. But when he cheated with Paris Hilton, Bush said, "I feel hurt, humiliated, and broken-hearted," and she then kicked the bastard out, just five months after they'd tied the knot. They still had to see each other every day on the set.

Years after their fling, Allman revealed that after hooking up with Paris he was so afraid of catching a disease that he ran to the bathroom and scrubbed his genitals with Tilex. Wouldn't a condom have been more comfortable?

Two weeks after splitting with his fiancée, Sophie Monk, Madden started dating Hilton, at the same time Madden's twin brother, Joel (pg. 92), was dating Hilton's then-BFF Nicole Richie (pg. 91). Double date!

💔 **1999**
💍 **2004–2005**
💍 **2001–2003**
💔 **2005–2007**
💔 **2006**
💔 **2004**
💔 **2004**

Carter didn't have nice things to say about Hilton after they split ("She was a drunken prude who ... did not really like sex," and "The only thing that made her happy was her own reflection").

Chad Michael Murray
Murray seduced both Lindsay Lohan (pg. 93) and Jamie Lee Curtis (their characters, anyway) in *Freaky Friday* before being cast in the WB's *One Tree Hill* and nailing the covers of *Rolling Stone* and *People* (in a cover story on TV's sexiest guys) that same year.

Elijah Blue Allman
Son of Cher and Gregg Allman

💔 **1997**
💔 **2001–2002**
💔 **2000**

Bijou Phillips p. 145
Heather Graham p. 47

Paris Latsis
Greek shipping heir

After they dated, Allman told Howard Stern (pg. 104) that Graham's "not in danger of being recruited by Mensa anytime soon."

Paris and Paris met over Memorial Day weekend and if they had connected in Paris, France, physicists agree that the space-time continuum would have collapsed in on itself. Fact.

Nicole Richie NEXT ▶

Yes, they dated. Yes, they were engaged. Yes, a sex tape leaked the year after they split up—this is Paris we're talking about, remember?

Jason Shaw
Fashion model

Stavros Niarchos III p. 92 ▶

Travis Barker
Drummer for Blink-182
💔 **2005**
2004–2008

Nick Carter
Carter performed his first gig with the Backstreet Boys (the top-selling boy band of all time) at Seaworld in Orlando, Florida, in 1993 and went on to become the band's "hot one."

Moments after his divorce to *One Tree Hill* costar Sophia Bush was finalized, Murray started dating high school senior Dalton, who had played an extra on the show.

Kenzie Dalton
Miss North Carolina Teen USA runner-up
💍 **2006–**

2° to Eric Dane
3° to Brett Ratner
4° to Serena Williams
Kari Ann Peniche p. 94
Shanna Moakler p. 144

Tila Tequila p.78 ▲

◄ p.85 **Lauren Conrad**

◄ p.85 **Lauren Conrad**

After *Laguna Beach*, Colletti and Conrad spent a few minutes attending college in San Francisco before returning to Hollywood to break up with each other and build up their careers. They briefly reconnected in 2007.

◄ BACK **Elijah Blue Allman**

◄ p.84 **Amanda Bynes**

Zano was Bynes's love interest on *What I Like About You*, but the couple went off book when they started dating in 2003. Bynes had good things to say about him—not so with her other relationships.

◄ p.99 **Jamie-Lynn Sigler**

Tony Soprano wouldn't approve of his daughter marrying her agent-manager, but that's exactly what Sigler did in 2003, two years after meeting DiScala at a basketball game.

2003–2005

Duff starred in an unreleased horror film called *I Remember* with DiScala's wife at the time, Jamie-Lynn Sigler (pg. 99). Defying cast loyalty, she dated DiScala for a few weeks after his marriage ended.

A. J. DiScala
Talent manager

They met on the *Gilmore Girls* set, where Ventimiglia played Bledel's on-screen bad-boy boyfriend, Jess. The real-life romance lasted longer than the scripted one; reports indicate she dumped him in 2006.

2006

2008

2006–2008

2006

Brody Jenner

Jenner comes from good Olympic decathlete stock (father Bruce Jenner won the gold in 1976) so who could be surprised that he was crowned one of *The Princes of Malibu* on the short-lived reality series. Bro had better luck with Bromance, but not by much.

Milo Ventimiglia
American actor

2003–2006

Alexis Bledel

Kimberly Alexis Bledel (she reserves "Kimberly" for family and friends, so don't call her that) got her start as a model before starring in *Gilmore Girls*. Her mother is Mexican and father Argentinean, so Spanish was her first language—a fact that came as a surprise to *Sisterhood of the Traveling Pants* costar America Ferrera.

❣ 2005–2006

2008–2009 ❣

This thousand-point Scrabble couple started dating on the set of *Heroes* (in which Ventimiglia plays her uncle) but reportedly broke up around Valentine's Day 2009 because of a pregnancy scare. Things only got worse when Panettiere supposedly refused to be on set with her ex.

Whether it was a real relationship (as Jenner would have us believe) or a publicity stunt (as Richie stated on her blog), these childhood friends got together for a brief period. Dad Lionel Richie approved, saying, "He's a great kid."

2004–2008

Nick Zano

He was born Nicholas Crapanzano in Nutley, New Jersey, so you can see why the kid changed his name. Nick was discovered by MTV while selling shoes, earning a gig hosting MTV's *Movie House*. A role on the sitcom *What I Like About You* soon followed, and Nutley's little Crapanzano was off!

2003–2004

❣

Haylie Duff

Older sister Haylie started acting before Hilary Duff (pg. 92), but she ultimately landed a small role on Hilary's show *Lizzie McGuire*. She had a recurring role on *7th Heaven* and joined Hilary again (at her insistence) as a character in 2009's *Barely Legal*.

Duff and Zano moved quickly from shagging to shacking up in a Toluca Lake, California, home right next door to neighbor Ashley Tisdale. Did anyone say block party?

Before letting Cavallari go to Miami for spring break in 2007, Zano branded her with a wrist tattoo that read *NZ*, a surefire way to destroy any celebrity relationship. A few months later they split, and she was off to her plastic surgeon to zap the tat.

♥ 2008–

❣ 2007

2007 ❣

❣ 2007

Hayden Panettiere

Panettiere was one of the youngest freaks on *Heroes*, but the daughter of soap star Lesley Vogel got her first steady acting gig at age five on *One Life to Live*. She's an active activist, filming a Funny or Die anti-McCain PSA and physically blocking dolphin fishermen in Japan with actress Isabel Lucas.

When Colletti and Panettiere broke up, she said, "I wanted to be single at the time. It just hit me like a ton of bricks—this is the time I need to be with myself." She then immediately started dating *Heroes* costar Milo Ventimiglia.

2006–2007

Stephen Colletti
American actor and reality star

2° to Wilmer Valderrama ▶
3° to Cameron Diaz ▶
4° to Jack Nicholson ▶

Lindsay Lohan NEXT ▶

2006 ❧ **Nicole Richie**

Born to a tour assistant and an unnamed father, Nicole was raised by Lionel Richie and his then-wife Brenda Harvey-Richie; they officially adopted her at nine years old (the saga is the basis for her novel, *The Truth About Diamonds*). She met BFF/nemesis Paris Hilton (pg. 89) at the exclusive Buckley School in Sherman Oaks, California.

2000 ❧

Madden got with Richie in a serious baby-making way, and the couple had their first child, daughter Harlow in 2008. Despite Ritchie saying "I make it a custom not to plan the future," they were engaged by 2010.

👤 2007– **Joel Madden** NEXT ▶

Brody and Kristin's on-again, off-again relationship switched off for good amid rumors that she was spending too much time with Nick Lachey (pg. 109), which, for some people, could be as little as twenty-five minutes.

2005–2006
2003–2005

Kristin Cavallari

High school junior Cavallari was dating senior Colletti when the first season of *Laguna Beach* began, creating a love triangle (the third vertex was Lauren Conrad, pg. 85) that continued for years. ❧ 2006

Cavallari may have dated DJ AM to get back at Nicole Richie, who had just started dating Cavallari's ex, Brody Jenner. That'll show her!

2004–2006
2006

Steve-O dated Richie during the short hiatus in her relationship with DJ AM. Later that year, at DJ AM's Vegas birthday party, Steve-O got trashed, stole the mic, and said, "I know you all expect me to say I fucked Nicole Richie." He didn't get kicked out until his drunk buddy "Wee Man" peed on the dance floor.

Stephen "Steve-O" Glover

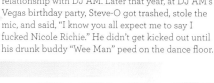

The London-born American freak attended Ringling Brothers and Barnum & Bailey Clown College and made his name on MTV's *Jackass* with shenanigans like stapling his scrotum to his leg in a stunt called "the Butterfly".

2006–2007 ❧

Kevin Connolly
Connolly's breakout role came at age six in the Chips Ahoy "Betcha bite a chip campaign." Not really—most people know him now in the iconic role of Eric "E" Murphy in *Entourage*.

Nicky Hilton

Nicholai Olivia Hilton, or "Nicky," as the proletariat calls her, is the younger, less pornographic of Richard Hilton's daughters. She worked as a fashion model and studied at Parsons School of Design (ex-domain of Tim Gunn of *Project Runway* fame) before launching her clothing line.

❧ 2004–2006

Adam "DJ AM" Goldstein p. III ▶
Adam "DJ AM" Goldstein p. III ▶

▲ p.76 Mary-Kate Olsen

They were America's Sweethearts—two heirs who taught us all how to love again. But when Niarchos began a side courtship with Lindsay Lohan, it was clear that there was trouble in paradise. Why do bad things happen to such good people?

2005–2007
💔

💔 2007
💔 2006

▲ p.89 Paris Hilton

Nemcova scooped up Niarchos after he split with Paris Hilton (pg. 89). Having survived a tsunami, Petra likely had no problem surviving anything Niarchos may have contracted after three years with Paris.

▲ p.102 Petra Nemcova

2005
💔

Stavros Niarchos III

Greek shipping heirs are a trillion dimes a dozen, but Niarchos III is special. He crashed Paris Hilton's (pg. 89) Bentley and drove off recklessly while leaving a club drunk, he offered a homeless man $100 to dump a drink on himself, and he started a wild "pillow fight" that led to the evacuation of the Las Vegas Hard Rock Hotel.

Niarchos was the cause of the infamous 2006 rift between Paris Hilton (pg. 89) and Lohan. When Paris went on vacation, her then-boyfriend Niarchos was seen exiting Lohan's hotel room at the Chateau Marmont. Paris was pissed.

While in rehab, Lohan sent a now-infamous text to Jenner claiming that all she wanted was "sex and McDonald's." They do have great fries.

◄ p.90 Brody Jenner

Joel Madden

Joel, the singing half of pop-punk band Good Charlotte, grew up with his twin brother and bandmate, Benji Madden (pg. 89, duh), in Maryland. They changed their last name from Combs to their mother's maiden name when Dad ditched the family.

2004–2006 💔

When Madden met Duff, he said, "I've found the perfect person." But they split, and five months later Nicole Richie (pg. 91) was pregnant with his daughter.

Mike Comrie
Hockey player

2007– 👤

Duff had to bone up on hockey when she started dating then—New York Islanders' center, Comrie. He scheduled couple's counseling for himself and Duff because "she has a lot of issues with her dad."

Hilary Duff

Duff was lauded as the new Annette Funicello when her series *Lizzie McGuire* premiered on the Disney Channel, but when Faye Dunaway heard Duff was reprising her role in *Bonnie & Clyde*, she said, "Couldn't they at least cast a real actress?" Duff responded by saying that her fans don't even know who Dunaway is. Touché.

💔 2007

Years after the feud between Duff and Lindsay Lohan (pg. 93) made headlines, gentleman Carter came clean about the love triangle. "I started dating Hilary on my thirteenth birthday . . . then I got a little bored so I started . . . dating Lindsay. Then I didn't want to do that anymore, so I got back with Hilary . . . then I ended up cheating on Hilary with her best friend."

💔 2000–2003

2007– 👤

Brooke Hogan

Hulk Hogan's daughter, Brooke, was *FHM*'s first cover model under twenty-one. They wanted to see her in a bikini so much that they were willing to sacrifice their liquor ads for that issue.

After meeting at an airport, fourteen-year-old Hogan started seeing Carter. But when her father, Hulk, met the guy, he said, according to Brooke, "No, dude. You are definitely not hanging out here," and kicked Carter out of the house.

2000–2003
💔

2002 💔

◄ BACK Nicole Richie

Samantha Ronson
Successful DJ Ronson was the first act signed by Jay-Z's (pg. 28) Roc-A-Fella Records. When pestered by paparazzi in 2008 about her pretty obvious relationship with Lindsay Lohan, Ronson gave the pithy response, "Are you retarded?"

Lohan tasted girl love for the first time with DJ Ronson, coming out to the press after two years of media speculation. In response to her ex-convict father's disapproval, Lohan tactfully posted an open letter on the *New York Post* Web site that read, "Samantha is not evil ... She loves me, as I do her."

Giles started seeing Lohan at the Cirque Lodge rehab center, where both were being treated for drug addictions. After the sixty-day program ended, according to Giles, Lohan replaced drugs with sex. "She'd demand sex again and again ... Sex became a key part of her recovery."

2008–2009

Riley Giles
Snowboarder

2006 💔

2007 💔

2006–2008 💔

Frank Delgado
Club promoter and Brody Jenner pal

Carter dated Lohan in the midst of his relationship with fellow Disney chick Hilary Duff, sparking a feud that boiled over when Duff tried to have Lohan thrown out of the premiere party for her film *Cheaper by the Dozen.* Film excs sided with Lohan (who had been invited!) and Duff and her mom stormed out in protest.

Lindsay Lohan
She was real cute in 1998's *The Parent Trap*, but little Lindsay grew up way too fast. Her crazy parents didn't help—their separations, lawsuits, and disputes exploded right along with her career. Multiple stints in rehab will hopefully set this girl straight.

2002–2003 2002–2003 2007

In a moment of randy weakness, Lohan permitted Best to shoot some "private" naked shots of her, but a "hacker" stole the snaps and Lindsay went off on her blog, saying, "My lawyer knows about it. If I ever find out who broke into my computer, he is in big shit."

Apparently the security camera loves Best. His sexual antics with Jagger outside a London club in 2005 were caught on tape and Best said, "We were both turned on and couldn't wait. I played around with her, and she played around with me."

💔 **2005**

Calum Best
British footballer George Best's son

Elizabeth Jagger
Fashion model

Jamie Burke ▲ p. 61

This couple made plans to visit their drink-happy homeland of Ireland, but the relationship was canceled before takeoff.

Jared Leto p. 99 ▶

💔 **2006**

💔 **2005–2006**

Harry Morton
Pink Taco founder

💔 **2005**

💔 **2003–2004** Wilmer Valderrama p. 110 ▶

This ultimate classic-rock coupling was created by none other than Keith Richards, who introduced Lennon and Jagger at a Rock and Roll Hall of Fame dinner. Her mother, Jerry Hall (pg. 51), approved, saying, "Sean's adorable. He looks so like John and writes beautiful poetry."

Sean Lennon p. 145 ▶

💔 **2004–2006**

Aaron Carter
Triple-platinum recording kid Carter was a huge hit in the early 2000s. He is now better known for getting arrested for marijuana possession (under two ounces, your honor!) and suing his mother for allegedly stealing his money.

💔 **2006**

Carter proposed to provocatively named Peniche on stage in Las Vegas after they had been together for five days. They called it off six days later, perhaps because she was his brother Nick Carter's ex-girlfriend.

Just one of the *Charmed* costars seduced by the witchy Milano (see Brian Krause), Dane was seen with Milano about town (the indicator of really serious relationships in Hollywood) throughout the summer of 2003.

Alyssa Milano

Carl Pavano
Baseball pitcher

A born and bred Yankees fan, Milano found new loyalty when she started dating Marlins pitcher Pavano (the first of her trio of starting pitchers). They split when Pavano couldn't handle the omnipresent paparazzi.

◀ p. 128 Lara Flynn Boyle   2002

2003

Eric Dane
"McSteamy" from *Grey's Anatomy* got his start with small parts on *Saved by the Bell* (who didn't?), *The Wonder Years*, and *Roseanne*.

🔒 2004–

💔 2009

Say it ain't so! Another sex tape leaked onto the Internet!? This one featured Peniche, Dane, and his wife, Rebecca Gayheart, smoking drugs and frolicking in a bathtub. Dane may have been right when he mumbled that he was with "two of the hottest girls this side of Mulholland," depending which side they were on.

Dane and Gayheart eloped to Las Vegas after deciding to get married over dinner. Referring to a storyline from his series *Grey's Anatomy*, Dane said, "If my wife said I had to go sixty days without sex? I think I could do it. But I don't think she'd ever make me."

Josh Shambaugh
Model

Justin Timberlake (pg. 98) revealed that a *J* pendant worn by Milano on the cover of *FHM* wasn't for him but was for her ex-boyfriend Josh Shambaugh.

Brian Krause
Actor

Krause started seeing recently divorced Milano on the set of *Charmed*—while he was still married to model Beth Bruce.

◀ BACK Aaron Carter   2006 💔

◀ p. 89 Nick Carter   2005 💔

Kari Ann Peniche
The former Miss Oregon Teen USA 2002 was shocked when her title was stripped for posing nude in *Playboy* in 2004. Was that in the manual?

When their sex-tape threesome went public in 2009, the world learned that Gayheart found Peniche to be "normal, funny, smart, fun," and Dane regarded her as a "good hang."   2009 💔

After Ratner allegedly picked fifteen-year-old Gayheart out of a lineup of models auditioning for his student film, the two dated for years and got engaged. They stayed together until she caught him with Jennifer Meyer (pg. 45), daughter of Universal Studios head Ron Meyer (who coincidentally was putting out Ratner's next movie, *Family Man*).

◀ p. 44 Brett Ratner

2004 🔒

Rebecca Gayheart
Gayheart was discovered (and hit on) by NYU student Brett Ratner (pg. 44) when he cast her in his student film *Whatever Happened to Mason Reese*. A stint as the facesplashing Noxzema girl brought exposure, but she got more than she wanted when she struck and killed a nine-year-old jaywalker and pleaded no contest to vehicular manslaughter in 2001.

Cinjun Tate
Lead singer for band Remy Zero

Milano married Tate on a Louisiana plantation on New Year's Day 1999, with her *Charmed* costars, Shannen Doherty (pg. 45) and Holly Combs in tow. They divorced less than eleven months later.

Barry Zito
This 2002 Cy Young Award winner landed the most expensive contract in baseball history (at the time) when he signed with the San Francisco Giants for $126 million over seven years. He went 6-9 at the start of the season.

1988–1999 🎤

Milano became a free agent after getting dumped by Carl Pavano, so she signed with Oakland A's pitcher Zito. Maybe she tired him out—when they started dating, Zito's ERA increased to just under 4.00.

Scott Wolf

Good old Bailey did so much to help the Salingers that it's hard to separate Wolf from his role on 1994's *Party of Five*. But the actor got his start much earlier with a role on *Kids Inc.* and as an extra on *Saved by the Bell*.

💔 2001

Milano fell for Wolf while shooting the video-game-inspired *Double Dragon*. They quickly got engaged and posed in a bubble bath for *People* magazine (don't all engaged couples do that?). But the wedding was called off a few months later and Milano's "SRW" tattoo was recast as an abbreviation for "Some Rad Woman."

2003 💔

Alyssa Milano

Milano was typecast as the result of a successful eight-year stint as sweet Samantha Micelli on *Who's the Boss?* She tried to shed her nice-girl image by getting naked and simulating sex in *Embrace of the Vampire* (1994), *Deadly Sins* (1995), and *Poison Ivy II: Lily* (1996). She succeeded.

2002 💔
2001 💔
1999 🔒
2004–2005 💔

Boston Red Sox fan Dushku started dating Penny back when he was pitching for the Los Angeles Dodgers. Penny signed with the Red Sox after they had split. Could it have been a desperate attempt to get her back?

When Dillon was launching his career in films like *The Outsiders*, Dushku was still in diapers. This didn't prevent him from pampering her at a 2006 pre-Oscars party.

2007 💔

Brad Penny
Boston Red Sox pitcher

Third in Milano's rotation of starting pitchers, Penny improved his stats during the relationship (unlike his predecessors). After three strikes, Milano said she was done with baseball players because "they're grown men playing a little boy's sport."

💍 1993–1994
💔 2003–2004
💔 2005
💔 1985–1986

Her career was just getting started when thirteen-year-old *Who's the Boss?* star Milano dated older-man Cameron, then fourteen. "He used to dedicate songs to me on the radio," she said.

Milano married her Creative Artists Agency representative Bugliari in 2009, snagging back that final 10 percent of her earnings.

🔒 2009–
💔 2002
💔 1987–1988

Haim and Milano dated in the late 1980s, right around the time she released her workout video, *Teen Steam*, which featured Milano in sports bra and Adidas high-tops, rapping fitness instructions.

Eliza Dushku

Dushku has always refused to appear in nude scenes, claiming that people have "a better chance of seeing God than seeing me naked." Unlike many starlets before her, she's actually held to her policy.

2006 💔

Matt Dillon

In his teens, Dillon was spotted by a casting director while he was cutting class. Since then he's been nominated for a Golden Globe and an Oscar for his role in the 2002 film *Crash* and has dated some of Hollywood's hottest, proving that sometimes it is cool to skip school.

💔 1995–1998

Cameron Diaz — p. 98 ▶

Kirk Cameron

Long before Cameron headlined the rapture film *Left Behind*, he was already a born-again Christian, causing trouble on the set of hit sitcom *Growing Pains*. Cameron demanded rewrites on episodes that featured Mike Seaver's girlfriend giving him keys to her apartment and had the actress fired because she had appeared in *Playboy*.

David Bugliari
Talent agent

Justin Timberlake — p. 98 ▶
Corey Haim — p. 100 ▶
Shoshanna Lonstein — p. 33 ▶

The Kids Are (Doing) All Right

If you want to sleep with the children of celebrities, it doesn't hurt to be the progeny of such a union yourself. Translation: Famous kids get it on with each other. Elijah Blue Allman (pg. 89), the result of a "duet" between Cher (pg. 140) and Gregg Allman, found love, or something like it, with Bijou Phillips (pg. 145, daughter of John Phillips, pg. 58, from The Mamas and the Papas) and both *Simple Life* heiresses—Nicole Richie (pg. 91, adopted daughter of Lionel Richie) and Paris Hilton (pg. 89, daughter of Richard Hilton). Bijou herself got it on with the big fish of famous kids, Sean Lennon (pg. 145, son of John and Yoko), who himself dated Elizabeth Jagger (pg. 93, yes, that Jagger), who went on to get it on in front of security cameras with Calum Best (pg. 93, son of British footballer George Best). Alison Eastwood (pg. 121), who was conceived during the *Dirty Harry* shoot, dated Chad McQueen (race-car-driving son of Steve McQueen). But Ahmet Zappa (pg. 39, son of Frank Zappa), bucked the trend by hooking up with Rose McGowan (pg. 38, daughter of an Irish artist) and Selma Blair (pg. 153, daughter of a Michigan judge).

Justin Timberlake's (pg. 98) grandmother, Sadie Bomar, knows her pecan pies, her squash relish, and a little too much about her grandson's sex life (or at least his romantic inclinations). Granny has never been shy about telling all to the press; in fact, they seem to seek her insight every time the singer meets a new girl. Of his 2002 fling with Alyssa Milano (pg. 95), this sage of the South said, "It's a relationship that's just started, I reckon. Alyssa . . . understands that he is busy." They split a few months later. When Britney Spears (pg. 33) hinted that her ex Timberlake had a wee "little" problem down there (using her thumb and forefinger to illustrate), Granny struck back, saying, "I helped raise him, and I can assure you there is nothing wrong with him physically." Go Granny!

In 2004, Granny Sadie said that Justin would never marry Cameron Diaz (pg. 98) because "she isn't that mature." That was three years before their traumatic public split. Right again! But Jessica Biel (pg. 98) got a blessing (and Diaz got a diss) in 2008 when Granny said, "Jessica is a sweet girl, and they really enjoy each other's company. She's his age and isn't possessive; Justin should get married in Lynn's backyard in Tennessee." From Grandma Sadie, that's about the highest praise you can get! Then again, Sadie later said "Justin does his own thing and he isn't ready to marry. As far as we're concerned, he's always been single."

Mario Lopez

Since his gig as Latin hunk A. C. Slater on *Saved by the Bell*, Lopez has been dogged by questions about his sexuality that were further fueled by his appearance in a Greg Louganis biopic and a starring role in the Broadway revival of *A Chorus Line*.

Josh Duhamel

American actor

1983

2004–

John Mayer p. 109

2007

While filming *Requiem for a Dream*, Leto refused to have sex with Diaz for two months, in preparation for his role as an emaciated junkie. Now that is some seriously committed Method acting.

Janet Jackson

The youngest child of the Jackson clan starred on *Good Times* and *Diff'rent Strokes* before signing her first record deal at sixteen. Her Super Bowl wardrobe malfunction (when Justin Timberlake ripped off her bodice, exposing a nipple) caused controversy and cost CBS $550,000.

Stacy "Fergie" Ferguson

California vocalist Fergie was a child star on *Kids Incorporated* along with Mario Lopez and Jennifer Love Hewitt (pg. 110). She began a crystal meth addiction when she turned eighteen and admits that her prolific sexuality got her into trouble during that time.

When Timberlake was a wee sixteen years old, he had a fling with twenty-three-year-old Fergie, who was addicted to crystal meth at the time.

1998–2002

Cameron Diaz

The San Diego–born third-generation Cuban American can't speak a lick of Spanish, but when you're gorgeous, it doesn't matter if you're multilingual. After modeling, her big break came when she was cast as human-hair-gel-stealing Mary in *There's Something About Mary*.

2007

1995–1998

◀ p. 95 Matt Dillon

2003–2007

Diaz and Timberlake met at the slime-filled Kid's Choice Awards in 2003 and embarked on an overly documented romance that ended with a formal press release citing their "love and respect for one another." Days later, when Timberlake arrived at a party with new girlfriend Jessica Biel, Diaz went off on the boy for forty-five minutes. Respect!

When asked if he'd gotten with his 2004 Super Bowl coperformer Jackson, Timberlake said "I think she's a lovely person . . . and if I did, how lucky would I be? . . . I would say in life that I was lucky." Hint, hint.

Things started off rough for this couple. Biel was verbally assaulted by his ex, Cameron Diaz, and then Timberlake, when asked about the love of his life early in the relationship, responded, "I haven't met her yet."

Biel and Evans dated for two years, during which time they played boyfriend and girlfriend in two films together, *Cellular* and *London*.

Danielle Ditto

Childhood girlfriend

At age fourteen, Timberlake fell for Ditto at a pizza place in Millington, Tennessee. According to her, they did it for the first time after her fifteenth birthday and were at it "like rabbits," eventually getting caught in bed by his mother.

1995–1996

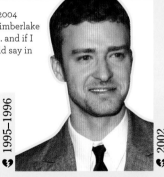

Justin Timberlake

From the ashes of *NSYNC (named by Timberlake's mother based on the last letters of the members' first names) rose a phoenix named Justin whose debut solo album, *Justified*, sold 7 million copies.

2002

1997

2003–2007

Jessica Biel

Biel was best known as a preacher's daughter in the family drama *7th Heaven*, a good-girl role she tried to ditch by posing topless for *Gear* magazine at age seventeen. Producer Aaron Spelling wouldn't let her out of her contract, despite the controversy.

2007–

◀ p. 95 Alyssa Milano 2002

◀ p. 33 Britney Spears 1998–2002

2002

1997–1999

Lindsay Lohan p. 93 ▲

Leto hated the attention that came with dating Lohan, allegedly telling her, "'Don't come over if you're going to bring fifteen fucking paparazzi.'" In fairness to Leto, the bedroom would be awfully cramped with even ten paparazzi squeezed inside.

1998–2002 💔

Jamie-Lynn Sigler
The half Jewish, half Cuban Sigler found fame as a very convincing Jersey Italian princess in the HBO series *The Sopranos* which began shooting when she was sixteen.

Jerry Ferrara
American actor

2008–2009 💔

In what seemed like a very special HBO crossover event, *The Sopranos* daughter Meadow started dating *Entourage*'s Turtle after playing herself in an *Entourage* cameo—in which she shared a mile-high club initiation with Ferrara.

2006–2008 💔

2005 💔

2003–2005 🔓

A. J. DiScala p. 90 ▶

Ashlee Simpson p. 85 ▶

After getting dumped by Ashley Olsen, Sartiano scooped up the next best Ashlee (Ashley Tisdale was not available).

Scott Sartiano
Club owner

2005–2006 💔

Jared Leto
At twenty-three, Leto embodied high school heartthrob Jordan Catalano on *My So-Called Life*. He continues to pursue his love of music with successful (for an actor's side-project) band 30 Seconds to Mars.

Eighteen-year-old Olsen didn't dump her thirty-year-old boyfriend Sartiano because he got her tangled up in a tale of bribery, drug dealing, and assault (which led to her $40 million defamation suit against the *National Enquirer*). Instead, according to her people, it was because she needed to clear her head for back-to-school.

Jenna Dewan
Dancer and actress

Justin and Britney Spears (pg. 33) officially split after Timberlake's sultry dance performance with Dewan at the 2002 Grammy Awards. At the time, Justin said, "I love Britney with all my heart, and I would never, ever do anything to disrespect her or degrade her," perhaps alluding to Britney's alleged affair.

2004–2006

Chris Evans p. 35 ▼

2004–2005 💔 / 2005–2008 💔

This couple got together briefly in 2005, and yet again in 2008. Despite the pair being spotted holding hands and making out at a gala in L.A., they insisted they were "just friends."

A year after breaking up with Leto, Johansson cut loose on allegations that she was promiscuous, saying, "There does seem to be a mistaken belief out there that I am sexually available somehow. I work really hard when I'm in a relationship to make it work in a monogamous way."

Timberlake met Finn while home for Christmas in 1997. When Britney Spears (pg. 33) dropped out of girl-group innosense, Timberlake's mother, the band manager, recruited Finn to replace her. Ironically, Finn would soon be replaced by Spears in Timberlake's heart.

Kelly Slater p. 29 ▼

Scarlett Johansson p. 46 ▼

Ashley Olsen
Ashley, the slightly more grounded half of the billion-dollar Olsen duopoly, lives in New York and attends NYU, while her sister lays claim to the West Coast.

2005–2008 💔

2004–2005 💔💔

There's a reason Columbia University has one of the worst football teams on Earth: Their quarterbacks are too busy dating grown-up child stars.

Matt Kaplan
Columbia University quarterback

2001–2004

2007

Lance Armstrong NEXT ▶

Ashley rolled into the strong arms of Armstrong, fifteen years her senior, at New York's Gramercy Park Hotel in 2007. On that fateful evening, the pair made out all night long, as onlookers wondered whether she was legal (she was!).

♥ 2008–

To some, Ashley Olsen is a national treasure. To Bartha, that's just the name of one of the movies he's starred in. Bartha, eight years Olsen's senior, has reportedly been planning their wedding in the South of France.

Veronica Finn
American singer

Justin Bartha
American actor

When the Spice Girl married the fledgling footballer they became a supercool couple known for sexiness, glamour, celebrity friends, and children with really, you know, interesting names (Brooklyn, Romeo, and Cruz).

David Beckham

Having played for the two biggest soccer clubs in the world, in 2007 Becks was signed to the L.A. Galaxy and hoped to raise the profile of the sport in the States. So far, soccer is still less popular than scabies.

1997–

Victoria Beckham

When Victoria Adams answered an ad looking for girls who were "street smart, extroverted, ambitious, and able to sing and dance," little did she know she was signing up for Posh Spice fame, fortune, and footballer David Beckham.

1995–1996

Corey Haim

Haim rocketed to *Tiger Beat* stardom in the 1980s with films like *Lucas* (Winona Ryder's [pg. 113] first picture) and eight films with Corey Feldman (pg. 78), but a long struggle with drugs derailed his career. "I smoked my first joint on *Lost Boys* [then started on downers] until at the end it was about eighty-five a day . . . and that was just the valium."

Rebounding after breaking up with Owen Wilson, Hudson had a very brief fling with Armstrong. How brief? It lasted about as long as *Bride Wars* played in theaters . . . okay, maybe it wasn't that brief.

Kate Hudson

PR executive Kristin Richards knew how to spread a viral message. Unfortunately, the Livestrong campaign was stronger than her marriage to Armstrong, which crumbled when he conquered cancer but failed to conquer a desire to cheat on his wife.

Haim dated Beckham back when she was Victoria Adams after the two met outside a London recording studio. While Haim reminisced about the unusual way she kissed, "[It felt] like a girl gnawing on your lip," Beckham said, "We didn't have sex or anything. In actual fact, he didn't seem to want to try."

They were already dating when Eggert starred in 1992's *Blown Away*, which featured a torrid sex scene with Haim—and another with Corey Feldman (pg. 78)! They got engaged, but the only thing that came out of the relationship was the straight-to-video movie *Just One of the Girls*, in which Haim disguises himself as a cheerleader.

1992–1993

Kristin Richards
Public relations executive

Nicole Eggert

Eggert's starring role as Jamie Powell on *Charles in Charge* led to a part on the international hit *Baywatch*, which led to implants, taking her from a modest 32A to a more bathing-suit-friendly 34C. These were reduced to 34B when the show ended. So how many passengers are on the bus?

2000–2002

Josh Charles
American actor

BACK Ashley Olsen

2008

2007

Lance Armstrong

Beloved by Americans, detested by Europeans, and tolerated by Tahitians, Armstrong is either a national hero or a world-class fraud. Let's let history be the judge and focus on the cyclist's sexual exploits.

1997–2003

2003–2006

2003–2006

Sheryl Crow

Crow began her career as a backup singer for Michael Jackson (pg. 13) on his Bad World Tour. In 1999 she played Casper, an asthmatic junkie, in *The Minus Man*, opposite then-boyfriend Owen Wilson. What? You don't remember that one? Lucky you.

Crow's quick relationship with Rock ended when he hooked up with Pamela Anderson (pg. 29) at a New York party. That didn't stop Anderson from promoting Crow and Rock's country duet "Picture" by personally handing it to radio host Rick Dees, who made it a hit.

"All I wanna do is Lance Armstrong, I got a feeling, this will not last that long." From power couple to celebs unified by their quest to combat cancer, this relationship seemed too good to be true.

2003

1998–2001

p. 29 Kid Rock

2001

Kristen Bell

The baby-faced star of *Veronica Mars* never thought of herself as "womanly," because she always played characters ten years younger than she was. In real life she is a good vegetarian girl who has stated, "I love nerds."

1988 💔

Lala Sloatman

Model-actress Sloatman's aunt Gail was Frank Zappa's widow, making her cousins with Ahmet Zappa (pg. 39), Dweezil Zappa (pg. 22), and all the other little Zappas.

1996–1998 🔒 **Chris Robinson**
Singer for band The Black Crowes

Getty moved in with Sloatman when he was sixteen and she was twenty-one. "It wasn't an act of rebellion," he said. "I'd fallen in love with a girl."

💔 **1991–1993**

Balthazar Getty
American actor

2007– 👤

1987–1988

They started dating in 2007, shortly after both split from their respective partners. If things work out, Shepard is in for a naughty treat: Bell has stated that she still has her Catholic school uniform and is planning to wear it on her wedding night!

Dax Shepard

After gaining exposure as part of Ashton Kutcher's team on *Punk'd*, Shepard landed a series of comedy roles in movies like *Without a Paddle* and *Employee of the Month*.

On the subject of her failed marriage to Chris Robinson, Hudson admitted, "We were so in love and passionate, and then we would just hate each other and throw stuff around." At least they kept things interesting.

2000–2006 🔒

2007 💔

Kate Hudson

The daughter of actress Goldie Hawn, Hudson won a Golden Globe for her role as rock groupie Penny Lane in *Almost Famous*. Since then she has moved from one romantic comedy (and one romantic costar) to another.

2008 Lance Armstrong 💔

♥ 2008–

Jennifer Connelly
American actress

Owen Wilson

Owen Wilson, the actor with a nose by Picasso and brother of Luke Wilson (pg. 79), has starred in some of the biggest comedies of the past ten years. The public caught a glimpse into Wilson's shockingly sad private life after a failed suicide attempt became front page news in 2007.

Connelly dumped Charles right before she won an Oscar for her performance in *A Beautiful Mind*. Apparently there was room for only one man in Connelly's life, and he's little and gold.

1998–2001 💔

Who would have guessed that fellow Texans Wilson and Lance Armstrong would share two of the same women? First Armstrong followed Wilson to Crow, and later he went after Wilson's other ex, Kate Hudson.

💔 **2006–2008**   **2006–2008**

💔 **2002**   Hudson broke off her yearlong liaison with her *You, Me and Dupree* costar in 2007 after it became clear to her that his partying took priority over their relationship. They briefly reconnected after Wilson's suicide attempt.

2009 Alex Rodriguez NEXT ▶

Few recall that, after Moore's marriage to Bruce Willis (pg. 138) ended, she got it on with somewhat-younger man Wilson before moving on to the significantly younger Ashton Kutcher (pg. 135).

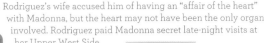

▲ p.54

Naomi Campbell

Cynthia Scurtis
Miami socialite

Rodriguez first saw Scurtis on the stair-climber at a Coconut Grove gym in 1996 and pursued her for six years before popping the question. She famously wore a tank top reading "fuck you" to ward off paparazzi after a photo of Rodriguez with a stripper surfaced, but after A-Rod was linked to Madonna, she filed for divorce.

P 1996–2008

Rodriguez's wife accused him of having an "affair of the heart" with Madonna, but the heart may not have been the only organ involved. Rodriguez paid Madonna secret late-night visits at her Upper West Side apartment, and they even attended Yom Kippur—the Jewish day of repentance— services together.

2008–2009

Madonna

Campbell was just one of the bumps in Sean Penn and Robin Wright's relationship when the actor spent time with the supermodel at the infamous Chateau Marmont.

Petra Nemcova
Fashion model Nemcova was featured in the *Sports Illustrated Swimsuit Issue* in 2001, 2003, 2004, 2005, and 2006. During an interview on *Jimmy Kimmel Live!* Nemcova said she speaks seven languages—Czech, Slovak, Polish, Italian, French, English, and body language. No doubt about that.

2007

Alex Rodriguez
A little of the luster came off Yankee third-baseman A-Rod's record as the youngest five-hundred home-run hitter and richest contract holder in baseball history ($275 million over ten years) when he admitted to using steroids.

◀ BACK **Kate Hudson**   *2009* ♥

◀ p.158 **Christy Turlington**

Patric and Turlington had an intense relationship (not unlike his film roles) in which Patric insulted her modeling friends and forced her to study business at NYU. "These girls are idiots. I keep telling Christy that looks don't last, but education does," he said, but when he got photographed with his ex, Julia Roberts (pg. 159), Turlington got educated and expelled him.

Jason Patric
Smoldering star Jason Patric broke out in 1987's vampire comedy *The Lost Boys*. He's the grandson of comedy legend Jackie Gleason and son of the Pulitzer Prize–winning playwright Jason Miller, who played the priest in *The Exorcist*. He's looking more and more like Dennis Miller every day.

1995–2000

Just a month after Penn announced his separation from Robin Wright, he arrived at Sir Elton John's post-Oscar party with Nemcova on his arm. When the Penns reconciled a few months later, they went to a Nemcova-hosted party together for reasons that are largely unfathomable—nothing good on TV?

When the Penns' marriage hit a rough patch in 2007, it was reported that Patric and Penn had rekindled their romance.

1989–1990

1990–2009   *1990–2009*

Robin Wright Penn
Give the girl a pat on the back for being the one to teach Forrest Gump about the birds and the bees, with her roommate a few feet away no less. But before that, she taught us all that death cannot stop true love—only delay it for a while—in the cult favorite *The Princess Bride*.

The couple were happily married until rumors of a dalliance with marriage-killer Sienna Miller (pg. 82) surfaced in 2007. Soon afterward, they announced that they were divorcing but called it off until rumors of his relationships with model Petra Nemcova and actress Natalie Portman led Robin Penn to file the paperwork in August of 2009.

Wright and Sheen dated when she was fifteen and he was sixteen. She was already working as a model and he was the star pitcher at Santa Monica High School.

◀ p.133 **Charlie Sheen**   *1981* ♥

Warren Beatty p.140

Beatty and Madonna costarred in the colorful 1990 film *Dick Tracy* in which she played Breathless Mahoney and he played the titular Dick. Madonna wanted the part so badly, she worked for scale ($1,440 a week) and said, "Dick Tracy is my life. You take that any way you want to take it."

Guy Ritchie
Film director

Their marriage produced a beautiful son named Rocco and a terrible film named *Swept Away* and ended when Madonna found a new guy named A-Rod.

1988–1990

1999–2008

Jewel
Perhaps the most famous Alaskan not named Palin, Jewel rose from bleak beginnings to become a Grammy-nominated chart topper.

Penn "discovered" the folk singer and gave her a big break when he asked her to contribute a song for the soundtrack of his film *The Crossing Guard*. He went so far as to anoint her "the female Bob Dylan."

2008–2009

Carlos Leon
Personal trainer

1994–1996

Madonna and personal trainer Leon were doing more than squat thrusts when her first child, Lourdes, was conceived and delivered in 1996.

Vanilla Ice
Rapper

1988 John F. Kennedy Jr. p.11 ▶

1992

Madonna

"Like" was the key word in sexy rocker Madonna's first number one hit, 1984's "Like a Virgin." From her early days as a dancer training in New York, Madonna has hooked up with the rich and powerful (and Vanilla Ice) on her journey to becoming the most successful female recording artist of all time.

Madonna and Vanilla Ice dated for eight months but split after she included pictures of him in her book *Sex*. "It was a moment in time, and I guess I was a part of it—I just didn't want to be a part of that slutty package," said Ice, a sentiment echoed by almost every man Madonna has been with.

1982

Mark Kamins
New York DJ

Most women would be happy if their boyfriends made breakfast or put the toilet seat down; but Kamins exceeded expectations when he helped launch Madonna's career.

1995–1996

2008 1994

1985–1988 1984 1994 1993–1995 1982

In the '80s, few couples were more infamous than Penn and Madonna. Their marriage was fraught with fights, one of which landed Penn in prison for sixty days for assaulting a photographer.

Sean Penn

The two-time Oscar winner first found success as the stoner Jeff Spicoli in *Fast Times at Ridgemont High*. During his acceptance speech at the 2009 Oscars, Penn admitted that his outspoken political beliefs often made him hard to like, and he said this right after he called everyone "commie homo-loving sons-of-guns."

🔒 1985–1988

Benitez owned the rights to the song "Holiday" and convinced Madonna to record what was to become her first hit single.

Jean-Michel Basquiat
Artist

Madonna respected Basquiat's talent, saying, "He was one of the few people I was truly envious of." Madonna in a relationship based on mutual respect? Imagine that.

Jellybean Benitez
DJ and music producer

Dennis Rodman p.40 ▼

Jenny Lynn Shimizu NEXT ▶

Stavros Niarchos III p.92

Naomi Campbell p.54

Mike Tyson
Professional boxer

Givens saw Murphy at a New York comedy club and, after the show, she asked him if he'd like her autograph. Thus began a one-year romance.

Eddie Murphy p.23

Givens dated Jordan at the start of his Chicago Bulls career after they met at a North Carolina golf tournament. She blamed their split on career demands, but she went on to play his future wife, Juanita Vanoy, in a 1999 TV biopic about him.

Timothy Hutton p.151

Michael Jordan
Basketball star

💔 1989

Givens's marriage to Tyson was a short one and ended predictably when she accused Tyson of spousal abuse and he claimed she was a gold-digger after his money.

1987–1989 🔒

1980

1986–1987

💔

Alison Berns
Howard Stern's college sweetheart

Robin Givens
Givens obviously had an eye for talent, because she dated Eddie Murphy (pg. 23) and Michael Jordan before anyone had ever heard of them.

They met on the set of 1997's *Playing God*, and Jolie tattooed an *H* on her arm in Hutton's honor. When they split up, she kept the tattoo but said it now referred to her brother James Haven.

Jonny Lee Miller
British actor

💔 1989

When Everhart's PR agent leaked information about this relationship, Stern blasted back on his radio show, denying the story and saying the leak "ruined his life." He later came clean and Everhart had no hard feelings—she told *FHM* magazine that Stern was the "best sex she's ever had."

◀ p.32 **Angie Everhart**

💔 2000

2000 💔

1978–2001 🔓

Pitt and Givens dated in 1989, when she was freshly separated from husband Mike Tyson. Givens said the heavyweight boxer would sometimes "show up in the driveway" and scare away her dates.

Stern met Givens on his show, and they started dating soon after his split from wife Allison Berns. According to a source close to Givens, he was "obsessed with her" and called her "ten times a day."

Miller married Jolie after meeting on the set of nerd thriller *Hackers* in 1995. The world got a glimpse of Jolie's more "inventive" side at their wedding, which she attended in skintight rubber pants and a white shirt inscribed with Miller's name in her own blood.

When they wed in 2008, Stern helped plan everything, down to the flower arrangements. Ostrosky said, "I think he's going to be the groomzilla."

2000– 🔒

Howard Stern
How did a gangly geek with a Jewfro make a career out of crank calling cripples and receiving porn star lap dances on the radio? Stern is just funny enough to make this shtick work and thus is the highest-paid radio personality in America.

Beth Ostrosky
Model

Jolie revealed her lesbian relationship (is there anything she can't do?) with *Foxfire* costar Shimizu, saying, "I would probably have married Jenny if I hadn't married my husband. I fell in love with her the first second I saw her."

💔 2000

Jenny Lynn Shimizu
Japanese American model

💔 💔

◀ BACK **Madonna**

◀ p.142 **Billy Bob Thornton**

1993–1995

Ione Skye p.181   1998–2001

1995

Timothy Hutton 1998–1999

Juliette Lewis

Lewis is Hollywood's go-to girl to play serial killers and psycho ex-girlfriends, and in 1996, she posed for a picture in *Us Weekly* which showed just a close-up of her filthy bare feet.

Pitt and Lewis met while working on the TV movie *Too Young to Die* when Lewis was just sixteen. They dated seriously for three years, costarring as serial killers in the 1993 film *Kalifornia*. Still, when asked in 2009 how Pitt fared in bed, Lewis reportedly said, "He was no *big* deal, if ya know what I mean."

Pitt and Schoelen met on the set of 1988's *Cutting Class* and were engaged for three months until Schoelen dumped him. Pitt later told the media that she was the only woman who had broken his heart.

Jill Schoelen
America actress

Uma Thurman p. 54

Gwyneth Paltrow p. 79

Thurman and Pitt arrived at the 1995 Golden Globe Awards alone but left together, so they can thank the Hollywood Foreign Press Association for providing at least one great night.

Jennifer Aniston p. 108 ▶

Shalane McCall
Child actress on *Dallas*

Pitt and McCall hooked up on the set of *Dallas* in the hunk's first smooching scene ever captured on film. "It was a real sweaty-palms time for me," said Pitt. "It was kind of wild, because I'd never even met her before."

Applegate described how their short relationship abruptly ended: "We went to the MTV Awards, and I ditched him! I left him there, and I felt really bad about it; I really, really do. I left with somebody else."

1988–1989 ♂
1990–1993 ♡
1989 💔

Brad Pitt

When he isn't rebuilding New Orleans by hand, Pitt is busy being *People* magazine's "Sexiest Man Alive"—at least he was in 1995 and 2000. But in his feature film debut, 1988's *The Dark Side of the Sun*, he played a guy with a really bad skin disorder. Ick.

1988–1989 ♂
1995 💔
1995–1997 ♂
1998–2005 🔒

1987 💔
1989 💔
1988–1989 💔

2005– ♥

Malone described her wacky "sex-capades" with Pitt, which included role-playing cowboys and Indians and public romps at concert venues. Despite all that, she said, "Jennifer [Aniston, pg. 108] could be in for a boring time. Sexually he certainly wasn't the best I have had."

Christina Applegate
American actress

Angelina Jolie

Jolie got her start as a model and music-video girl for Meat Loaf and Lenny Kravitz (pg. 69) before breaking out in 1998's *Gia*, described by a critic as "the most beautiful train wreck ever filmed." She remains estranged from father, Jon Voight (pg. 57), despite his appearance in her *Lara Croft* film.

1995–1999 🔒
1999–2003 🔒

2005– ♥

Jolie was accused of being the spark that started the fire that burned Pitt's marriage with Jennifer Aniston (pg. 108) to the ground. Jolie admitted that they "fell in love" on the set of *Mr. & Mrs. Smith* although she claimed they never got it on.

Simon Cowell

Cowell has proven that all you really need to succeed on TV is a sharp tongue and a tight shirt. The British A&R exec is best known to American audiences as the hardest nut to crack on the ratings power-house *American Idol*.

Sinitta Malone
Pop singer

1982–1999 ♂

Cowell discovered Malone and signed her to a record label. It can only be assumed that Malone got sick of the constant critiquing, leading to the end of their seventeen-year union in 1999.

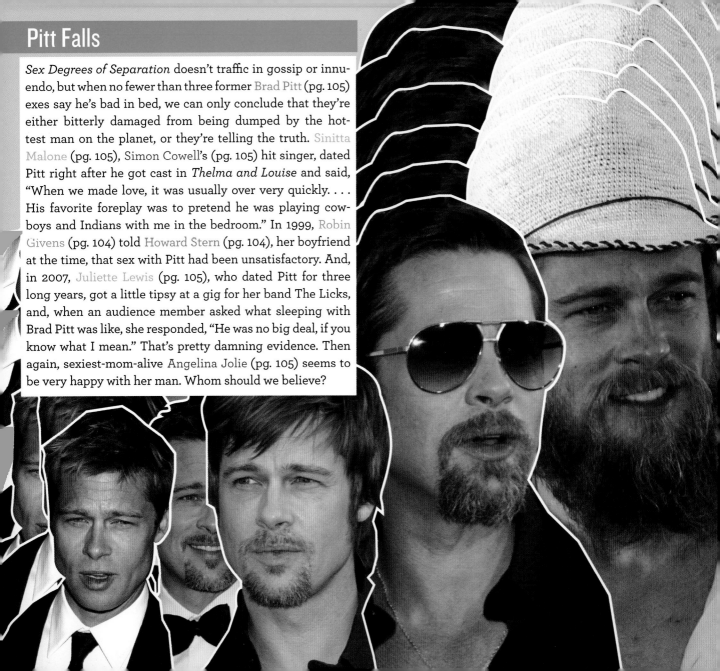

Pitt Falls

Sex Degrees of Separation doesn't traffic in gossip or innu-endo, but when no fewer than three former Brad Pitt (pg. 105) exes say he's bad in bed, we can only conclude that they're either bitterly damaged from being dumped by the hot-test man on the planet, or they're telling the truth. Sinitta Malone (pg. 105), Simon Cowell's (pg. 105) hit singer, dated Pitt right after he got cast in *Thelma and Louise* and said, "When we made love, it was usually over very quickly. . . . His favorite foreplay was to pretend he was playing cow-boys and Indians with me in the bedroom." In 1999, Robin Givens (pg. 104) told Howard Stern (pg. 104), her boyfriend at the time, that sex with Pitt had been unsatisfactory. And, in 2007, Juliette Lewis (pg. 105), who dated Pitt for three long years, got a little tipsy at a gig for her band The Licks, and, when an audience member asked what sleeping with Brad Pitt was like, she responded, "He was no big deal, if you know what I mean." That's pretty damning evidence. Then again, sexiest-mom-alive Angelina Jolie (pg. 105) seems to be very happy with her man. Whom should we believe?

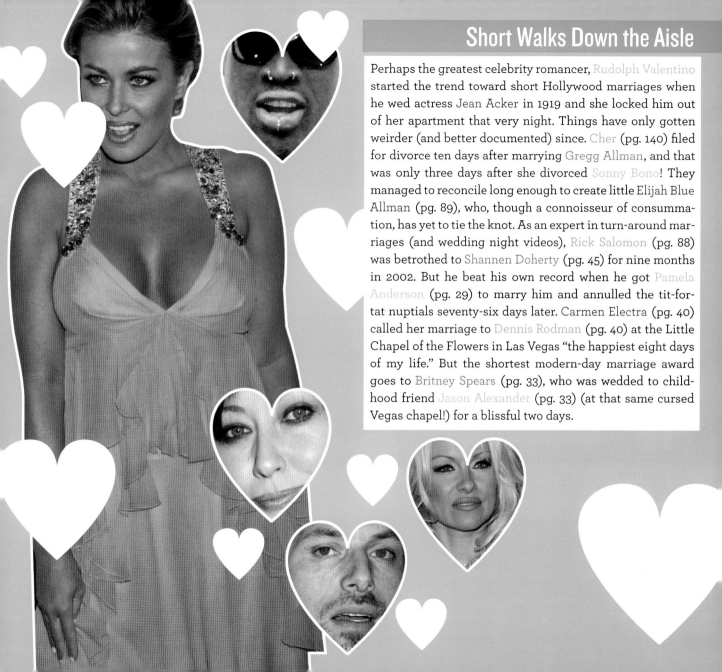

Short Walks Down the Aisle

Perhaps the greatest celebrity romancer, Rudolph Valentino started the trend toward short Hollywood marriages when he wed actress Jean Acker in 1919 and she locked him out of her apartment that very night. Things have only gotten weirder (and better documented) since. Cher (pg. 140) filed for divorce ten days after marrying Gregg Allman, and that was only three days after she divorced Sonny Bono! They managed to reconcile long enough to create little Elijah Blue Allman (pg. 89), who, though a connoisseur of consummation, has yet to tie the knot. As an expert in turn-around marriages (and wedding night videos), Rick Salomon (pg. 88) was betrothed to Shannen Doherty (pg. 45) for nine months in 2002. But he beat his own record when he got Pamela Anderson (pg. 29) to marry him and annulled the tit-for-tat nuptials seventy-six days later. Carmen Electra (pg. 40) called her marriage to Dennis Rodman (pg. 40) at the Little Chapel of the Flowers in Las Vegas "the happiest eight days of my life." But the shortest modern-day marriage award goes to Britney Spears (pg. 33), who was wedded to child-hood friend Jason Alexander (pg. 33) (at that same cursed Vegas chapel!) for a blissful two days.

◀ p.19

Vince Vaughn
Everyone's favorite everyman, Vinny Vaughn is part of the annoyingly named Hollywood "Frat Pack" along with friends Owen Wilson (pg. 101), Will Ferrell, and Ben Stiller (pg.122).

After Aniston split from Brad Pitt (pg. 105), Vaughn was the man who got to spend a year rebound-dating the gorgeous actress after they met filming the *The Break-Up* in 2005.

Joey Lauren Adams
American actress

💔 1997–1998

Adams dumped her director boyfriend Kevin Smith to date Vaughn after they costarred in 1998's *A Cool, Dry Place*. Years after they split, she would play Vaughn's girlfriend's best friend in *The Break Up*.

Teri Hatcher ▲ p.128

While shooting the movie *Marley & Me* with Owen Wilson (pg. 101) in Miami, Aniston had an intimate lunch with Mayer. The two spent an entire weekend together (we know this because paparazzi documented their every move), which was the start of a long on-and-off association.

Jennifer Aniston
Of all the *Friends*, Aniston made the most successful transition from television to film, and from celebrity to superstardom. Her split with husband Brad Pitt (pg. 105) and subsequent Jolie-related stories fueled tabloids for years, but her career boomed, placing her between Jennifer Lopez (pg. 81) and Britney Spears (pg. 33) in the list of the ten richest women in entertainment (Angelina didn't make the list!).

💔 2005–2006
💔 2008–2009
💔 1995

Adam Duritz
Bearing more than a passing resemblance to Sideshow Bob from *The Simpsons* hasn't stopped Counting Crows lead singer Duritz from dating some of Hollywood's hottest. The soulful rocker suffers from depression, insomnia, and a dissociative disorder that he says "makes the world feel unreal"—just like his dating triumphs.

River Phoenix
The dreamy teen actor grew up in the religious cult Children of God with his parents and siblings Leaf (later changed to Joaquin), Rain, Summer, and Liberty (apparently his parents were ahead of the bizarre-celebrity-baby-naming trend). His life was cut short by a drug overdose outside the Viper Room (which was owned by Johnny Depp [pg. 114] at the time).

Duritz's first Friend was Aniston, whom he dated for a few months in 1995 before moving on to Courteney Cox. The relationship was quick, and Duritz bragged, "We never even slept together."

1998–2005
1995–1998

◀ p.105

Donovan blamed the failure of this three-year romance on their personality differences. "[Aniston] likes top-notch hotels and luxury, and I like bed-and-breakfasts and riding my bike. That's the most shallow version of it, but it's indicative of our personalities."

💔 1995
💔 1995–1997
💔 2004

Samantha Mathis
American actress

💔 1995–1996
💔 2005
💔 1992–1993

Mathis found herself in the center of a media firestorm following the death of her boyfriend River Phoenix. She took a role in the film *Jack and Sarah* which was shot in London so that she could leave the country and escape the press.

◀ p.155

1992–1995

Bullock met Donovan on the set of *Love Potion No. 9*. The couple split right before Bullock catapulted to the A-list with her role in *While You Were Sleeping*.

Tate Donovan
Actor

Jennifer Aniston got "Cox-blocked" when her *Friends* cast mate Cox started dating her ex, Duritz. This relationship lasted longer and ran deeper. Duritz wrote songs for Courteney, including "A Long December"—she later appeared in the music video.

Brandon "Bam" Margera
Skateboarder and TV personality

After Margera's father told a radio station that Bam had slept with the then-married Simpson, Margera denied the claim, but in 2007 he undenied it, revealing they had drunk a few margaritas and "it went from there. I left at eight in the morning . . . We were seeing each other for a while."

Nick Lachey
Lachey hit the big time when his boy band, 98 Degrees, disbanded in 2002 and he married Jessica Simpson.

The pair married in 2002 and invited MTV to film their lives in a reality show called *Newlyweds*. On camera their love seemed to know no bounds, but off camera there were arguments about Lachey's partying. They divorced in 2006 due to irreconcilable differences, but their memories survive on DVD.

♥ 2006– Vanessa Minnillo
♥ 2006 Kim Kardashian

After divorcing Jessica Simpson, Lachey dated Kardashian, who'd experienced a failed marriage of her own with music producer Damon Thomas.

Jancan met Mayer while working as a waitress but they only dated for a couple of months. She revealed that "John was devastated at the breakup with [Jennifer Aniston] . . . He's been playing the guitar alone at night, pining over her." Mayer dumped her for talking to the press.

Scheana Jancan
Waitress

2008–2009

John Mayer
Mayer hit it out of the ballpark on his first big-label release when he won the Grammy for "Your Body Is a Wonderland" in 2003. He said, "This is very, very fast, and I promise to catch up," in his acceptance speech.

2009

♥ 2002 Jennifer Love Hewitt NEXT ▶
♥ 2007 Cameron Diaz p. 98 ▶

Mayer pins his success with beautiful women on his advanced bedroom technique. "I have great balance and coordination. Inventiveness," he said. Did they do it on a Segway?

2005

📖 1998–2006

Jessica Simpson
When Simpson first appeared, she was derided as the poor man's Britney Spears (pg. 33). But she turned her trailer-park style into an asset, opening up her life on the MTV series *Newlyweds* to expose her Lucille Ball-sy antics. The show was a hit but the marriage to Nick Lachey wasn't.

Although Simpson had been out and about after her separation from Nick Lachey, Mayer was her first official new beau.

♥ 2006–2007
♥ 2007–2009

2005–2006

Simpson's presence at Cowboys games seemed to lead to losing matches, and fans began referring to her as Yoko Romo. But she had an embarrassing nickname of her own for Tony—Simpson called him "FBD" for "Future Baby Daddy."

2006–2007 ♥

♥ 2007 Sophia Bush p. 88 ▶
♥ 2006–2007 Carrie Underwood p. 153 ▶

After breaking up with Romo following rumors that he had been cheating with Jessica Simpson, Underwood said the Dallas QB still called her. His new girlfriend, the aforementioned Simpson, said, "We got a chuckle out of [that]." When asked how she could be sure Romo wasn't calling, Simpson responded, "I looked at his call log."

This affair allegedly began before Simpson's divorce from Nick Lachey and continued into 2006, when they made so much noise in a Chateau Marmont room that staff had to shush them. Levine broke things off the old-fashioned way—with a text message that read, "Really busy. Need space."

Tony Romo
Dallas Cowboys quarterback

Adam Levine
Having so many biblical names is a lot to live up to, but Adam Noah Levine realized his potential when he nailed a game-winning basketball shot at age seven. The lead singer of Maroon 5 likes his music videos sexy (their videos have featured his girlfriend Kelly McKee, Kelly Preston (pg. 114), and other metaphorical Kellys getting it on with him), which is fine with us.

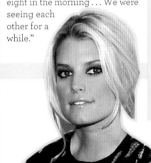

Mary-Louise Parker p. 152 ▶

Kip Pardue · 2003

Carson Daly p.63 · 1997–1999

Rich Cronin

Cronin was the lead singer for pop-rap group LFO (which stood for Lyte Funky Ones), who dubiously rhymed "I like girls that wear Abercrombie and Fitch" with "I'd take her if I had one wish" in his 1999 hit "Summer Girls."

In 2001, Cronin saw a story about his then-girlfriend Hewitt in a tabloid and called her up to ask about it. Her reported response? "Don't you fucking call me up like this when I am at work.... I am out of this relationship. Goodbye. I have to go do *The Tonight Show*."

1999

Cronin and DeLoach had a brief fling when both singers worked in Orlando, Florida, at Lou Pearlman's pop music boot camp—despite the fact that the strict manager discouraged hookups because they took time away from rehearsals.

Jamie Kennedy

Scream star Kennedy was his own agent when he started out, disguising his voice in the persona of "Marty Power" and tricking real agents into attending his stand-up shows.

1994–2000

Katherine Heigl
American actress

1999–2001

Jennifer Love Hewitt

Actress and singer (she's huge in Australia!) Hewitt performed on Disney's *Kids Inc.* with Fergie (pg. 98), but America fell in love with Love on *Party of Five*, where she played Scott Wolf's (pg. 95) girl for five seasons. *Maxim* called her the "Sexiest Woman in the World" in 1999.

♥ **2009–**

Joey Lawrence

Joseph Lawrence Mignogna Jr. got his break on *Gimme a Break!* when his character, Joey Donovan, was adopted by Nell Carter and family in the show's third season. He starred in *Blossom*, on which his signature "Whoa!" was born.

1996

They dated briefly in 1996 when he was on sitcom *Brotherly Love* (with his two real brothers!) and she was just starting on *Party of Five*.

1999

Valderrama told Howard Stern (pg. 104) that Hewitt rated a respectable eight out of ten in the sack. Hewitt responded, saying, "I was told that we had all these very steamy encounters and I was like, 'Really! Well, I would have loved to have been there!'"

◀ BACK **John Mayer** · 2002

1998–1999

2000–2001

Hewitt starred in the literally tongue-in-cheek video for boyfriend Iglesias's biggest hit, "Hero," in 2001 (it also featured a pre-comeback Mickey Rourke).

In 1999, rumors of an on-set affair alleged that Hewitt was getting with her married and soon-to-be-dad *Party of Five* costar Bairstow, while she was supposed to be seeing Carson Daly (pg. 63). Bairstow and wife divorced soon after.

Enrique Iglesias
Latin music star

Four years after they broke up, Mayer, who occasionally does stand-up comedy, cracked that he never got to have sex with Hewitt because of a case of food poisoning. He immediately felt bad about the joke and sent her an apology.

Scott Bairstow

Actor Bairstow played Neve Campbell's (pg. 122) abusive boyfriend on *Party of Five*. In 2003 he pleaded not guilty to charges of child rape amid allegations that he'd had sex with a twelve-year-old female relative of his then-wife from 1998 to 2001.

2000

Lohan claims that Valderrama was her first love but she dumped him when he wouldn't stop flirting with other women. After they parted, Lohan said, "My life was too out of order. I was too depressed," clearly oblivious to what her life would soon become.

1999

Wilmer Valderrama

Born in Florida and raised in Venezuela, Valderrama found fame as the foreign-exchange student of ambiguous origin on sitcom *That '70s Show*.

Christina Aguilera p.44 ▼

◀ p.93 **Lindsay Lohan**

2003–2004 · 2000–2002

Nikki DeLoach

DeLoach was a cast member on *The New Mickey Mouse Club* and sang in the girl-group innosense with Britney Spears (pg. 33) and Justin Timberlake's (pg. 98) girlfriend Veronica Finn (pg. 99).

1994–1997 Josh "J. C." Chasez

Richie started dating Goldstein at the height of his obesity, saying, "He's always been an amazing, sexy person, no matter what his size." They got engaged, split up, and got back together, parting ways for good in 2006.

Nicole Richie

Lauren Hastings

The model is most famous for accusing Lindsay Lohan (pg. 93) of stealing clothes and accessories worth $10,000 from her. She also played the Britney look-alike that Justin Timberlake (pg. 98) hides from in the music video for "Cry Me a River."

Drew Barrymore p.78

Matthew Perry p. 123 ▶

Shia LaBeouf p. 132 ▶

When Goldstein's new girlfriend Hastings showed up at a *Teen Vogue* party in Los Angeles, Nicole Richie (his recent ex) allegedly had club security "clear her area," trapping Hastings on the wrong side of the velvet rope.

2004–2006
2006

Adam "DJ AM" Goldstein

Goldstein scratched for the biggest in the biz including Madonna (pg. 103), Will Smith, and Jay-Z (pg. 28). In 2004, the big guy had gastric bypass surgery and went from a hefty 324 pounds to a healthy 185 pounds. Four years later, his Learjet crashed on takeoff, killing everyone on board except for Goldstein and his performance partner, Travis Barker. He died of a drug overdose in 2009.

DJ AM and Moore ended their relationship in 2007, but following his horrific plane crash the pair reunited. In October 2008, Moore said, "I like this guy a lot and I want to see where it can go again. Life is too short to not be with someone you really care about."

2007–2008

2008

2007
2008–

Mandy Moore

Moore made the leap from teen pop star to movie headliner with her role as the cancer-suffering preacher's daughter in *A Walk to Remember*, a role she later parodied in the religious satire *Saved!*

Ryan Adams NEXT ▶

2007

Zach Braff
American actor

2007–2008
2002–2004
2000–2002
2004–2006

Sources said this couple was really happy but split after two years because Moore wasn't quite ready to settle down.

But Moore had this to say: "…when the relationship ended, it was a bummer," and the split was the icing on "the really bad cake. The burned cake."

2005 Kirsten Dunst p. 71

A beach…a boat…a babe. Such is romance on St. Barts, where Braff and Dunst shared a special night on real estate mogul Jeff Green's yacht.

2006

In 2006, Valderrama reported to shock jock Howard Stern (pg. 104) that he was the proud owner of Moore's virginity. Wilmer claims that he knew Moore had the hots for him, because her mother told him that she had changed her shirt three times in preparation for their first date.

Kristin Cavallari p.91 ▼

Andy Roddick
Tennis pro

Moore thought Roddick was cute and sent her mom to a tournament with an invitation for Roddick to visit her film set. Thus began a beautiful mingling of music and fuzzy balls that lasted for two years.

Parker Posey

p. 124

Moore and Adams eloped in Savannah, Georgia, in early 2009 amid rumors of pregnancy. She joked about a collaboration, saying, "You know, if he ever needs a job or something, maybe he can audition for my band."

2003–2005

2008–

Joffe earned her keep by helping Adams kick a sick drug habit. "I snorted heroin a lot—with coke. I did speedballs every day for years," he says. With her help he went cold turkey, sort of. "I got some valium, which sounds like cheating, but it really wasn't."

2005–2007

Dave Pirner
Pirner's 1990s slacker soundtrack band Soul Asylum was so big that in 1993 President Clinton invited them to play their hit single "Runaway Train" at the White House.

Jessica Joffe
New York writer

This short relationship went public when Grohl's fresh ex, Louise Post of the band Veruca Salt, told a concert audience that she just "found out my boyfriend has been fucking around on me."

Dave Grohl
The Nirvana drummer had already toured the world with the band Scream before joining up with Kurt Cobain (pg. 61) and Krist Novoselic for Nirvana's breakout album, *Nevermind*. In 2006, unfounded rumors of his death spread across the Internet, and Grohl's wife received condolence calls from friends and family.

◄BACK   Mandy Moore

Ryan Adams

Ryan Adams freakishly shares a birthday with fellow musician Bryan Adams (*Summer of '69*), but he nevertheless came up with his own signature country-rock music style. In January 2009, Adams said he was quitting music because of Ménière's disease, an affliction of the ear and not a preparation for sole.

Touring folk rockers Næss and Adams got engaged in 2003 but split when he started dating Parker Posey (pg. 124). She put out an album titled *He's Gone*, and he released one called *Love Is Hell*, so at least the heartbreak was productive.

2002–2003

Ben Lee
One of a mere one hundred thousand Jews in Australia, Lee became friends with Beastie Boy Mike D., whose label released several of Lee's albums in the United States. His catchy tunes have appeared on *Grey's Anatomy* and *Scrubs*, and they have been enjoyed by nontelevision doctors as well.

2001

Hugh Dancy
British actor and tweedy Burberry model Dancy received an Emmy nomination for his work on the miniseries *Elizabeth I*, so we can overlook his performance in *Basic Instinct 2* in 2006.

Leona Næss
Singer-songwriter Leona is the daughter of Arne Næss Jr. (pg. 57), the Norwegian mountaineer and shipping magnate who married Diana Ross (pg. 57) after divorcing Leona's mother.

2008–

Ione Skye p. 18

After announcing their engagement in 2009, Danes had this to say about monogamy: "I resolved that there isn't really a better model . . ."

2006–

1997–2003

2003–2006

Claire Danes

Yale dropout Danes beat out Alicia Silverstone (pg. 27) for the part of Angela Chase in *My So-Called Life* and earned a Golden Globe at age fifteen for her performance. The short-lived show also provided her first kiss—on-screen, before her first in real life.

1995–1996

Danes dumped longtime boyfriend Lee to get with Billy Crudup (pg. 152), who split with his seven-year mate Mary-Louise Parker (pg. 152). But Lee turned his pain into double platinum with a soulful album about romance that came out after the split.

1997

Billy Crudup p.152

Dead center in Ryder's tour of rocker boyfriends, this relationship damaged the grunge cred of Pirner and Soul Asylum. But it wasn't all bad—he scored a cameo in young director Ben Stiller's (pg. 122) *Reality Bites*, and Ryder boosted his image as a brainy savant, telling *Rolling Stone* that "During dinner, he uses the word 'cognitive' twice in five minutes."

1993–1995

David Duchovny p.23

Ryder must have really upset Jay Kay when she dumped him, because he went on record with some obnoxious, unrepeatable comments that we're happy to highlight here: "She did have this habit of constantly wanting to play hide the sausage," and "She has these enormous breasts—bigger than they look on film."

1996

2004

Jay Kay p.17

Michelle Williams p.77

Luciana Barroso
Miami bartender

Damon met, then married, civilian bartender Barroso while filming the comedy *Stuck on You* in Miami in 2003.

1999–2001

Winona Ryder

Born Winona Horowitz to hippie friends of Timothy Leary, Ryder made her debut in the nerd romance *Lucas*, which had her character falling for a football star played by Charlie Sheen (pg. 133). Quirky roles in *Beetlejuice* and *Heathers* established her outsider status, but a shoplifting conviction in 2001 cemented it.

The Bright Eyes indie rocker had a brief tryst with Ryder, despite being quoted in 2002 saying, "I don't think I would date Winona Ryder. She's kind of old. I like Natalie Portman."

Connor Oberst
Emo musician

2003

1989–1992

1998–2000

1997
2001

Johnny Depp NEXT ▶

Andrew Dorff
Singer and Stephen Dorff's brother

Whitmire worked as Billy Bob Thornton's (pg. 142) personal assistant before becoming Ben Affleck's (pg. 80) personal assistant and, ultimately, Damon's very, very personal assistant.

Odessa Whitmire
Personal assistant

Fueling rumors of their buddy love, Matt Damon started dating Gwyneth Paltrow's (pg. 79) best friend, Winona Ryder, at the same time Paltrow was dating Ben Affleck (pg. 80), who summed it up by saying, "It was so gay." Damon almost got into a brawl with Russell Crowe (pg. 143) at a Hollywood party when the gladiator hit on Ryder.

Scandal ensued when Damon reportedly broke up with his *Good Will Hunting* costar Driver during his appearance on *The Oprah Winfrey Show*, then re-ensued when both actors denied the story.

1997
2001–2003
1998–2000
2003–

1998–2001

Minnie Driver
Driver is the daughter of a financial adviser to the British royal family, Ronnie Driver, whose London United Investments collapsed in the 1990s, losing billions in value. But, as his fortunes faded, her acting career bloomed, with success on British television and an Oscar nod for *Good Will Hunting*.

Driver and Brolin reportedly broke up their engagement due to some diva-class meddling by his stepmother, Barbra Streisand (pg. 118). Streisand insisted her friend Donna Karan should design Driver's dress, while Driver preferred Vera Wang.

Josh Brolin p.150

Matt Damon

Damon and his close friend Ben Affleck (pg. 80) grew up in the pricey Newton neighborhood of Boston, not the rough South Boston of their *Good Will Hunting* characters. But Damon did attend Harvard (though he never graduated).

1997

Lori Allison
Makeup artist

Allison introduced Depp to Nicolas Cage (pg. 12), who in turn suggested he quit music to pursue acting. Allison was the sister of Depp's bandmate in Six Gun Method, and they were married for two years while the band pursued a record deal in Los Angeles.

1983–1985

Helen Mirren

Despite her wild youth (Mirren grew up on a marijuana-growing commune and showed a fondness for cocaine and acid trips), she has said, "I was always a good girl. I was never Amy Winehouse."

Long before their Oscars, Mirren and Neeson lived together for four years in London, and she claims to have shot his first head shots.

When the couple split in 1992, Depp famously had his "Winona Forever" tattoo reduced to "Wino Forever." Depp was Ryder's first—"I hadn't even had a boyfriend then; never had anything serious at all."

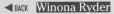

◄ BACK **Winona Ryder** 1989–1992

◄ p. 60 **Kate Moss** 1994–1997

◄ p. 11 **Matthew Broderick**

Johnny Depp

Depp came to Los Angeles to pursue a career in music, but a breakout role in 1984's *A Nightmare on Elm Street* changed all that. Depp has continued to dabble in music—his band P, with bassist Flea, was performing at Depp's L.A. club The Viper Room in 1993 at the very moment River Phoenix (pg. 108) collapsed outside the venue.

1988–1989

Depp's rush to get engaged could have been the result of peer pressure from *21 Jump Street* costars Peter DeLuise and Gina Nemo, who got engaged around the same time. Nine months later the wedding was off, however, and Grey said she was done dating actors. "In the words of my people," she said, "Never again."

Depp met Paradis in a Paris restaurant and said he had "this feeling—I can't really explain what it was." But whatever it was, it got Paradis pregnant almost immediately, and the couple had their first child, daughter Lily Rose, in 1999.

1998–

Preston was so excited about her wedding plans that she told *Entertainment Tonight*, "We plan to invite about two hundred of our closest friends [to the wedding] and then we plan to have some babies. We're practicing right now." But they ended up eloping and having a second ceremony when they learned that their Paris vows weren't legal in the States.

Princess Diana
Princess of Wales

1997 ♥ **Dodi Fayed**
Son of Harrods' owner

John Travolta

Disco star, bumbling assassin, dreadlocked alien—Travolta has played them all. But he'll always have a place in our hearts as Vinnie Barbarino in *Welcome Back, Kotter*.

1991– 🔒

1998– ♥

Vanessa Paradis

Beautiful French crooner Paradis topped the charts with her hit "Joe le taxi" (about a particularly knowledgeable driver) in 1987 at the age of fourteen, but she is best known here for her long-term romance with Johnny Depp and her incongruous candy-corn teeth.

Kelly Preston
American actress

Dean Cain
Actor

Chris Henchy
Sitcom writer

Future television *Lois & Clark* star Cain was a "super man" at Princeton, too, where he played football and dated Shields, who described him as "the very first love of my life" and admitted she lost her virginity to him.

Michael Bolton

Kravitz wooed the nineteen-year-old Paradis in Hoboken, New Jersey, and produced her self-titled album. The relationship lasted a couple of years, during which Kravitz was always stoned and "kept a guy whose specific job it was to roll joints."

1992–1995

1989–1990

1987–1989

◄ p. 69 **Lenny Kravitz**

◄ p. 133 **Charlie Sheen**

◄ p. 125 **George Clooney**

Natasha Richardson
British actress

Jennifer Grey
Grey followed her roots (her grandfather was Jewish comedian Mickey Katz) back to the Catskills for the classic dance romance *Dirty Dancing*. Grey's biggest regret? A nose job that made her face unrecognizable at the height of her career.

Roberts was nineteen years old when she dated the thirty-five-year-old Neeson, whom she met on her debut film, *Satisfaction* (a film about Justine Bateman's [pg. 128] rock band). Neeson later said, "she had great charisma, but I also thought she should get acting lessons."

Julia Roberts p.159 ▲
Janice Dickinson p.139 ▲

The always-classy Dickinson revealed in her memoir that Neeson has "the biggest penis of any man alive." She continued demurely, "He unzipped his pants and an Evian bottle fell out. It was insane!"

Grey fell for Stephanopoulos early in the campaign and got her chance after the Clinton win, securing a private White House tour that included a visit to the Oval Office while Clinton delivered his weekly radio address.

George Stephanopoulos
President Bill Clinton's communications director

🔒 1994–2009
💔 1980–1984
💔 1987–1988
💔 1993

1993
1987–1988
1992
1991–1992
1991–1992

Liam Neeson
💔 Neeson's Oscar-nominated portrayal of Oskar Schindler in Spielberg's *Schindler's List* was just the lead up to the pinnacle of his career—playing Jedi Master Qui-Gon Jinn in the surreal and incomprehensible art film *The Phantom Menace*.

💔 1991

Barbra Streisand p.118 ▶

Brooke's mother, Teri, arranged for Travolta to meet Shields at the studio of photographer Patrick Demarchelier. Of their encounter, Brooke said, "I wasn't disappointed." Making a subtle reference to *Grease*, mother Teri said it was "a sixteen-year-old's first summer love."

Both Shields and Neeson were on the rebound from musical divas (he from Streisand, she from Michael Jackson) when they found each other for a brief, but probably blessedly quiet, romance.

Shields was spotted touring colleges with John F. Kennedy Jr. in 1982, but the relationship didn't graduate to the next level. Shields described it as "Brief, short-lived. It was a good diary entry, that's all."

The wedding of Shields and Agassi foreshadowed the troubles their relationship would face—she almost bit the dust after tripping on her train and he accidentally threw out his wedding band before they left on their honeymoon.

Andre Agassi p.118 ▶
JFK Jr. p.11 ▶

1985

🔒 1997–1999

💔 1989

💔 1988

Brooke Shields
Shields launched her career at eleven months old, modeling in an Ivory Soap ad, just the first of many controversial nude scenes. Fans cheered when she took on Scientologist Tom Cruise (pg. 70) over the issue of psychiatric medications and forced him to apologize for his (crazy) comments.

2000– 🔒
1992 💔
1985–1986 💔

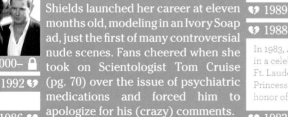

In 1983, Albert and Shields participated in a celebrity tennis tournament in Ft. Lauderdale, Florida, to benefit the Princess Grace Foundation, named in honor of Albert's mother, Grace Kelly.

💔 1983

1997–2001
💔

Woody Harrelson p.10 ▶

Prince Albert of Monaco II
Prince Albert II rules the .76-square-mile city-state of Monaco, has his own stamps, and is really, really rich. But even a sparkly crown can't distract from the rumors of his homosexuality, which continue despite two bastard children (that's what they're officially called!), confirmed via DNA tests by Swiss technicians.

Angie Everhart p.32 ▼

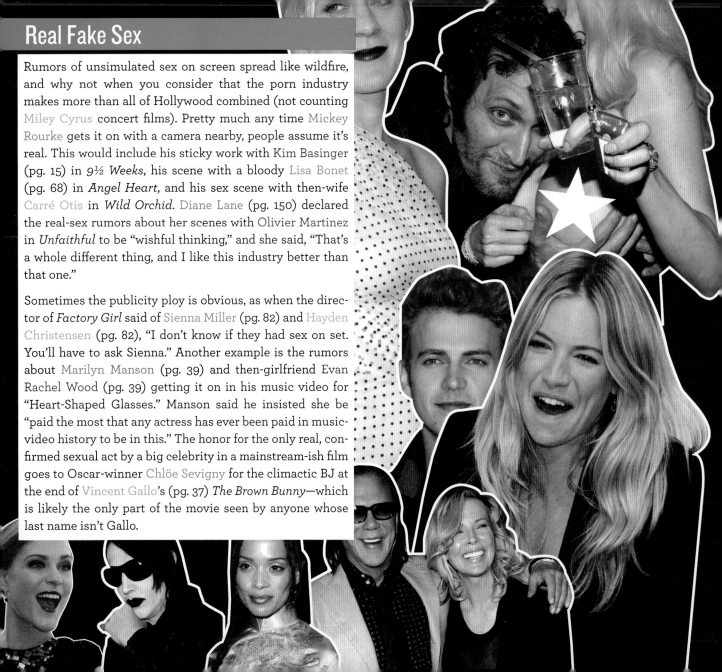

Real Fake Sex

Rumors of unsimulated sex on screen spread like wildfire, and why not when you consider that the porn industry makes more than all of Hollywood combined (not counting Miley Cyrus concert films). Pretty much any time Mickey Rourke gets it on with a camera nearby, people assume it's real. This would include his sticky work with Kim Basinger (pg. 15) in *9½ Weeks*, his scene with a bloody Lisa Bonet (pg. 68) in *Angel Heart*, and his sex scene with then-wife Carré Otis in *Wild Orchid*. Diane Lane (pg. 150) declared the real-sex rumors about her scenes with Olivier Martinez in *Unfaithful* to be "wishful thinking," and she said, "That's a whole different thing, and I like this industry better than that one."

Sometimes the publicity ploy is obvious, as when the director of *Factory Girl* said of Sienna Miller (pg. 82) and Hayden Christensen (pg. 82), "I don't know if they had sex on set. You'll have to ask Sienna." Another example is the rumors about Marilyn Manson (pg. 39) and then-girlfriend Evan Rachel Wood (pg. 39) getting it on in his music video for "Heart-Shaped Glasses." Manson said he insisted she be "paid the most that any actress has ever been paid in music-video history to be in this." The honor for the only real, confirmed sexual act by a big celebrity in a mainstream-ish film goes to Oscar-winner Chlöe Sevigny for the climactic BJ at the end of Vincent Gallo's (pg. 37) *The Brown Bunny*—which is likely the only part of the movie seen by anyone whose last name isn't Gallo.

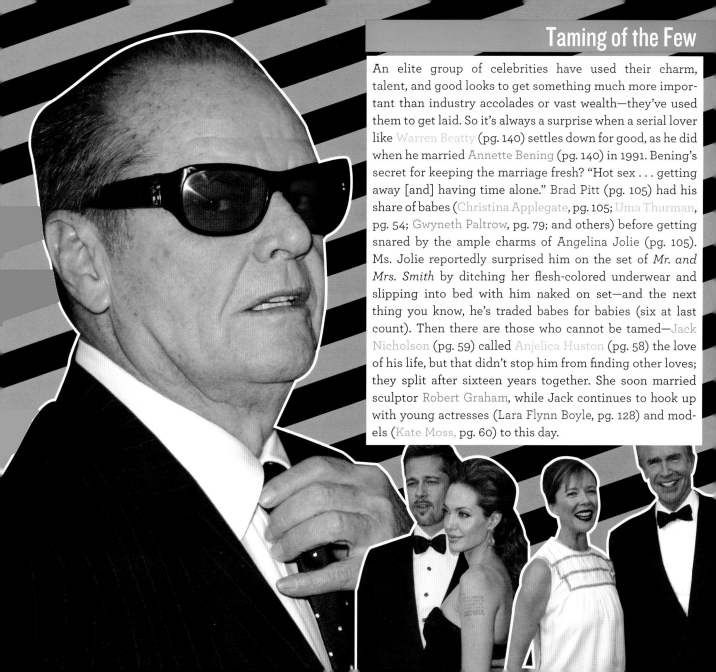

Taming of the Few

An elite group of celebrities have used their charm, talent, and good looks to get something much more important than industry accolades or vast wealth—they've used them to get laid. So it's always a surprise when a serial lover like Warren Beatty (pg. 140) settles down for good, as he did when he married Annette Bening (pg. 140) in 1991. Bening's secret for keeping the marriage fresh? "Hot sex . . . getting away [and] having time alone." Brad Pitt (pg. 105) had his share of babes (Christina Applegate, pg. 105; Uma Thurman, pg. 54; Gwyneth Paltrow, pg. 79; and others) before getting snared by the ample charms of Angelina Jolie (pg. 105). Ms. Jolie reportedly surprised him on the set of *Mr. and Mrs. Smith* by ditching her flesh-colored underwear and slipping into bed with him naked on set—and the next thing you know, he's traded babes for babies (six at last count). Then there are those who cannot be tamed—Jack Nicholson (pg. 59) called Anjelica Huston (pg. 58) the love of his life, but that didn't stop him from finding other loves; they split after sixteen years together. She soon married sculptor Robert Graham, while Jack continues to hook up with young actresses (Lara Flynn Boyle, pg. 128) and models (Kate Moss, pg. 60) to this day.

Andre Agassi

Agassi's father began grooming the future tennis star the moment he left the womb, by hanging tennis balls over his crib and making him hit thousands of volleys per day.

◀ p.115 Brooke Shields   1997–1999

1999–

Steffi Graf
German tennis champion

Agassi got Graf pregnant, and the two eloped in 2001. The pregnancy wasn't planned, but it shouldn't have been entirely unexpected—Agassi has one hell of a serve.

1992

This May–December romance made headlines when Streisand, his senior by almost thirty years, commented that Agassi played "like a Zen master." Agassi showed up at Wimbledon with a shaved chest, which he said made him more aerodynamic; however, most people assumed this was meant to satisfy some other, Streisand-related, need.

1991

At the time, sources claimed that Neeson was "all but moved in" with Streisand, but her publicists said they were just "good friends," like her other good friends Elliot Gould (pg. 118), Ryan O'Neal (pg. 56), and Neil Diamond. Okay, she was actually just friends with Neil.

◀ p.115 Liam Neeson

◀ 2° to Helen Mirren
◀ 3° to Lyle Lovett
◀ 4° to Robin Wright Penn

Right before marrying Tommy Lee (pg. 32), and immediately after divorcing him, Anderson fell into the arms of Peters for comfort, and possibly some career advice.

◀ p.29 Pamela Anderson   1995

◀ p.15 Kim Basinger   1988

Jon Peters
The hairdresser-turned-Hollywood-mogul got his start shampooing celebs (inspiring Warren Beatty's *Shampoo*), including Barbra Streisand, who helped him launch a producing career that included a stint as head of Sony Pictures. Steven Spielberg disliked him so much that he had Peters banned from the set of *The Color Purple*.

Gould's marriage to Streisand disintegrated when her career took off and his appeared to stagnate. That, and she was dating Omar Sharif.

1992

1963–1971

Barbra Streisand

Streisand, a singing, dancing, acting "triple threat" who has earned a Grammy, Oscar, Tony, and Emmy, posed another kind of threat to her male costars—at first they were not attracted to her, but they all inevitably fell in love.

1974–1976

They met at his Rodeo Drive salon but soon became lovers and, more important in Hollywood, business partners—Peters managed Streisand's career and produced her hit remake of *A Star Is Born* in 1976.

1970

Warren Beatty
p.140

1970

Ryan O'Neal
p.56

1970

Ryan O'Neal
p.56

Elliot Gould
American actor

James Brolin
A childhood friend of Ryan O'Neal (pg. 56), Brolin started acting on TV in the 1960s, including the role of Ralph Staphylococcus on *Batman*, but his role as Pee-Wee Herman's suave alter-ego "PW" is a fan favorite.

A million dollars buys a lot of stephanotis blossoms (twenty-five hundred, to be exact), but that's the low estimate of what Streisand spent for her top-secret wedding to Brolin at her Malibu mansion. She successfully sued the helicopter pilot who swooped to steal photos in the middle of the ceremony.

🔒 1998–

💔 1970

💔 1967

💔 1988

During a whirlwind six-month relationship, Streisand and Johnson recorded a duet as the title track for her album *Till I Loved You*, which was universally panned as one of the worst duets in music history. A critic said, "What's next—an Eddie Van Halen album with Valerie Bertinelli?"

According to the biography *Streisand: Her Life*, Streisand had a torrid affair with O'Neal while he was married to Leigh Taylor-Young (pg. 56) and living in Malibu, where he was known to jog naked on the beach.

Kris Kristofferson
💔 1969–1970

Country singer
and actor

In 1976's ***A Star Is Born***, Kristofferson and Streisand share a romantic bathtub scene that was difficult to shoot because producer Jon Peters (who was dating Streisand at the time) wanted Kristofferson to wear a wet suit. Kristofferson claims to have compromised and worn boxers.

Leonard Cohen once pretended to be Kris Kristofferson when he bumped into Joplin in the Chelsea Hotel in order to get with her. After she met the real Kris, she recorded his song "Me and Bobby McGee," and they dated until her death by a heroin overdose in 1970.

Omar Sharif
Egyptian actor

Janis Joplin
American singer

Funny Girl was shot in 1967 while Streisand was married to Elliot Gould (pg. 118) and the Six Day War was raging between Egypt and Israel. When Sharif told Streisand that the Arab press had called him a traitor for kissing a Jewish woman, she responded, "You should see the letter my aunt wrote me about kissing [you]."

This February–April romance featured alleged tongue-tied nights on the town in Manhattan. Crawford denied the claim (and possibly made things worse) when he said, "She's like our little sister. We really take her under our wing . . ."

Taylor Momsen
At age seven, Momsen got her start as the apple-cheeked, disturbingly coiffed creature Cindy Lou Who in 2000's *How the Grinch Stole Christmas.*

2008–2009 💔

Chace Crawford

Crawford dropped out of Pepperdine University for the role of Nate Archibald in *Gossip Girl* and lived with costar Ed Westwick (pg. 78) in New York City. Crawford rebutted claims that they were dating, saying when they first heard the rumor, "We're kind of like, okay, you want to go play pool and have a beer?" Which is what straight guys would do.

💔 **2007–2008** Country and city came together when Underwood and Crawford started dating, but it all fell apart when Crawford dumped her with the lamest breakup text ever, "Peace out."

Carrie Underwood p. 153 ▶

Don Johnson NEXT ▶

Following Bauer's success in ***Scarface***, this couple got into the Hollywood drug scene, until Bauer got "addicted to free and easy sex" and Griffith gave him the boot in 1985—a few weeks after their son, Alexander, was born.

Steven Bauer
You may picture Bauer in his final scene as Manny Ribera in 1983's *Scarface*, standing in a towel about to get shot by a strung-out Al Pacino (pg. 10). It should have been the start of a great career, but a dive into addiction killed his prospects, until he managed a comeback—playing, you guessed it, a drug dealer in 2000's *Traffic*.

🔒 **1981–1985**

Melanie Griffith
Griffith's breakout role was as an over-sexed runaway teen in Arthur Penn's *Night Moves*—a film in which the teenager had a bunch of hot nude scenes, cementing her reputation as a sexpot.

Johnson met the fourteen-year-old Griffith on the set of 1973's ***The Harrad Experiment***, about a fictional college that encourages students to experiment with free love and sex. They married in Vegas in 1976, divorced six months later, remarried in 1989, and finally redivorced in 1996 because of Johnson's drug problems.

🔓 **1973–1996**

Don Johnson NEXT ▶

Antonio Banderas
Spanish actor

🔒 **1996–**

In 1995's ***Two Much***, Banderas played a guy who pretends he's a twin in order to date the two women he loves, Melanie Griffith and Daryl Hannah (pg. 10). Banderas chose Griffith, and they've been happily married ever since.

1973–1974 💔

Think O'Neal's relationship with half-his-age Griffith was sketchy? His daughter, Tatum O'Neal (pg. 13), took the freak factor one step further by revealing that Griffith had brought her to an opium-fueled Hollywood orgy when she was twelve.

Des Barres had a sexual encounter with Keith Moon in 1969, the year of the **Apollo** mission. At one event, a dirty object touched down on a Moon and then blasted off, and the other was the NASA moon landing.

Although Johnson dumped her after a year of living together, in favor of fourteen-year-old Melanie Griffith (pg. 119), Des Barres fondly reminisces in her memoirs about Johnson's handsome looks, which "could have prevented World War II," and his "huge cock," which . . . oh, never mind.

Pamela Des Barres
Self-proclaimed rock-and-roll "muse," Des Barres definitely amused some rockers as the ultimate 1960s groupie. She got sucked onto the Sunset Strip while still in high school, ultimately nannying for Frank Zappa and getting with every classic rock legend this side of Ringo Starr.

Keith Moon
The Who drummer

1969 ❥

Jimmy Page
Led Zeppelin guitarist

1971–1972 ❥

1970

❥ **1971**

1988 ❥

Don Johnson
Long before he and Philip Michael Thomas (aka Tubbs) strutted the streets of South Beach in Versace pastels, Johnson was a struggling actor starring in a series of bad 1970s movies including *Zachariah* (with Country Joe and the Fish) and the postapocalyptic sci-fi *A Boy and His Dog*.

1988

Des Barres said, "Mick was . . . the most gorgeous, androgynous man. I loved androgyny in a man, and he sort of invented that, really."

1967

Jim Morrison
The Doors singer

◀ p.118
Barbra Streisand

◀ p.50
Mick Jagger

1973–1996

1981–1986

Johnson, who proposed with a 5.5-carat square-cut diamond ring, met Phleger at a party for San Francisco's then-mayor Willie Brown, who ended up presiding at their wedding.

1998–

Kelly Phleger
San Francisco socialite

1970 ❥

Patti D'Arbanville
D'Arbanville grew up in New York's Greenwich Village, clubbing until midnight by the time she was thirteen and starring in Andy Warhol's sexual fetish dream *Flesh* at sixteen. She followed up with a career in nude and lesbian cinema, leading to the ultimate surprise—respectable starring roles on *The Guiding Light* and *Third Watch*.

◀ p.50
Mick Jagger

While they were dating, Johnson and D'Arbanville shared a Santa Monica house with Pamela Des Barres (his ex-girlfriend) and her husband, and Melanie Griffith (Johnson's ex-wife) and her husband, Steven Bauer, (pg. 119). As Des Barres said, "It was incestuous and close and great."

❥ **1993–1997**

Newsom and Phleger were one of the Bay Area's best known power couples until she ditched him for Don Johnson.

Simon's song "Anticipation" was written about waiting for Stevens to pick her up for a date. She opened for Stevens in her first concert, where (ironically) James Taylor (pg. 50) was in the audience and went backstage to meet her, simultaneously sowing the seeds of love (for Taylor) and destruction (for Stevens).

Melanie Griffith

◀ BACK

1968–1970

Their two-year relationship inspired Cat Stevens's "My Lady D'Arbanville" (duh) and also "Wild World," written about D'Arbanville dumping the Cat and moving on to that other rocker—what's his name? Oh yeah, Mick Jagger (pg. 50).

Cat Stevens
Before he became Yusuf Islam and murkily supported a fatwa against Salman Rushdie, Stevens was a teen pop star in Britain, touring with Hendrix and Humperdinck. But a life-threatening case of tuberculosis in 1968 changed his perspective, and, when he recovered, his signature spiritual sound topped the charts.

Gavin Newsom

p.124

◀ p.50
Carly Simon

1971–1972 ❥

In 1997, Johnson's PR squad went into overdrive, denying rumors that the forty-seven-year-old actor had dropped $30,000 on an engagement ring for eighteen-year-old **Nash Bridges** star O'Keefe, who played his daughter on the show. They eventually came clean: Yes, they were getting it on; no, Johnson wasn't making it legal.

1997

Jodi Lyn O'Keefe
O'Keefe modeled for Gitano jeans and acted in *Another World* before landing her breakout role as Don Johnson's daughter on *Nash Bridges*.

Cusack and O'Keefe dated for six years before she dumped him in 2009, because biological clocks keep ticking, even when you're twelve years younger than your guy.

2003–2009

John Cusack
Young Cusack broke every girl's heart with the most romantic teenage gesture imaginable in *Say Anything*, the boombox serenade. He has worked with his sister Joan Cusack on seven films, including the cult hit *High Fidelity*.

1997–1998

Cusack and Clint's daughter Alison shared an offscreen romance while shooting 1997's **Midnight in the Garden of Good and Evil**. When he directed their kissing scene, her father and director Clint Eastwood said, "I told John, 'Think of me as your chaperone.' Then I whispered to him, 'Son, my advice to you would be to do this in one take.'"

Cusack dated Campbell after meeting in Canada when she was filming **Three to Tango** and he was shooting **Pushing Tin**. He appeared on **The View** and told Barbara Walters he was more interested in older women, shortly before breaking up with Campbell.

1997

1998–2002

Claire Forlani
The British-born star of *The Rock* and *Meet Joe Black* made her debut in a film classic called *Police Academy: Mission to Moscow*, the seventh in the series.

1998–1999

Alison Eastwood
Conceived by Clint Eastwood and swimsuit model Maggie Johnson during the production of *Dirty Harry*, Alison Eastwood acted in dad's thriller *Tightrope* and posed nude in *Playboy* in 2003 above the caption "Wanna get lucky?"

Neve Campbell NEXT ▶

Ben Stiller NEXT ▶

Ben Stiller NEXT ▶

1999

2002–

After five years of dating, Flockhart finally captured the fugitive when Harrison proposed in 2007. Together, they have a son, Liam, whom she adopted as a newborn in 2001.

Calista Flockhart
Flockhart is well known for playing the title character in the quirky TV series *Ally McBeal*, though she might be better known for her super-slim figure.

Harrison Ford
Ford invented two of the most iconic characters of the 1980s—Han Solo and Indiana Jones. He continued to play romantic leads late into his career, stealing twenty-seven-years-younger Anne Heche (pg. 152) from her boyfriend played by David Schwimmer (pg. 66) in *Six Days Seven Nights*.

Although they denied their romantic relationship, Stiller and Flockhart were seen together for weeks after meeting at a charity event. A year later, Stiller defended his ex against rumors that she was anorexic. "All these rumors about her being underweight are trash. She's gorgeous," he said.

Back in the days before prenups, Ford married Mathison, had two kids, and settled down for seventeen years. But when Han went solo, the divorce settlement set a Hollywood record of $85 million—not counting $300,000 a year in child support!

 1983–2004

Melissa Mathison
Screenwriter of *E.T.*

This couple met on the set of 1999's **Mystery Men**, in which Stiller played the always-angry Mr. Furious (better than performing as Paul Reubens's anti-superhero, the flatulent Spleen).

◀ BACK Claire Forlani 1998–1999

Billy Burke and Neve dated briefly and vacationed together in Paris. The pair met while filming 2002's **Lost Junction**.

Billy Burke
American actor

2001–2003

💔 1998

Ben Stiller

Stiller may forever be known for his zipper scene in *There's Something About Mary*. The 1998 film launched him to the next level—going from indies like *Flirting with Disaster* and *Reality Bites* (which he also directed) to starring in *Meet the Parents* and writing and directing *Tropic Thunder*.

Neve Campbell

💔 1988
💔 1998

Born in Guelph, Ontario, to a yoga instructor and high school drama teacher, Campbell began turning heads at the age of twenty-one while playing the fifteen-year-old Julia Salinger on *Party of Five*. In 1998 she and costar Denise Richards raised more than just eyebrows in the film (and we use that term loosely) *Wild Things*.

◀ BACK Calista Flockhart

1999 💔

Tripplehorn appeared on **The Ben Stiller Show** numerous times when the two began dating. If it hadn't been for a fling with a stuntman while she was shooting Kevin Costner's (pg. 51) **Waterworld**, their engagement might have turned into a marriage.

◀ BACK John Cusack

◀ 2° to Alison Eastwood
◀ 3° to Don Johnson
◀ 4° to Amanda Peet

C 1992–1996

🔒 1999–

This classy Hollywood couple met when Stiller directed her in a TV pilot called **Heat Vision and Jack**. The show starred Jack Black as a supersmart astronaut with a talking motorcycle voiced by Owen Wilson (pg. 101). They have two kids named Ella Olivia and Quinlin Dempsey.

💔💔 1997–1998 | 1998–2002

Peet and Perry dated while shooting **The Whole Nine Yards**, but by the time the sequel rolled around, the spark was gone. Also absent from the sequel: comedy, originality, and topless Amanda Peet holding a gun.

2002

💔

Jeanne Tripplehorn

Once considered the younger Rene Russo, Tripplehorn studied acting at Juilliard before breaking out as the bisexual shrink in *Basic Instinct*, a movie she didn't let her Oklahoma grandmother see, for what she calls "obvious reasons."

1995
💔

Christine Taylor

Taylor is probably best known for her role as Marcia Brady in *The Brady Bunch Movie*, after which she was tortured by witch Neve Campbell in *The Craft*.

Matthew Lillard p. 38

Matthew Lillard p. 38

1998 💔

There's something about Stiller—the funnyman has an undeniable knack for bagging beautiful babes, including Peet, whom he dated in 1998. Just be warned, ladies: That's not hair gel.

Amanda Peet

Peet has had more success on the big screen than the small—her series *Jack & Jill* and *Studio 60 on the Sunset Strip* didn't last long. But we'll always remember her as the hitman-loving dental hygienist in *The Whole Nine Yards*, a part she aptly described as "… a G-spot role."

Pat Mastroianni

At age fourteen, Pat launched his career as Joey on *Degrassi Junior High*, a role he continued to play for the next twenty years.

Mastroianni dated Campbell when they were on *Degrassi High* and she was an unknown. He later joked, "I had to dump her because she held me back."

The two Canucks got together in their homeland while filming the romantic comedy *Three to Tango*. This quintessential Canadian love story ended all too quickly when Perry had to get back to his real *Friends*.

2002 ❦

2006 ❦

2002 ❦

Joey costars and lovers Matt LeBlanc and Andrea Anders were responsible for setting Caplan up with Perry. He was thirty-seven. She was twenty-four.

Lizzy Caplan
Actress

Jennifer Capriati
Tennis champion

David Benioff
Screenwriter

🔒 2006–

Selma Blair p.153

2003

Matthew Perry

Canadian-born Perry became a darling of international living rooms when he morphed into Chandler Bing on *Friends*. Known for picking up women at bars, nightclubs, and rehab centers throughout Los Angeles, this die-hard Ottawa Senators fan has befriended more than his share of Hollywood hotties.

As the world's top female tennis player in 2002, Capriati could have had anyone, but this courtside courtship should come as no surprise. Perry was a top-ranked junior tennis player in Canada and regularly played doubles with John McEnroe (pg. 13).

❦ ❦

2002–2008

❦ ❦
Rachel Dunn
Fashion student

2003–2005

Dunn broke it off with Perry soon after she moved in with him in L.A. because he couldn't keep himself sober.

After dating briefly in 2002, the pair reunited in 2008 at Ellen DeGeneres's (pg. 152) fiftieth birthday party. Maybe they reconnected to commiserate about their failed 2007 series, *Studio 60 on the Sunset Strip* (she guested as a host on the fictional show within a show).

Lauren Graham
She might be best known for her role as Lorelai Gilmore in the award-winning *Gilmore Girls*, but there's a legion of fans out there who will always remember her for playing the naughty bar maid with the sexy Santa fetish in *Bad Santa*.

Yasmine Bleeth
Bleeth started on soaps *Ryan's Hope* and *One Life to Live* and turned down a part on *90210* before landing the more artistic, serious role of lifeguard Caroline Holden on *Baywatch* in 1993. She struggled with cocaine addiction in 2001 (veering onto the median of a Michigan highway) but has stayed sober since.

Piper Perabo
Actress

Perry was introduced to Perabo by his ex (and future) girlfriend Lauren Graham at the Polo Lounge in Beverly Hills after he broke up with Rachel Dunn.

2006

As a recent graduate of a school called "Rehab," Perry took a strong liking to Moore for one reason: She doesn't drink. But it turned out that a mutual love of sobriety isn't enough to make a relationship last.

❦ 2007   Mandy Moore p. 111 ▶
❦ 2002   Lara Flynn Boyle p. 128 ▶
❦ 2002   Heather Graham p. 47 ▶
❦ 2007   Meg Ryan p. 144 ▶

In a strange twist of fate, Ryan's ex-boyfriend Craig Bierko (pg. 144) was offered the role of Chandler on *Friends* but passed on it, giving the job to Perry. When he met Ryan, Perry was quickly swept off his feet and even asked *Friends* costar Courteney Cox (pg. 155) for advice on how to talk to Ryan's children.

Zellweger and Perry met at a party hosted by Amanda Peet, Perry's costar in *The Whole Nine Yards*. Despite his recent trips to rehab, three nights later they were out on a date.

1996   1995–1996   2002

❦   ❦ ❦

Renee Zellweger   NEXT ▶

After her breakup with Richard Grieco, Bleeth started to get it on with Perry. Grieco may have been down, but he was not out, and he continued to send Bleeth hundreds of flowers every day, ultimately winning back her heart.

Julia Roberts p. 159

Whether he ever found out if her body was a Wonderland is still a subject of speculation, but we do know that she cheered him on at his concerts, and they were seen together in public.

2003 ❦

Vanessa Carlton
Pop singer

◀ p.109 John Mayer

2002–2007

"She learned to play the drums faster than anyone I've ever seen," said beau Jenkins of Theron after they met while she was vacationing in Hawaii with her family.

Stephan Jenkins
Lead singer for Third Eye Blind

1997–2001 ❦

Indie rocker met indie film star in 2003, leading Adams to cite Posey as his "Exe-*cute*-ive Producer" on his album *Rock N Roll*. After they split, Posey kept their dog, Gracie.

◀ p.112 Ryan Adams

◀ BACK Matthew Perry

2005

Parker Posey
Posey's first big role was the bitch-queen cheerleader in *Dazed and Confused*, followed by roles in countless indie films including *Best in Show*, *Party Girl*, *Kicking and Screaming*, and *Clockwatchers*.

2000

Charlize Theron
South African Theron was the rare hyphenate model–ballet dancer until she injured her knee at nineteen and headed to L.A. to launch her acting career.

❦ 2001–2010

Stuart Townsend
Irish actor Townsend happily attended the Gaiety School of Acting in Dublin. After training for two months, he lost the role of Aragorn in *The Lord of the Rings* to Viggo Mortenson two days before shooting began.

Townsend met Theron while shooting 2002's *Trapped*. Though Townsend said, "I don't need a certificate . . . I consider her my wife and she considers me her husband," she ditched him and the commitment ring in 2010.

The couple met on the set of 1999's *The Venice Project*, and the relationship was a revelation for Posey. "My previous relationships have all been disasters," said the actress. "But being with Stuart has made me realize that's not necessarily my fate."

❦ 1998–2001

Talia Balsam
Talia Balsam is the daughter of Joyce Van Patten (Dick Van Patten's little sister) and Martin Balsam, who played the private investigator killed by Norman Bates in *Psycho*. She's had a long career, starting with appearances on *Happy Days* and on AMC's *Mad Men* as her real-life husband's screen wife, Mona Sterling.

Clooney's passion for pigs took a toll on his marriage to Balsam and caused a major custody battle during this couple's 1993 divorce proceedings. Balsam said, "I think George feels more at ease with a pig than he does with a woman." Oink!

Clooney fell for underwear model Balitran while she was studying law in Paris and he was in town for a film shoot. Though the pair split amicably, Balitran became enraged in 2002 when Clooney began dating her best friend, Jennifer Siebel (pg. 125).

Celine Balitran
French model

1993–1997 ❦

Gavin Newsom
Somewhat self-made millionaire Newsom started the PlumpJack Wine Shop in San Francisco with the help of billionaire family friend Gordon Getty. But he sold it all (well, almost all) in order to avoid a conflict of interest when he became mayor of San Francisco in 2004.

Kelly Phleger p.120

Kelly Preston p.114
Julia Roberts p.159

1987–1989 — Kelly Preston

The worst thing about Clooney's breakup with Preston was that she lost custody of Max, the black potbellied piglet he had bought for her. The lucky pig lived with Clooney until 2006, oftentimes sharing his bed.

2001 — Julia Roberts

George Clooney

Clooney's rugged charms have always attracted women but since divorcing his first wife in 1993 he has vowed to remain the lovable bachelor forever. He even bet both Nicole Kidman (pg. 69) and Michelle Pfeiffer (pg. 155) that he would still be unmarried and childless at the age of fifty in 2011.

2000

1989–1993 🔒

1996–1999

2000–2006

Jennifer Siebel
San Francisco socialite

Clooney noticed Siebel at a friend's barbeque, and she noticed him noticing. "I think he liked that I could hang with the guys, play sports, and wasn't that impressed by his celebrity," she said.

2002

🔒 **2008–**

Three months after Mayor Newsom met Siebel on a blind date, his campaign director resigned after discovering that Newsom was having an affair with his wife. The scandal wasn't enough to split up Newsom and Siebel, and they got married in 2008.

In 2001, after his split from Lisa Snowden and hers from Jim Carrey (pg. 16), Clooney invited Zellweger over for a home-cooked meal, and she was soon showing up at his pad three or four times per week. Those are some mashed potatoes!

2001

Lucy Liu

David Kelly wrote the part of Ling Woo on *Ally McBeal* for Queens native Liu. She experienced big-screen success post-McBeal, kicking ass as one of *Charlie's Angels* with Drew Barrymore (pg. 78) and Cameron Diaz (pg. 98).

Ellen Barkin p.156

After his character treated her character's child on an episode of **ER**, the couple dated openly in real life for a while, split up, and then smooched around again five years later.

Barkin costarred in **Ocean's 13** and Clooney said he was "electrified by her." Recently divorced from Ron Perelman (pg. 156), Barkin needed a shoulder to cry on, and single Clooney was in the right place with the right shoulder.

2006

2006

2002–2009

Teri Hatcher p.128 ▶

Clooney was heartbroken after Allen dumped him two years into the relationship. But in October 2008, Allen and Clooney quietly began seeing each other again. Will Krista Allen ever be Mrs. George Clooney? Only time will tell.

Krista Allen p.128 ▶

The pair met at a Tsunami relief concert in 2005. They married five months later, only to have the marriage annulled after four weeks. The pair cited different marriage objectives as the reason for the split. That's the problem with a whirlwind romance: Nobody ever takes the time to write down their long-term goals.

Kenny Chesney
Country singer

2005 🔒

After meeting on the set of **Cold Mountain** in 2003, the couple began an on-again, off-again relationship. Zellweger was drawn to White's music, but in 2004 the couple split, with Zellweger looking forward to being "just a girl." So what exactly was she in their relationship?

Jack White
Rock musician

2003–2004

Matthew Perry

2000 🔒

2002

The couple met on the set of **Me, Myself & Irene** and, true to Carrey form, were soon engaged. But the engagement was broken in December 2000. A possible reason for the breakup: Carrey proposed while in character as the schizophrenic star of the film.

Jim Carrey p.16

2001

Renee Zellweger

The A-list actress twice beefed up her skinny physique to play the chubby British lead in the *Bridget Jones's Diary* films. Despite the films' message, Zellweger slimmed down as soon as shooting was finished.

Say It with T-Shirts

When you're constantly followed by paparazzi and featured in tabloids, your life is an open book. It's also a powerful propaganda machine that just needs a customized T-shirt to communicate with the masses. When Alyssa Milano (pg. 95) started dating Justin Timberlake (pg. 98), his bitter ex Britney Spears (pg. 33) was photographed in a T-shirt that read "Dump Him." When A-Rod (pg. 102) was caught with a stripper, his then-loyal wife (pg. 102) sent a subtle message to paparazzi by wearing a shirt that read "Fuck You." Jessica Simpson (pg. 109) was a little more subtle when she took a poke at her boyfriend Tony Romo's (pg. 109) vegetarian ex-girlfriend Carrie Underwood (pg. 153) by sporting a T-shirt with the phrase "Real Girls Eat Meat." And when Serena Williams (pg. 41) dumped director Brett Ratner (pg. 44), she and her also-single sister celebrated. "We're going to get T-shirts that say, 'I'm single,' and on the back it says, 'So is my sister.'"

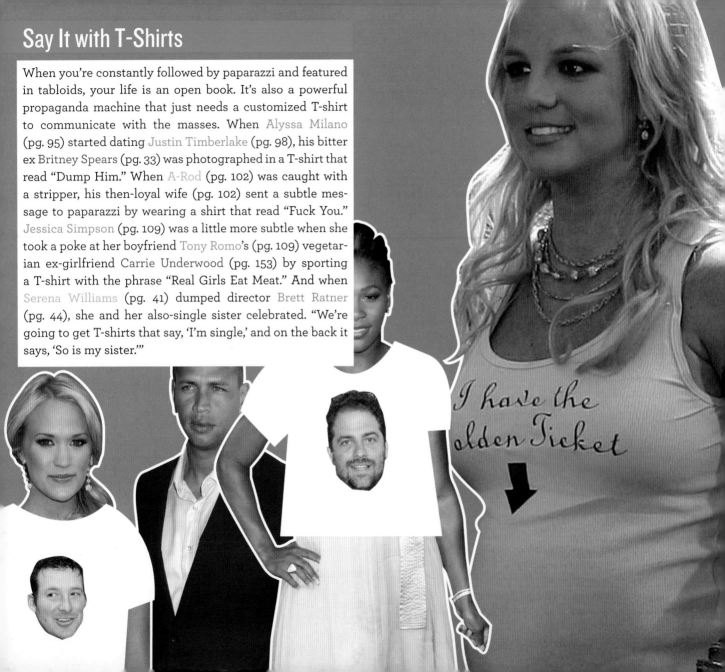

Life Cycle of a Celebrity Relationship

It starts with a spark—the flash from a paparazzo's camera. And with that first picture published, the celebrity relationship begins a predictable decay, not unlike a radioactive isotope.

PHASE 1: Their publicists deny any relationship, insisting that they are "just friends." That's what Tobey Maguire's (pg. 45) people said when he was seen all over New York with Heather Graham (pg. 47) in 2002.

PHASE 2: The couple begin to gush about each other and their love to the press (just prior to revealing their matching tattoos). That's what Johnny Depp (pg. 114) and Winona Ryder (pg. 113) did in 1989.

PHASE 3: Their reps quash rumors of their engagement, despite the fat ring photographed on her finger. Nicolas Cage's (pg. 12) people said, "Nicolas is definitely not engaged," after he popped the question, pricey pink diamond in hand, to gorgeous girlfriend Kristen Zang (pg. 72).

PHASE 4: They separate due to "distance" or "busy schedules." It's not you, it's not even me—it's just geography. That's what split up Orlando Bloom (pg. 71) and Kate Bosworth (pg. 70), not to mention Brooke Burns (pg. 138) and Bruce Willis (pg. 138), Tom Cruise (pg. 70) and Penelope Cruz (pg. 70), and many many more.

PHASE 5: One partner or the other is spotted at the Chateau Marmont, typically with Lindsay Lohan (pg. 93)—regardless of gender—the flashbulb bursts, and the cycle begins anew!

With Affleck on the rebound from J.Lo (pg. 81) and Allen on the rebound from George Clooney (pg. 125), this couple had nothing but chips to lose when they met at a Vegas poker table and retired to his suite at the Bellagio. Oddly, Allen had been flown to Vegas by ex-boyfriend David Spade (pg. 129), who wanted to cheer her up over the loss of Clooney.

◀ p.80 **Ben Affleck**

Krista Allen
On her way to Los Angeles to pursue an acting career, Allen stopped in Vegas and won $2,500 while playing a slot machine, which persuaded her that she was on the right track. As luck would have it, her first role was as a kinky ambassador for the human race in soft-core series *Emmanuelle in Space*.

2004 ♥

♥ 2004

Things were fine for the first six months of Spade's relationship with stunner Allen, until he found out that she'd hacked into his voicemail and was checking on his every move. After they split, he was overheard saying, "The truth of the matter is Krista is insanely jealous."

Boyle began dabbling in older actors when she began dating two-decades-wiser Anderson in 1995. But the couple split, with Anderson citing his need for "solitary time."

1995 ♥

Lara Flynn Boyle
Boyle had her scenes cut from *Ferris Bueller's Day Off* and *Dead Poets Society*, but her role as Laura Palmer's best friend in *Twin Peaks* was a first step toward the creepy, psycho femme fatales she played in numerous other films.

2002

♥

🔒

♥

Sources spotted Hatcher and Clooney smooching around Southern California, but she said, "If I went on a date with George Clooney I would not be talking about it." As Hollywood's most eligible bachelor, stealthy dating is high on Clooney's priority list.

2002–2009

◀ p.125 **George Clooney**
◀ p.125 **George Clooney**
◀ p.108 **Adam Duritz**
◀ p.62 **Stephen Kay**

Richard Dean Anderson
If you have a Swiss Army Knife and some duct tape, you can figure out Anderson's signature role—that's right, it's MacGyver. He also played Jack O'Neill on *Stargate SG-1* for eight years, ultimately being made an honorary Brigadier General by the U.S. Air Force to honor his positive portrayal of the service.

Hatcher met Anderson when she played flaky Penny Parker, a friend of MacGyver who was regularly rescued with a clever magnetized paper clip or a lentil hourglass time bomb.

Dane dated Boyle at the same time she was seeing Jack Nicholson (pg. 59), but they soon split. Dane said, "Jack Nicholson is Jack Nicholson. But my take on the whole thing was, I'm thirty. He's seventy. This is not going to go down like this."

1999

2002

Bateman and Anderson dated briefly while shooting the movie of the week *In the Eyes of a Stranger* in Vancouver.

1992

Ryan Seacrest
The host of *American Idol* and *Dick Clark's New Year's Rockin' Eve* was dogged by rumors that he was gay until he set the record straight—he just likes shopping and a clean-cut appearance. This led *Stuff* magazine to call him the "American poster boy for metrosexuality."

2006–2007

2005

♥

2006

♥

In 2006, these two were photographed kissing in Malibu. Hatcher later admitted to Oprah that they were on their third date when they were "caught" making out but, an hour after the photos were published, Seacrest called her up and said it wasn't going to work.

1985–1991

2006

♥

♥

Teri Hatcher
Teri "They're real and they're spectacular" Hatcher kicked things off as a San Francisco Forty-Niners cheerleader but *Desperate Housewives* took her career to the next level. Her real life features more scandal than that series ever could.

Justine Bateman
Sweet but stupid Mallory Keaton of *Family Ties* was played by Bateman from 1982 to 1989. She reappeared years later in *Arrested Development* as a prostitute accidentally hired by real brother Jason Bateman's character on the show.

♥ 1992
♥ 2005
🔒 1994–2003

Jon Tenney
American actor

Jack Nicholson p.59

Eric Dane p.94

Matthew Perry ▲ p.123

Perry and Boyle first met at the premiere of her flick *Men in Black II*, and the highlight of their relationship was false tabloid speculation that she was pregnant with his child.

Donald Ray Thomas II
Texas real estate mogul

Bolton met Shields at the recording session for "Voices That Care," a super-group song intended to boost morale for Operation Desert Storm troops (because nothing boosts morale like Bolton, Kenny G, Celine Dion, and Little Richard). Future Boltonite Nicollette Sheridan was in the choir!

Brooke Shields p.115
Ashley Judd p.55 ▶

After she supported him through two failed solo albums (as "Michael Bolotin") and several bad haircuts, Bolton split with McGuire, mother of his three daughters, in 2001. The girls stayed with Dad in his posh Westport, Connecticut, pad.

Maureen McGuire
Fitness instructor

2002
2006–

1992
1996–1997
🔒 1975–1990
☾ 2006–2008

1991–1992

1992 💔

Michael Bolton

Believe it or not, soft-rock mullet man Bolton was a heavy metal singer in the early 1980s and his band, Blackjack, toured with Ozzy Osbourne. He penned songs for Barbra Streisand (pg. 118) and won a Grammy for his cover of "When a Man Loves a Woman," which completed his transition to the adult contemporary rack.

Before Bolton got engaged to Nicollette Sheridan (pg. 130) in 2006, he had already dated her *Desperate Housewives* costar Hatcher, who appeared in his music video for "Missing You Now" in the 1990s.

With *Ed* shooting in New Jersey and *Just Shoot Me!* filming in Los Angeles, this couple was dating at a distance of three thousand miles, but Spade made Bowen's thirty-fourth birthday special by getting Stevie Nicks to call her and sing the birthday girl's favorite song, "Landslide," over the phone.

After rekindling a failed 1990s romance in 2006 and getting engaged, Sheridan called things off and kicked Bolton out of their $4.4 million house (formerly owned by Melissa Etheridge). He'd already put his Connecticut estate up for sale, and a source said, "He's basically homeless . . ."

Nicollette Sheridan NEXT ▶
Nicollette Sheridan NEXT ▶

2002–2003

Julie Bowen
American actress

Krista Allen 2004 💔

David Spade

Spade didn't know Boyle was cheating on him with Jack Nicholson (pg. 59) until he read about it in the *National Enquirer*. But he quickly found his sense of humor, saying, "When David Spade makes it into a supermarket publication, it's a mighty slow news week."

1999 💔

2005 💔

When Spade left *Saturday Night Live* after six years, he said, "You can't stay there forever—it kills you inside." His Laurel and Hardy partnership with Chris Farley ended with Farley's overdose death in 1997.

💔
💔

In late 2007, after they had already split, Locklear was set to appear on Spade's sitcom *Rules of Engagement* as a girl the other characters think is too good for Spade. "It's like even on my show that's the angle," said Spade about the cameo.

2009
2008–2009
2006–2007

Kyle MacLachlan

💔
2007–2008

Jillian Grace

Heather Locklear p.134 ▶

p.67 ▶
p.143 ▶

In 1988, Woods sued ex-girlfriend Young for allegedly harassing him by leaving bloody, disfigured dolls on his doorstep. Maybe she was hinting she wanted kids? Rumor also had it that she super-glued Woods's penis to his leg.

Sean Young
Actress

When Woods's publicist was asked if Sheridan was dating the actor after they were spotted out together at the Golden Globes, the smartest publicist in Hollywood said, "According to my dictionary, that would be apropos."

◄ BACK **Michael Bolton** 2006–2008 ♂

Despite denials from both sides, members of the press reported that Sheridan and Spade were "full-on making out" on her forty-fifth birthday. Spade romantically quipped, "We've gone out a few times as friends. I think it's less dating and more her killing time."

◄ BACK David Spade   2008–2009

Heather Graham p. 47 ▲

Ashley Madison
Actress

This relationship ended when Madison showed up to the funeral of Woods's brother "in a three-inch miniskirt, and chain-smoking," according to a friend of Woods.

2006–2007

1988 ♥

1993 ♥

1995–1996

Tom Cruise p. 70 ▲

Gilbert dated Cruise when she was seventeen, and refutes rumors that he's asexual, contending, "there was a lot of making out on the couch in my mom's living room." She hasn't said, however, if they jumped on the couch as well.

James Woods
The aptly named Woods, born in aptly named Vernal, Utah, is well known for his high IQ (184) and love of the ladies (a friend said, "There is no one in Hollywood who manages to outrage dumped lovers more than [Woods]"). He reported the suspicious activity of the 9/11 hijackers doing a practice flight a month before the attacks took place.

Lisa Rinna
The sexy star of *Days of Our Lives* and *Melrose Place* has admitted to overdoing her plastic surgery, saying, "I had Juvederm put in my cheeks. That's what I overdid, big time . . . I look like a freak!"

1995–1996

1995–1996

Nicollette Sheridan
British-born Sheridan, the stepdaughter of Telly Savalas, played the role of *The Sure Thing* in the John Cusack (pg. 121) film of the same name before landing her career-making role on *Knots Landing*. She reportedly stole a chandelier from her *Desperate Housewives* trailer when she didn't get a going-away party on her last day of shooting in 2009.

1988

In her pre-*Desperate Housewives* days, Sheridan was desperately in love, but Baio said it wasn't meant to be: "That relationship was more of a speed bump."

🔒 1991–1993

1978–1982 ♥

Hamlin married his third soap star in 1997, the year before she posed naked in *Playboy* while six months pregnant with their daughter, Delilah Belle.

1997–

Harry Hamlin
"Release the Kraken!" is what you should yell if you ever meet Hamlin dressed in a loincloth, as he was in 1981's *Clash of the Titans*. He was playing a different kind of hero (or monster, if you dislike lawyers) in *L.A. Law* when he was named *People* magazine's "Sexiest Man Alive" in 1987.

Ursula Andress p. 146 ▼

Geraldo Rivera p. 50 ▼

2004–2005

Rob Lowe p. 131

1981–1987 ♻
1981 💔
1990 💔

Melissa Gilbert

Gilbert is best known for her nine-year role as Laura Ingalls Wilder on *Little House on the Prairie*.

Teen magazines in the late 1970s fought for photos of Baio and Shields together. "[They] were all over us," said Baio. Of his relationship, he said, "We were both puppies."

Brooke Shields p. 115
Pamela Anderson p. 29
Heather Locklear p. 134

In 1983, Baio told *People* magazine that Locklear was his first true love. He later said, "If she had come into my life when I was forty, I may have been ready for something that fantastic."

Dylan McDermott

Stepson of *The Vagina Monologues* playwright Eve Ensler, McDermott has always had a way with the ladies. He broke out playing a do-gooder lawyer on David Kelley's (pg. 154) *The Practice*, but budget and "creative realities" led to his firing.

♻ 1988–1990

Their engagement was born when they worked on *Steel Magnolias*, but McDermott always knew where he stood. He said dating actresses is all about "How long are you going to be around?" and "When is my number up?" His was up when Roberts met Kiefer Sutherland (pg. 159).

When Baio appeared on the *Howard Stern* (pg. 104) *Show* in 2007, he rated his lovers from 1 to 10. Gilbert topped his charts with a perfect 10. Score!

Renee Sloan
Body double

Denise Richards NEXT ▶

1990 💔

1978 💔 1990–1993 💔 1983 💔

1994 💔

Scott Baio

2007– 🔒
1988 💔
2005 💔

Baio may have peaked in the 1980s with the series *Charles in Charge* beginning its run, and the feature film *Zapped!* bringing his charm (and naked girls) to the big screen. It was during this time that Baio was banned from the Playboy mansion for scamming on too many of Hugh Hefner's Playmates.

Liza Minnelli

Minnelli continued mother Judy Garland's legacy as a world-class performer, drug addict, and gay icon, going as far as marrying a gay Broadway songwriter (Peter Allen), just as her mother reportedly did with husbands Mark Herron and Liza's father, Vincente Minnelli.

💔 1986

Rivera boasted of a fling with Minnelli in his 1991 autobiography, *Exposing Myself*, a book he later referred to as "the colossal error of my adult life."

Baio claimed that Minnelli wanted him to father a child for her using artificial insemination and a surrogate mother, but, unfortunately for the human race, that never happened. Sources alleged that they "bumped uglies" as recently as 2005.

1997–2003   Al Pacino p. 10
💔

Beverly D'Angelo

D'Angelo won critical acclaim for portraying Patsy Cline in *Coal Miner's Daughter*, but her big break was as Ellen "Oh, God, the dog wet the picnic basket" Griswold in *National Lampoon's Vacation*—she also dated more Hollywood hotshots than Christie Brinkley, her adversary in the film.

Joanie really did love Chachi. Baio told *People* in 1982 that he had lost his virginity to *Happy Days* costar Moran. He says, "She was an important woman in my life."

💔 💔
1995
1980–1982

Julia Roberts p. 159

Sheridan split from personal trainer–fiancé Soderblam in 2005, and he immediately sold his story in the book *Desperate Houseman*. The kiss-and-teller wrote, "She is a very troubled woman . . . just a lost, angry little girl who has never grown up." Someone else sounds a little angry, too.

Nicklas Soderblam
Personal trainer

Erin Moran
American actress

Baio told this story about meeting D'Angelo at a party: "I walked right over to her and confessed, 'You know, you have one of the sexiest qualities a woman can ever have.' 'Oh yeah? What's that?' she asked. 'You have an overbite.' 'I don't have an overbite, dear,' she said. 'I have a cocksucker's mouth.'"

Carey Mulligan

Mulligan was rejected from three drama schools before appearing in 2005's *Pride & Prejudice* with Keira Knightley (pg. 84). She broke out in 2009's *An Education* in which the twenty-two-year-old played a mean sixteen.

Rihanna said she and Hartnett were "just good friends," and we all know what that means. She later confirmed the obvious, and rationalized the lies by saying, "It's good to be friends first. When I hang out with Josh, it's lovely."

Josh Hartnett p. 72 ▲

Chris Brown

Brown hit the top of the Billboard charts at age sixteen with his 2005 self-titled debut album. A year later he said, "In 10 years' time, I'll also be making movies, owning my own company and my own clothing line." And he's well on his way, except for one little domestic abuse conviction in 2009.

It's not Megan Fox, but Shia is dating a costar. The man for whom love is always a bull market got together with Mulligan when they shot Oliver Stone's *Wall Street* sequel.

— 2009 ♥

Shia LaBeouf

LaBeouf started out as a Disney child actor but by 2006 he was taking roles in which he could curse as much as possible, in order to age himself up. It worked, and after impressing as a youth under house arrest in *Disturbia*, he signed on to star as the lead human in three *Transformer* films.

2007 💔

Shia and Rihanna went out briefly while LaBeouf was shooting *Indiana Jones*—just long enough for Chris Brown to ice his knuckles.

The teenage romance ended tragically when Brown assaulted Rihanna in a rented Lamborghini on the way home from a pre-Grammy party. She had to cancel her Grammy performance, and he was sentenced to six months of community service and five years probation.

Brittany Ashland
Porn star

Sheen pleaded no contest to smashing then-girlfriend Ashland's face into the marble floor of his home, knocking her unconscious, then threatening to kill her if she told anyone what had happened. But don't worry, justice was served—the millionaire was fined $2,800 and ordered to attend counseling.

LaBeouf met Hastings through a mutual friend and thought she was one of the "most beautiful girls he's ever seen," according to a "source." But when you're a hot, young superstar, there's always another most-beautiful-girl-you've-ever-seen around the corner. LaBeouf later admitted that he was only interested in "dating and messing around."

♥💔 2008

2007 💔

2008 💔

2008–2009 💔

Lauren Hastings p. III

Rihanna

The Barbados native R&B singer got her start as a sex symbol young. Like, before-she-was-legal young. Barbados created a national holiday to honor the Grammy winner.

This affair only came to light when Baio rated sex with exes on Howard Stern's (pg. 104) show in 2007. Richards ranked a three on his scale, just below Liza Minnelli (pg. 131).

Peele and Sheen were married six weeks after they met; four months and twenty-four days later, they split. Sheen reportedly explained the divorce by saying, "You buy a car; it breaks down." He should have married Yoko Ono—very reliable.

Donna Peele
Model

Ginger Lynn

Lynn was one of the biggest porn stars of the 1980s but quit the business (temporarily) in 1986 to try her hand at mainstream entertainment. A few years later she added another vice to her repertoire and spent four months in jail for cheating on her taxes.

Robin Wright Penn p.102

2° to Jason Patric
3° to Madonna
3° to Naomi Campbell

Dupre, known then as "Victoria," and another girl were allegedly sent to Sheen in cheerleader role-play attire for a well-documented birthday celebration. Their pimp alleged that "Sheen got the girls ... chanting 'Charlie! Charlie! He's our man. If he can't do it, nobody can! ... They loved Charlie.'"

Ashley Dupre

If you were "Client 9," you knew her as "Kristen," but the woman *The Village Voice* called the most famous hooker in America was born Ashley Youmans. Her call-girl activities brought down New York's governor and led to her new career as a *NY Post* sex advice columnist.

1981 💔

Charlie Sheen

We won't list all five thousand of Sheen's alleged conquests here, but, suffice it to say, the guy's a player. But that doesn't mean he's above paying for it—the one place he may be listed more frequently than the trades is Hollywood madam Heidi Fleiss's infamous black book.

2002–2006

Sheen and Richards met while working on *Scary Movie 3*, but things really got scary after they married. Richards alleged that Sheen threatened to have her killed and was so paranoid about 9/11 conspiracies that he kept guns under their coffee table. Scarier still, he posted a photo of his erect penis on his online profile.

2008

New York governor Spitzer sealed his fate as a political has-been in 2008 when he got caught paying $4,300 for a night with pricey call girl Dupre. The FBI recorded one call in which Spitzer placed his order and another in which Dupre told her booker "I don't think he's difficult ... I'm here for a purpose."

Eliot Spitzer
Former New York governor

John Stamos NEXT ▶

1996 💔

1995–1996 🔓

Porn star Lynn once said, "When Charlie's sober, he's sweet, kind, loving, generous. When he's drinking and using, he's out of control." After they split up, she sold the pearl necklace he gave her on eBay. You can't make this stuff up.

1990–1995

1983–1984

1989–1990

2006–

At age nineteen, Sheen fathered a child, Cassandra Jade, with sixteen-year-old Profitt, his girlfriend at the time. Grandfather Martin Sheen, a good Catholic, set the young mother up with a house and trust fund so she wouldn't abort the baby.

Paula Profitt
High school girlfriend

Sheen and Preston were engaged and living together when she was shot in their home by a loaded gun that Sheen had left in the pocket of his crumpled-on-the-floor pants. When she moved the pants, the gun went off and shot her in the leg. That's what you get for helping someone with his laundry.

Kelly Preston p.114 ▼

2002–2006

2006

2006–2007

Denise Richards

Admit you rewound her Neve Campbell (pg. 122) kissing scene from *Wild Things* and you'll be well on your way to accepting the perennial appeal of Denise Richards. She shone on-screen in the late 1990s and dominated tabloids in the early 2000s, culminating in her own reality show on E!

Richard Sambora NEXT ▶

Brooke Mueller
Real estate investor

Sheen's third marriage was to Mueller, who was introduced to Sheen by her best friend, Rebecca Gayheart (pg. 94). "This feels like my first real marriage," said Sheen, "The first one was a show, the second one was a con, and this one is the real deal." Despite that sentiment, Mueller called the cops on Sheen in 2009, claiming he had threatened to kill her.

1994

Stamos and Richards had dated before, but he reconnected with her and provided support during her rocky divorce from Charlie Sheen (pg. 133). But not too much support—Stamos and Richards split for good because her kids were too much for him to handle.

◀ p.40 Sky Nellor   2000–2002 💕

◀ p.34 Michelle Dupont   2002–2006 💕

As Hannibal Lecter said, we covet what we see every day, and Sambora saw Richards when she became best friends with his wife, Heather Locklear. But instead of dropping her in a pit and making her rub lotion on her body, Sambora dated Richards after ditching Locklear and their eleven-year marriage.

◀ BACK Denise Richards   2006–2007

◀ BACK Denise Richards 💕

Richard Sambora
Guitarist for band Bon Jovi

The pair met at an REO Speedwagon concert in 1985 and married in 1986. Locklear once said, "Tommy doesn't worship the devil, he worships me," but that didn't stop him from sinning while on tour with Mötley Crüe, leading to their divorce.

Locklear surprised her husband of eleven years right before Valentine's Day in 2006 when her publicist spread the word that she was filing for divorce. "It's completely untrue," said Sambora, who was on tour at the time. Ouch.

1994–2006

1983

◀ p.32 Tommy Lee   1985–1993 💕

In the series finale of *Melrose Place*, Locklear's Amanda Woodward and Wagner's Dr. Peter Burns faked their own deaths to elope. The actors connected in real life (minus the fake deaths) after Locklear's divorce with Sambora.

Jack Wagner
Soap opera actor

2007– ❤

◀ p.129 David Spade   2006–2007 💕

Heather Locklear

Locklear made a big impression on Aaron Spelling and earned a permanent role on the soap opera *Dynasty* before appearing in series *T. J. Hooker*, *Spin City*, and the short-lived *LAX*. She was arrested for driving under the influence of controlled substances in 2008.

Scott Baio   p.131 ▲

Adrien Brody

Brody was the youngest actor to ever win a Best Actor Oscar for his role in Roman Polanski's *The Pianist*. He barely survived a motorcycle accident when he was nineteen, just like his on-screen brother's character played by Owen Wilson (pg. 101) in *The Darjeeling Limited*.

Dave Navarro   p.40 ▲

2001–2002

Navarro and Monet dated for about a year, and he played bass and guitar with her band Nancy Raygun in 1999.

1996–1997 💕

Monet Mazur

Monet made out okay in the Mazur family's naming system when compared to her siblings, Matisse and Cezanne. The actress appeared in *Blow* with Johnny Depp (pg. 114) but really filled out the role as the evil Playmate in 2008's *The House Bunny*.

Josh Groban

Groban is best described as the young Kenny G of opera. David Kelley (pg. 154) featured him on *Ally McBeal* and, the next thing you knew, his debut album had gone double-platinum.

Groban said the magically seductive powers of opera helped him snare Ms. Jones: "Let's face it, opera is one of the most romantic forms of music. It's certainly helped me out."

2003–2006

January Jones

The all-American Abercrombie & Fitch model made the perfect 1960s suburban housewife in AMC's *Mad Men* (she could be Doris Day's sexy sister) but she was already a familiar (pretty) face from the *American Pie* sequel, *American Wedding*.

Kutcher likes girls who wear Abercrombie & Fitch and look like fellow model Jones. He met her when both were striking poses in New York City. The relationship ended shortly after Kutcher's film career began to take off.

Brittany Murphy

It's hard to believe that the same Murphy who creeped us out with her psycho "I'll never tell" performance in 2001's *Don't Say a Word* also provided the voice for sweet Luanne on *King of the Hill*. She died in 2009.

2002–2003

In 2001, Kutcher went to pick up girlfriend Ellerin for a Grammy party. When she didn't answer the door, he left. The next morning, Ellerin's roommate found her; she had been stabbed to death. Serial killer Michael Gargiulo was linked to the murder in 2008 when he tried to stab another woman in Santa Monica.

Kutcher wooed Murphy on the set of the film *Just Married*, with romantic lines like, "I chose you; it's not like you're my sister and I have to be with you."

Ashley Ellerin
Model

Rebecca Romijn ▲ p. 36

Owen Wilson ▲ p. 101

1994–2005

2007

1982

♥ 2006

John Stamos

Stamos frequently toured with The Beach Boys as a drummer but it took eight seasons on *Full House* to make him a sex symbol and role model for kick-ass uncles everywhere.

Stamos and Moore dated after he made a guest appearance on her soap opera, *General Hospital*. Remember, kids: What happens in the ER stays in the ER.

Emma Heming
Victoria's Secret model

🔒 2008–

1998–1999

Flavio Briatore p. 17 ▶

2° to Heidi Klum ▶
3° to Mike Tyson ▶
4° to Uma Thurman ▶

Bruce Willis p. 138 ▶

Bruce Willis p. 138 ▶

Bruce Willis (pg. 138) may not have been happy with his ex Demi Moore dating the tattooed Kiedis, but some onlookers thought it was pretty great. "At least he's a better musician than Bruce," joked one Hollywood insider.

Anthony Kiedis p. 17 ▶

Freddy Moore
Singer-songwriter

Demetria Gene Guynes got her professional name when she married musician Moore in 1980.

1982 ♥

♥ 2002

1980–1985

🔒 1987–2000

♥ 2002

♥ 2002

Demi Moore

Moore dropped out of Los Angeles's Fairfax High (leaving behind schoolmates Anthony Kiedis, pg. 17, and Timothy Hutton, pg. 151) and lived near friend Nastassja Kinski as she pursued her career. She got a break on *General Hospital*, leading to the 1980s "Brat Pack" hits (and cocaine addictions) that made her a star.

🔒 2005–

America thought it was being "punk'd" when Moore shacked up with Kutcher, but the joke was on us—they have been together longer than most marrieds. And they have matching Twitter accounts (hers is @mrskutcher).

Ashton Kutcher

2002

1998–2001

♥ ♥

♥ Kutcher grew up in Cedar Rapids, Iowa, not far from the fictional Wisconsin home of his hit series *That '70's Show*. But the dopey-seeming Calvin Klein–undies model and star of *Dude, Where's My Car?* has quietly built a media empire producing *Punk'd*, *Beauty and the Geek*, and more.

♥ 🔒
2001 2005–

Years before she married Ashton Kutcher, Moore was snagging younger guys, including Farrell. He hooked up with the mother of three at a Golden Globes party, despite his being quoted around that time saying, "Have you ever been with a girl with fake breasts? It's like groping a rock."

Colin Farrell
Farrell may have had a traditional Irish Catholic upbringing, but that didn't stop him from shooting a sex tape with *Playboy* model Nicole Narain or propositioning his seventy-year-old costar, Dame Eileen Atkins, for "sex with no strings." Dude loves the ladies.

The Worst Sex Scenes Ever

If filmmakers can create convincing dinosaurs and blow up entire planets with special effects, you'd think they'd be able to deliver a sexy sex scene. But it's apparently harder than it looks (just ask Paris Hilton, pg. 89). The following moments have to be some of the least arousing ever captured on film. In *Alexander*, Colin Farrell (pg. 135) battles a naked Rosario Dawson (pg. 151) in a slap-happy girl fight that somehow inspires sweet tender love in front of the fire. Stanley Kubrick capped off a life's worth of weird sex scenes (see Pig Mask Couple in *The Shining*) with *Eyes Wide Shut*, in which Tom Cruise (pg. 70) attends the world's most uptight orgy. *Gigli* was a flop, but the sex scene between Jennifer Lopez (pg. 81) and Ben Affleck (pg. 80), which should have been full of passion, was the worst. It starts with a discussion about dirty nails, continues with some Affleck titty twisters, and really kicks off when Lopez hints for him to go "down there" by saying, "It's turkey time . . . gobble, gobble." But the very worst might be *Saved by the Bell* starlet Elizabeth Berkley's (pg. 158) "wild" pool moment with Kyle MacLachlan (pg. 143) in camp classic *Showgirls*. This classic bad sex scene begins with some underwater passion and ends with a splashy, thrashy, eggbeater-style orgasm.

The book you're holding has been assembled through exhaustive research by a team of trained scholars from our nation's finest universities, but the same cannot be said of the "facts" you'll find on the Internet. The Web is a wild and dangerous place, a place where no one can be trusted and truth is as elusive as a photograph of Heidi Klum's (pg. 17) kids. It's the place where a fellow named Jeff Smeenge makes his home. Go ahead and Google him. You'll find entries saying that "playwright Jeff Smeenge" has dated Kate Winslet, Kirsten Dunst (pg. 71), Rachel McAdams (pg. 46), Zooey Deschanel (pg. 153), Chloë Sevigny, and Mischa Barton (pg. 84). These facts are everywhere and prove that, besides having great taste in women (we'll let Mischa slide), Smeenge has mastered the art of rewriting history on the Web. By planting his seed on several Web sites (not celebrities), Smeenge's story was picked up and spread to dozens more and soon became Internet "fact." And thus, the term a "Smeenge" was coined:

smeenge \'sménj\ noun
a fabricated "fact" that floats across the Internet until it's repeated by enough Web sites to be accepted as truth.

Watch out for smeenges! And stick to safe, dependable sources (hint: you're holding one) for all your celebrity-gossip needs.

Julian McMahon
p. 45
1999–2001

p. 36
Estella Warren

p. 135
Emma Heming

Brooke Burns
Blonde babe Brooke Burns jiggled her way to notoriety on the TV series *Baywatch* and continued to light up the small screen on shows like *Dog Eat Dog* and *Miss Guided*.

Bruce beat out Demi Moore (pg. 135) when he hooked up with Burns, who's a full month younger than Ashton Kutcher (pg. 135)!

Willis was casting for the role of future wife while shooting the erotic thriller *Perfect Stranger* in 2007. "He personally went through head shots and when the girls were called in to 'read,' he was there," said a source.

2001–2002
2003–2004

2008–2009

Willis and Moore married in 1987 to become the ultimate Hollywood power couple. After thirteen years of marriage, three kids, and a divorce, they're still close enough (and confident enough!) to vacation together with his-and-hers hot young significant others.

1974–1985

Sasha Czack
Photographer

After meeting on the set of *Rocky IV* in 1985, Nielsen loomed over height-impaired husband Stallone until their divorce in 1987 (he's 5'9"; she's 6'1" without the hair).

1985–1987

1995
1997–

Jennifer Flavin
Skin products entrepreneur

1993–1994

Talk about rocky relationships—Dickinson falsely accused Stallone of fathering her child (DNA tests proved otherwise), then claimed he injected her with steroids in her sleep. "He juiced me. I'd wake up and . . . was as big as Popeye," she said.

Sylvester Stallone
When the newborn Italian Stallion was delivered in a Hell's Kitchen charity ward, the forceps severed a facial nerve, leading to his characteristic snarl and slur. But that early injury and a first role in a soft-core porn flick didn't stop Stallone from become one of the biggest stars of the 1980s and 1990s, and his *Rocky* and *Rambo* roles (at least the first episodes) were praised by critics and fans.

Bruce Willis
Harmonica huffin', head shavin' Willis came to Hollywood after a brief stint off-Broadway and won the role of a lifetime opposite Cybill Shepherd in *Moonlighting*. He reinvented himself as an action star in *Die Hard*, performing most of his own stunts and generally kicking ass with a "Yippee ki yay, motherfucker!"

2006
2007

According to reports in 2009, Willis test dated both Feldman and Emma Heming before settling on Heming and marrying her.

Tamara Feldman
American actress

Tamara Witmer
Playboy Playmate

1987–2000
1983

The self-proclaimed "world's first supermodel" told her fellow *I'm a Celebrity . . . Get Me out of Here!* contestants that she'd had an affair with Bruce. Dickinson bragged, "I was twenty-eight and single, so I had him on speed dial."

Willis's second Tamara (after he split up with Tamara Feldman) was this twenty-three-year-old Playboy Playmate, who said, "He's got the sexiest voice . . . I don't mind the bald head."

p. 135
Demi Moore

Angie Everhart ▲ p. 32

Brigitte Nielsen

The sultry Dane with the body of a linebacker starred with Stallone in *Rocky IV* and *Cobra* and had a reality TV resurgence when she slurred her way through VH1 hit *Strange Love* with Flavor Flav in 2005.

Dickinson insisted that Sylvester Stallone had impregnated her in 1993 and that her daughter, Savannah, was his. He thought she was crazy. A paternity test proved that Savannah was actually the daughter of Hollywood producer Birnbaum.

Michael Birnbaum
Film producer

1993

Jon Lovitz
Comedian

Want proof opposites attract? Consider the strange case of Dickinson and Lovitz, who dated for a year. "Jon is . . . the funniest, sexiest, most well-put together man that walks the earth. He's hot, he's a hunk," contended Dickinson. By bagging a supermodel, Lovitz gives hope to the short, fat, balding man in us all.

1994

Ron Levy
Pianist for BB King

1976–1978

Mick Jagger ▲ p. 50

Dickinson caught Jagger's eye at Hollywood's Roxy Theatre while he was dating model Jerry Hall (pg. 51). Their forbidden love didn't end until a phone call from Hall, who allegedly told Dickinson, "Stay the fuck away from Mick! I've got a gun in my purse and I know how to use it!"

1981

Mick Jagger ▲ p. 50

Janice Dickinson

Janice Dickinson claims she invented the word *supermodel*, but, because she appears to be crazy, this seems unlikely. After an admittedly successful modeling career, she proudly slept her way around Hollywood before transforming into a reality TV star on Tyra Banks's (pg. 15) *America's Next Top Model*.

1993–1994

1992–1994

Galotti stole Dickinson from Sylvester Stallone after meeting the couple in Paris while they were in the middle of an argument. Galotti said, "Fuck him, come with me," and she did. They shared a passionate affair, and, according to Dickinson, sex on the twelfth floor of *Vogue* headquarters: "I notched on the floor above Anna Wintour's office! That was a first!"

Ron Galotti
Galotti was the publisher of *Vogue*, *GQ*, *Talk*, and *Vanity Fair*, friend of she-devil Anna Wintour and the model for *Sex and the City*'s "Mr. Big" (he dated Candace Bushnell). The fast-talking schmoozer drove his Ferrari off to retire on a Vermont farm in 2004.

1995–1997

Candace Bushnell

Bushnell is the prototype of Carrie Bradshaw (portrayed by Sarah Jessica Parker, pg. 12) of *Sex and the City*—she was a New York party girl and columnist for the *New York Observer*, and she wrote the book that became the HBO series.

1983 **1993**

Liam Neeson ▲ p. 115

Simon Fields
Film producer

1983 Warren Beatty NEXT ▶

1993 John F. Kennedy Jr. p. 11 ▶

Dickinson was set up on a blind date with JFK Jr. by New York hairstylist Frederic Fekkai at Cefe Un Deuk Trois in Manhattan. They made out by the bathroom before Kennedy bailed on the date because Janice was allegedly obsessing about the blood on Jackie O's Chanel suit when JFK was assassinated.

1980 Jack Nicholson p. 59

Dickinson's marriage to real estate developer Gerston took a turn for the worse when he drove their car off a cliff on a St. Barts vacation. Both survived the crash. When they split, Dickinson got to keep her twenty-three-karat diamond engagement ring worth $180,000, but she had to give back the Mercedes (not the car from the crash, of course).

1987–1992 **1994–1996**

Albert Gerston
Real estate developer

Cher

Cher has the honor of being the first woman to show her belly button on TV. Her penchant for eye-popping fashions culminated in the music video for her hit "If I Could Turn Back Time," which was banned from MTV because of her V-neck-meets-G-string wardrobe.

Annette Bening
American actress

Many doubted that Hollywood's "most eligible bachelor," or "man-whore" in the modern nomenclature, could ever settle down, but Beatty's marriage to Bening remains one of Tinseltown's rare romantic success stories.

Carole Mallory p.55

Diane Von Furstenberg p.154

Peter Sellers
British actor

1964–1968

Rod Stewart p.27

Britt Ekland
Swedish actress

💔 1975–1977

Laws of probability dictate that two people who get around as much as Beatty and Cher will inevitably hook up. "Warren has been with everybody, and unfortunately I am one of them. I was sixteen at the time and had pretty low self-esteem," said Cher.

◄ p.103 Madonna

◄ p.50 Carly Simon

◄ p.118 Barbra Streisand

As Streisand later recalled, Beatty was one of her "flings."

Joan Collins
Actress and author

At twenty-six, Joan Collins embarked on a serious affair with a then-unknown Beatty. Once asked if the claim that she and Beatty made love seven times a day was true, she responded, "Maybe he did, but I'd just lay there!" Always the bitch, eh, Alexis?

🔒 1991–

1962

1988–1990

💔

1970 💔

1970 💔

Warren Beatty

If Shirley MacLaine, his sister, had multiple lives, Beatty had many lives' worth of romances before settling down with Annette Bening in 1991. Most of his exes remember him fondly, stating that he was "the love of [her] life" (Michelle Phillips, pg. 58) or "the most divine lover of all" (Britt Ekland).

💔 1976

💔 1978

💔 1970

💔 1981–1986

💍 1959–1961

◄ p.58 Michelle Phillips

1991 💔

Phillips claimed that she was "madly in love with [Beatty]," and says she "fell off the couch laughing" when Beatty told Barbara Walters in a TV interview that his relationships with women often ended because they broke up with him. "That is what Warren makes his women do!" said Phillips.

Christie had a high-profile but intermittent relationship with Warren Beatty, who described her as "the most beautiful and at the same time the most nervous person I had ever known."

💔 1967–1974

Julie Christie
Actress

In her memoir, Janice Dickinson rated the sexual prowess of each of her many beaus. Of Warren Beatty, she said, "He was great. He knew where everything was and just what to do with it."

💔 1983

💔 1986

1993–1999

💔

1991 Stephanie Seymour p.155

1961 💔

Isabelle Adjani
French actress and singer

Daniel Day-Lewis p.16

Wood became mesmerized with Beatty when they costarred in *Splendor in the Grass* and left her husband Robert Wagner for him.

Natalie Wood

Wood was with Robert Wagner (whom she married twice) and Christopher Walken when she drowned near Santa Catalina Island, California, in 1981.

◄ BACK Janice Dickinson

Mia Farrow

Maria de Lourdes Villiers-Farrow fell into film as the daughter of Oscar-nominated director John Farrow and Irish star Maureen O'Sullivan. She gained fame on *Peyton Place* right as her private life began to super-cede her stardom, with marriages to Frank Sinatra and Andre Previn.

Though Farrow and Allen never married, they adopted two children together during their twelve-year relationship and had one biological child. Their relationship ended when Farrow found nude photographs of her adopted daughter Soon-Yi Farrow Previn (from a previous marriage) in Allen's possession.

Brought together for each *Godfather* film, Pacino and Keaton dated on and off for two decades before splitting (and never speaking again) when he knocked up Jan Tarrant (pg. 10). Keaton said, "Now that I'm older, time is valuable. You just think, gee, it would have been nice if we had parted a little earlier."

Al Pacino p. 10 ▶

1981–1986 ❧

1972–1991

Diane Keaton

There's a lot of Keaton in her Oscar-winning portrayal in *Annie Hall*—the quirky mannerisms, the mannish fashions. She dated some of the biggest names in Hollywood but, like her role model, Katharine Hepburn, has always maintained her independent lifestyle. "I understand that these are episodes we go through with people, and they don't all last."

1980–1992

Woody Allen

If nebbishy septuagenarian Woody Allen can still play with starlets like Scarlett Johansson (pg. 48), imagine what he was like in his early years. But if the thought of Allen dressed as a giant sperm in 1972's *Everything You Always Wanted to Know About Sex But Were Afraid to Ask* gets you hot, then that's something to discuss with your therapist.

1970–1979 ❧

Keanu Reeves

Although critics question his acting acumen, there is no doubting Keanu's superstar status. The Dogstar band member has been dogged by rumors of a secret wedding to David Geffen, but whatever the truth is, he clearly is *The One*.

The pair became romantically involved when Allen cast Keaton in his successful Broadway play, *Play It Again, Sam*. And, of course, they starred together in what is considered by many to be the best romantic comedy of all time, *Annie Hall*.

Steve Jobs

Technology mogul Steve Jobs made a fortune as cofounder of Apple Computers, turning white earbuds and sleek silver notebooks into must-haves for cool kids everywhere. He's also the bastard who cut the price of the iPhone two days after you finally bought one.

❧ ❧

1982

2003–2005   2003–2005 ❧

In 2003, Reeves and Keaton met on the set of *Something's Gotta Give*. Despite the nineteen years between the two, they started dating, and Keaton was photographed visiting Keanu's L.A. house after hours.

❧ ❧ 2008

China Chow p. 27 ▶

❧ 1981

1998–2000

After Wood's mysterious drowning death in November 1981, rumors of an affair with her then-costar Walken swirled. Husband Robert Wagner admitted years later that he had fought with Walken about issues of "emotional infidelity," but there is speculation that Wood uncovered an affair between Walken and Wagner and threatened to out them both.

Christopher Walken

Walken has been impersonated by everyone from Johnny Depp (pg. 114) to Eddie Izzard to the entire cast of *SNL*. Not to be forgotten are Walken's substantial acting achievements—he won an Oscar for *The Deer Hunter*, that movie about Vietnam you never saw.

Syme got pregnant while dating Reeves—a pregnancy that ended in the stillbirth of their daughter, Ava Archer Syme Reeves, around Christmas 1999. After Syme died in a tragic car accident in 2001, she was buried next to her daughter at the Westwood Village Memorial Park Cemetery in Los Angeles.

Jennifer Syme

The *Lost Highway* actress was killed in 2001 when she crashed her SUV into a row of parked cars in Los Angeles after a party at Marilyn Manson's (pg. 39) home. Her mother unsuccessfully sued Manson for wrongful death, alleging he had given her "various quantities of an illegal controlled substance."

Connie Angland
Special effects technician

Danielle Dotzenrod
Model

After getting dumped by Angelina Jolie (pg. 105), Thornton dated the much-younger Dotzenrod, who, despite the name, is a model, not a porn star. Jolie dropped out of that year's Academy Awards (attended by Thornton), first saying that her gown had been stolen and then saying it was inappropriate to attend considering the war.

Boyle met MacLachlan on the set of *Twin Peaks* and they started dating, despite the fact that she had love scenes with another actor on the series. Boyle said "...sometimes I'll have, like, this huge kissing scene with James and, like, Kyle'll be sitting in the trailer like this, you know?"

Lara Flynn Boyle p.128 ▲

Ben Harper
College-radio favorite Ben "Burn one down" Harper toured with blues legend Taj Mahal after mastering the ultrafolksy lap slide guitar.

◀ p.105 **Angelina Jolie**

Jolie met Thornton on the set of the underrated *Pushing Tin* in 1999 and they married in 2000, waiting only moments to do weird things like wearing vials of each other's blood (really just single drops, they later explained) and adopting Cambodian child Maddox. Both Maddox and her blood went with Jolie in the divorce.

1999–2003 🔒

2003– ♥

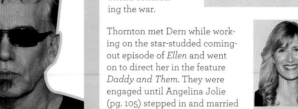

Thornton met Dern while working on the star-studded coming-out episode of *Ellen* and went on to direct her in the feature *Daddy and Them*. They were engaged until Angelina Jolie (pg. 105) stepped in and married Thornton only months later. "I left our home to go and make a movie and while I was away my boyfriend got married and I never heard from him again," said Dern.

2002–2003 💔

Dern started dating slide guitar ace Harper in 2000 while he was married and living with his then-wife and children.

2005–

Laura Dern
Dern got emancipated from her parents, Bruce Dern and Diane Ladd, at age thirteen when they refused to let her star in the cult classic girl-punk film *Ladies and Gentleman, The Fabulous Stains*.

1993–1997 🔒

Billy Bob Thornton

Thornton is a real-deal Arkansas native—his mother was a psychic, his cousins are pro wrestlers Dory and Terry Funk, and his grandfather was named Otis. He moved to Los Angeles to be an actor, but legendary director Billy Wilder advised him to consider screenwriting. Thus came his Oscar-winning *Sling Blade*.

Cherniak and Thornton had two sons before the drama began. She got a restraining order after accusing Billy Bob of biting her. When he said it was just sexual fun, she responded, "I never once claimed he bit me during sex . . . Quite frankly, our sex life was pretty dull." Years later, Angelina Jolie (pg. 105) split from Thornton after he was seen with Cherniak.

Pietra Cherniak
Aspiring model and actress

🔓 *1997–2000*

Dern and Goldblum got engaged after meeting on *Jurassic Park*, with Goldblum saying, "I had been discreetly casting glances across the dinosaur. It's mysterious what attracts you to a person."

1994–1996 🔓

At the height of his success, Harlin produced *Rambling Rose*, which earned then-girlfriend Dern an Oscar nomination for best actress.

1990 💔

Renny Harlin
Finnish film director

Jeff Goldblum
Goldblum is freakishly tall (six feet, four and one-half inches), quirky, and charming, and he has made a living playing the characters who figure things out before anyone else (*Jurassic Park, Independence Day*). He's also a nudist, at least according to Hollywood delivery folks.

2002 💔

After he fell for Helena Bonham Carter (pg. 157), Burton split from his longtime girlfriend/fiancée, Lisa Marie, with a phone call to say, simply, "It's over." Marie filed a lawsuit claiming that Burton owed her more than the $5.5 million he gave her when he broke it off, which a judge finally dismissed in 2008.

◀ p.157 Tim Burton

1991–2001

Lisa Marie
Model and actress

🔓

2002 💔

During this brief relationship, Goldblum and Marie displayed their affinity for having sand in their cracks by frolicking nude on the beaches of St. Barts.

Kristin Davis p.141 ▼

Kyle MacLachlan

You'd think they'd find it disturbing, but women never seemed to mind that the Kwisatz Haderach (from the movie *Dune*) has specialized in playing the creepiest characters on film (see *Blue Velvet*, *Twin Peaks*, *Showgirls*).

1991–1992

1985–1989

1992–1998

François-Henri Pinault p. 60

Evangelista left her husband, Gerald Marie, who happened to run her modeling firm's Paris office, to get with MacLachlan after meeting him on an ad shoot.

2005–2006

Linda Evangelista

Evangelista formed the powerful "trinity" of modeling in the 1980s and 1990s with fellow supermodels Naomi Campbell (pg. 54) and Christy Turlington (pg. 158). She's the one who said, "We don't wake up for less than $10,000 a day," famously misquoted as "I don't get out of bed for less than $10,000 a day."

1993–1998

This couple was responsible for the biggest flop in Hollywood history when Harlin cast Davis opposite Michael Douglas in the 1985 pirate flick *Cutthroat Island* and then enlarged Davis's part until Douglas dropped out. Production company Carolco was decimated by the flop, and both of their careers were hurt.

Davis married Goldblum after meeting on the set of *Transylvania 6-5000*, and they costarred in *The Fly* and *Earth Girls Are Easy*. Davis said she "didn't mind at all the fact that we were sort of living it twenty-four hours a day," but while they were getting divorced she posted a sign on her office bulletin board saying, "No movie projects with Goldblum."

Geena Davis

Davis was working as a model when Sydney Pollack cast her as the soap star in 1982's *Tootsie*. She produced the megaflop *Cutthroat Island* with husband Renny Harlin (pg. 142) but don't get her mad— she's one of the top archers in the country.

1987–1990

2001

Nicole Kidman p. 69

Erica Baxter
Australian model

Peta Wilson
Australian actress from *La Femme Nikita* television series

Crowe dumped Meg Ryan (pg. 144) for fellow Aussie Wilson because she was "less Hollywood." Soon after the short fling, she was pregnant with previous boyfriend Damian Harris's child.

2001

2000

2003–

Russell Crowe

Crowe got his first acting gig in an Australian production of *The Rocky Horror Show*. When he isn't making movies or running his rugby team, Crowe is throwing phones at hotel employees (see Naomi Campbell, pg. 54, for more phone attacks) or punching people from Australia to Japan.

Right before he started seeing Meg Ryan (pg. 144), Crowe hooked up with Australian model Baxter, who later married the third richest man in Australia, James Packer.

Danielle Spencer
Australian singer

Crowe married longtime on-and-off girlfriend Spencer on his thirty-ninth birthday (better not forget that anniversary!). They met in the 1990s while working on his first film, *The Crossing*.

Ryan left her husband, Dennis Quaid (pg. 144), for the high-strung Australian actor when they met on the set of box-office flop *Proof of Life* in 2001. As a result, Ryan's spotless, girlish image was tarnished, and she became known as a "scarlet woman." Is there anything celebrities won't do to reinvent themselves?

2000–2001

Meg Ryan NEXT ►

p.124 ▲

Jeanine Lobell
Founder of Stila cosmetics

Matthew Perry p.123 ▲

1994– 🔒

Anthony Edwards
We'll never forget Edwards's need-for-speed performance as Tom Cruise's (pg. 70) pilot buddy Goose in *Top Gun*. But he'll always be known as Dr. Mark Greene from his 181 episodes of *ER*.

Charlize Theron

Billy Idol
British rock star

Gerard Butler
After showing off his half-faced singing skills in the film version of *The Phantom of the Opera*, Butler starred as King Leonidas in the homoerotic action blockbuster *300*.

Moakler had a brief fling with action star Butler while her ex, Travis Barker, was in the hospital after surviving a plane crash. Fate is a cruel mistress, but she's got nothing on Moakler.

2008

Though Moakler is quick to point out how great his personality is, she also claims, "[Idol's] horrible in bed." That must mean that in the midnight hour, instead of crying "More, more, more," Moakler cried, "No, ow, stop!"

1997

1996–1998

They met on the set of *Top Gun*, in which they played husband and wife, but their relationship went into a flatspin when Ryan fell for Dennis Quaid on the set of *Innerspace*.

Craig Bierko
American actor

Bierko was destined to date Ryan. He turned down the role of Chandler Bing in *Friends*, which later went to Matthew Perry (pg. 123), a future Ryan beau. And he was cast to fight Russell Crowe (pg. 143), a former Ryan love, in *Cinderella Man*.

2002

1986–1987

2000–2001

2007

Meg Ryan
Although the characters she plays almost always find romance, offscreen the queen of the romantic comedy has not enjoyed a fairy-tale love life. This might have something to do with her unfortunate habit of falling for her costars.

Russell Crowe

◀ BACK

Shanna Moakler
Miss USA and *Playboy* Playmate Moakler claims that she had a premonition that kept her from getting on the plane that crashed with her husband Travis Barker (and Adam Goldstein, pg. 111) onboard in 2008.

1997–2000

All seemed to be going well between Moakler and De La Hoya until she was watching the Latin Grammys and inexplicably saw her fiancé and baby daddy with another woman—yet another case of a couple torn apart by the Latin Grammys.

Oscar De La Hoya
Champion boxer

Moakler said Quaid was better in bed than Oscar De La Hoya "by a landslide! And he's got a better body." That's right—the dad from *The Parent Trap* is a demon in the sack.

2004–2008

2001

1991–2000

Their relationship endured the low of Quaid's coke addiction and the high of the birth of their son. But, after nine years of marriage, in which Ryan claims Quaid repeatedly cheated on her, it all unraveled when she fell for *Gladiator* star Russell Crowe (pg. 143).

1991–2000

Kimberly Buffington
Texas real estate agent

Moakler married Barker on Halloween in a ceremony inspired by the film *The Nightmare Before Christmas* (Barker proposed in front of the Haunted Mansion at Disneyland) and their lives were profiled on the MTV series *Meet the Barkers*.

◀ p.89
Travis Barker

Dennis Quaid
While battling anorexia and cocaine addiction, Quaid has managed to maintain a successful thirty-year film career and get married thrice. He likes to keep busy!

🔒 2004–

Quaid and Buffington received the scare of a lifetime in 2007, when their newborn twins were given 1,000 times the correct dosage of a blood thinner. The babies did not suffer any lasting ill effects, but Quaid and his wife received a $500,000 settlement from the hospital.

Yuka Honda
Japanese musician and Cibo Matto cofounder

Honda met Lennon while she was remixing Yoko Ono's song "Talking to the Universe" and she invited him to play bass on tour with Cibo Matto. She later produced his debut album, *Into the Sun*, and lived in his Manhattan apartment until 2000.

💔 1996–2000

Elizabeth Jagger p. 93 ▲

💔 2004–2006

💔 2004–2005

♥ 2004–

Model Muhl and Lennon started dating soon after his harsh split with Bijou Phillips. In 2008, they were photographed on the streets of New York in poses and clothes that bore a striking resemblance to those of John and Yoko forty years earlier.

Kemp Muhl
Fashion model

Danny Masterson
Known for playing the chronic pot smoker Steven Hyde on *That '70s Show*, actor Masterson has never touched the stuff, or even taken aspirin, in line with his Scientology beliefs.

Milla Jovovich

NEXT ▶

Sean Lennon
Starting in high school, Lennon had his own apartment in the Dakota building and was frequently involved with older women. As the son of John and Yoko, he brought a wee bit of baggage to his own music career, which began with his debut album *Into the Sun* in 1998 and *Friendly Fire* in 2006, the latter of which was inspired by his breakup with Bijou Phillips.

Things couldn't have been better when these longtime Dakota building neighbors and musical offspring started dating—Phillips even named her pet Chihuahua "Yoko." But that couldn't make up for the revelation that she had cheated on Lennon with her best friend, Max LeRoy.

💔 2000–2003

Though Masterson and Phillips are happily engaged, it was probably odd for him to watch his fiancée perform a sex scene with his brother, actor Chris Masterson, on the set of *Made for Each Other*.

2003–2004

Max LeRoy
The only son of Tavern on the Green owner Warner LeRoy, Max was best friends with Mark Ronson (pg. 44) and Sean Lennon. He died in a motorcycle accident in 2005 in Los Angeles.

🐍 2004

Courtney Wagner p. 28

Wagner and LeRoy were set to get married when he died. Bijou Phillips had this to say about her best friend Wagner dating LeRoy: "Courtney is such a ho! She dates everyone I date!"

This relationship killed two birds with one stone when it was revealed to Sean Lennon, the longtime boyfriend of Phillips and lifelong best friend of LeRoy. Lennon and Phillips split up immediately, and Lennon and LeRoy didn't have a chance to make up, because LeRoy died soon after.

💔 2000–2003

♂ 2004–

Bijou Phillips
Bijou is the youngest daughter of The Mamas and the Papas front man John Phillips (pg. 58). She was born during a "rough patch," a year before he was arrested for dealing cocaine.

Wild child Phillips ended her affair with Allman, son of Cher (pg. 140), by throwing all his crap out the window of her apartment.

💔 1995

💔 1997

Evan Dando p. 62 ▶

Elijah Blue Allman p. 89

Phillips lost her virginity to Dando in 1995 at age fifteen and he dumped her four days later. But the young starlet was tough enough to tell *Talk* magazine, "It was horrible. But I learned later that he's never been good in bed. He'll [perform a certain sex act] for forty-five minutes, but he's bad at it. You just want him out of there."

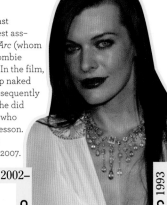

Paul W. S. Anderson
Director-writer-producer Paul W. S. Anderson began using his middle initials to avoid being confused with *Boogie Nights* director Paul Thomas Anderson.

Director Anderson cast Jovovich as the hottest ass-kicker since *Joan of Arc* (whom she also played) in zombie thriller *Resident Evil*. In the film, he shot her waking up naked in a lab, and they subsequently fell in love, just like she did with the last director who tried that shot, Luc Besson. They had a daughter named Ever Gabo in 2007.

2002–

Hayden Christensen p. 82

While filming *Dazed and Confused* in Texas, Andrews and then-sixteen-year-old Jovovich skipped to Las Vegas and got married. The union was quickly annulled by her mother.

Shawn Andrews
Andrews starred in *Dazed and Confused* as Kevin Pickford, the guy throwing the keg party. He highlighted a 2008 comeback with an intense role as a heartbroken gambler in indie film *Big Heart City*.

1993

1997–1999

Supermodel and singer Jovovich dated Frusciante after his triumphant return to the Red Hot Chili Peppers, and the two collaborated on a potential follow-up album to Jovovich's 1994 album (she sings too) *The Divine Comedy*.

Jon Frusciante
Guitarist for Red Hot Chili Peppers

2000 ❣

◀ BACK Sean Lennon

2004–2005 ❣

Milla Jovovich
Supermodel Jovovich was born in the Ukraine during the Soviet years but grew up in Los Angeles, where she was called "Commie" and "Russian spy" and never fit in. She signed as a model at eleven and got her first cover at twelve. She was cast in the Brooke Shields (pg. 115) role in *Return to the Blue Lagoon* (in which she also performed nude).

Bilson rated her boyfriend and *Jumper* costar Christensen a "ten when it comes to kissing" but told Regis and Kelly that simulating sex on camera, even with your main squeeze, is "always a bit awkward." Despite the awkwardness, they got engaged in December 2008.

2008–

Rachel Bilson
Bilson's grandfather directed *Get Smart*, which is just cool. She made it big on *The O.C.* and made waves with her distinctive fashion sense. Her take on dating costars (she's dated two so far): "They say, 'Don't date your costar,' but that's who you're around!"

James Dean
Dean has the sad honor of winning the first posthumous Oscar after his love of cars did him in when he crashed his Porsche 550 Spyder on September 30, 1955.

According to Dennis Hopper (pg. 58), not only was Dean straight but he also had great taste in women. The only reason he didn't marry Andress when she asked was that he wanted to "wait until he saw how his career was going."

1955 ❣

According to some reports in the 1990s, Brando couldn't remember whether or not he'd gotten it on with Andress in the 1950s, so he phoned her up in Rome to ask. "Yes," she replied, "but I dumped you for James Dean." Click.

❣ 1955

Ursula Andress
The original Bond girl, Swiss actress Andress made her American film debut rising out of the sea in a wet, white bikini, to Sean Connery's (pg. 55) delight in 1962's *Dr. No*.

❣ 1978–1982

Harry Hamlin p. 130

Hamlin wooed Andress, and the two starred in *Clash of the Titans* (she as Aphrodite, technically Perseus's sister by Zeus). They had a son, Dimitiri, in 1981 before the film premiered.

Marlon Brando
Brando was blacklisted in the 1960s for supporting the Black Panthers and Native Americans, and he ended his life obese, hanging out with best friend Michael Jackson (pg. 13) in Neverland.

2003–2006

Bilson and Brody followed the script and dated in real life while their characters were falling in love on *The O.C.* They adopted two dogs during their relationship (Penny Lane and Thurmen), which were split up along with their other stuff when they separated.

2003–2006

◀ p. 56 Ryan O'Neal 1971

Luc Besson

French writer-director Besson traveled the world with his Club Med scuba-instructor parents as a child and wanted to be a marine biologist, but a diving accident forced him to change plans. If it weren't for that accident we wouldn't have *Nikita*, *The Fifth Element*, or any of the twenty-seven *Transporter* films.

Just watch the opening scenes of *The Fifth Element* and you'll understand why Besson fell for Jovovich, the bandage-bedecked star of his sci-fi film/fashion show. They married and made the ill-fated *Joan of Arc* (which should have been burned at the stake) before splitting amicably.

Imogen Thomas

Star of *Big Brother* U.K.

Brand briefly dated Thomas, Miss Wales, whose stint as a *Big Brother* (UK) housemate became extra special when her sex tape (with a different dude) appeared online while she was in the house.

2006

Sadie Frost p.83 ▶

Following a fling with her best friend Kate Moss (pg. 60), Brand hooked up with Frost. A witness reported that "Kate is a free spirit and cool with that. They're one big happy family."

2006

Kate Moss p.60 ▶

Russell Brand

British comedian, actor, and self-professed sex addict (among other addictions), Brand was fired by the BBC for crank calling a seventy-eight-year-old actor with messages that he'd screwed his granddaughter, and by MTV for dressing up as Osama bin Laden shortly after 9/11.

2006

2008

Palmer and Britain's two-time "Shagger of the Year" (according to the *Sun*) were inseparable, with Brand saying he was "a changed man." After he hosted the MTV Music Awards (and possibly hooked up with Britney Spears, pg. 33), his tune changed to the following: "I really wanted to go mental after the awards and fuck everyone—but it is difficult when your girlfriend's in the bed."

Katy Perry

American singer-songwriter

2009– ♀

Just another in the string of *Big Brother* (UK) starlets bedded by Brand, the two were joined by a shared interest. "I love sex!" said eloquent Kate.

2006

Kate Lawler

U.K. *Big Brother* winner

Teresa Palmer

The Adelaide model burst onto the scene as Daniel Radcliffe's pigtailed lover in 2007's *December Boys*, followed by roles in big comedies *Bedtime Stories* and *Young Americans*.

Stuart Dew

Australian footballer

2005–2007

After they started dating, Palmer revealed that she had fallen for the footballer when she was thirteen years old and her father took her to a Port Adelaide game where she had her picture taken (wearing a silly jester hat) with the then-nineteen-year-old Dew.

2007–2009

Topher Grace p.59 ▶

Adam Brody

One of Brody's first roles was playing big Brady brother Barry Williams in 2000's television tell-all *Growing Up Brady*. That was before he topped numerous magazine lists as hottest TV geek for his role as Seth Cohen on *The O.C.*

2008

This couple was seen together all over Australia, where shooting was supposed to begin for the troubled production of comic book feature *Justice League: Mortal*. (The shoot was canceled.)

2007

Grace and Palmer started dating on the set of the comedy *Young Americans* in 2007 and then, after a short jaunt with her *Bedtime Stories* costar Russell Brand, she reconnected with Topher and took him Down Under (not metaphorically) saying, "He's everything I could ask for."

Kirsten Dunst p.71 ▶

What's My Type?

We all have our preferences, but when you're a celebrity those preferences are a whole lot easier to satiate. Take George Clooney (pg. 125) whose girlfriends tend to have two big things in common (not counting their hair color).

Lisa Snowden

Krista Allen (pg. 128)

Kelly Preston (pg. 114)

Lisa

Krista

Kelly

Paris Hilton (pg. 89) has very strict requirements for her boyfriends—namely that they make great-grandfather Conrad Hilton roll over in his solid platinum coffin.

Benji Madden (pg. 89)

Travis Barker (pg. 89)

Rick Salomon (pg. 88)

Benji

Travis

Rick

Then there's Bruce Willis (pg. 138), who dated plenty but has only married twice—to Demi Moore (pg. 135) in 1987 and to her (seeming) organ-harvesting clone Emma Heming (pg. 135) in 2009.

Demi?

Emma?

With celebrities' busy production schedules and love lives, you'd find it hard to believe that they have the time to go Grape-Ape crazy and threaten their lucrative careers—yet the busiest and most dedicated seem to find the time. In 2002, a year after she signed the biggest record deal in history ($100 million for six albums), Whitney Houston (pg. 24) told Diane Sawyer on *ABC Primetime* that "Crack is cheap. I make too much money to ever smoke crack. . . . We don't do crack. Crack is whack." And that was just the opening salvo in a sweaty descent to reality television D-lister. But she isn't the only one to flip out. At the top of his game, two years after the record-breaking success of *The Passion of the Christ*, Mel Gibson was arrested for driving under the influence and managed to make the PR disaster even worse by going on a psycho, anti-Semitic rant during his arrest. A kind of madness struck Mariah Carey (pg. 25) a few months after she was named Billboard's "Artist of the Decade" when she handed out popsicles on MTV's *TRL* and started a strip tease that had Carson Daly (pg. 63) covering his eyes. And then there's Tom Cruise (pg. 70) who will be remembered for all time for pouncing on Oprah Winfrey's couch and declaring his love for Katie Holmes (pg. 150).

◀ p.113 Minnie Driver

Christopher Lambert

Lambert grew up in Geneva and Paris as the son of a French diplomat to the United Nations. He appeared as Tarzan in 1986's overnamed *Greystoke: The Legend of Tarzan, Lord of the Apes* but is best known for his brooding, undying portrayal in *Highlander*.

1998–2001

Life with Brolin can't be easy for Lane: He was arrested in 2007 for suspicion of domestic battery, he had to get in character for *W.*, so it must've been like living with Dubya, and her mother-in-law is Barbra Streisand (pg. 118).

When they divorced in 1994, Lane joked that she would never again have to read a story about them with the headline "Me Tarzan, You Lane."

1988–1994

Diane Lane

Lane had the genes—her mother was *Playboy*'s Miss October 1957 and her father was an acting coach—so it's not surprising that she debuted with the best, starring in *A Little Romance* opposite Laurence Olivier. She was soon cast by Francis Ford Coppola in *The Outsiders* and *Rumble Fish*.

1988–1992

Josh Brolin

The son of James Brolin (pg. 118), Josh got his first big role as the hunky older brother in *The Goonies*. He turned down Johnny Depp's (pg. 114) role on *21 Jump Street* but made up for that mistake in recent years with killer roles in *No Country for Old Men* and the George W. Bush biopic, *W.*

2002–

Chris Klein

Seemingly sweet Klein showed his unendearing side after his split from Katie Holmes when he said, "When a woman isn't feeling good about herself and you combine that with her period . . . eventually she'll ask you if you like her body. You have to say no . . . . I don't placate." Some blame his sudden personality change on a Scientology conspiracy to help the public accept Holmes's new relationship.

Holmes and Klein broke off their engagement seemingly moments before Tom Cruise (pg. 70) fell madly in love with her. Klein claimed Cruise had nothing to do with their split and said of Holmes "Are we friends? Absolutely. Do we talk? No."

Alice Adair

American actress from *Beverly Hills Cop II*

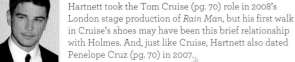

Hartnett took the Tom Cruise (pg. 70) role in 2008's London stage production of *Rain Man*, but his first walk in Cruise's shoes may have been this brief relationship with Holmes. And, just like Cruise, Hartnett also dated Penelope Cruz (pg. 70) in 2007.

◀ p.72 Josh Hartnett

2006–2008

2000–2005

Ginnifer Goodwin

The Boston University graduate plays Bill Paxton's youngest wife, Margene, on HBO's *Big Love*. She appeared in Comedy Central's first original movie, *Porn 'n Chicken*.

Long met Goodwin on the set of television's *Ed* back in 2001, when their characters dated too. They reunited for 2009's *He's Just Not That Into You*, in which they played potential lovers.

When Klein started seeing Goodwin after parting ways with Katie Holmes, people compared the two women. Both Goodwin and Holmes have short brown hair, cute smiles, prominent cheekbones, and the same birth year. But Holmes is three inches taller.

2002

2005

2005–

Tom Cruise

p.70 ▼

◀ p.78 Justin Long

Katie Holmes

These days, Holmes's history seems to begin with her "quirky" 2005 romance and subsequent marriage to couch-jumpingly ecstatic Tom Cruise (pg. 70), but she did have a life pre-Tom. A role in Ang Lee's *The Ice Storm* launched her career, and the innocent-yet-sultry girl next door from *Dawson's Creek* was born.

Lane was nominated for her first Oscar in 2003, but she'd attended the Academy Awards ceremony in 1981 with then-boyfriend Hutton. When he was whisked away after winning the first Oscar of the night, Lane spent "The rest of the evening . . . next to a seat filler."

1980–1981

Angelina Jolie p.105

Uma Thurman p.54

Rosario Dawson

Dawson's childhood was eerily similar to the experience of her character in *Rent*—her young parents squatted in an abandoned Lower East Side building and she grew up surrounded by HIV-positive family and friends. It may have been on that very stoop that she was discovered by Harmony Korine and Larry Clark and cast in her breakout role in 1995's *Kids*.

During the short time they dated, Jackson and Dawson were plagued by false rumors that they were either breaking up or engaged. Dawson said, "It was so funny because [we'd get calls] from people saying, 'Are you okay? Oh, that really sucks, man. You must be so down.' I was like, 'What are you talking about?'"

Holmes and Jackson dated during the first season of the show. After they split, she said, "It was something so incredible and indescribable that I will treasure it always," while Jackson said, "I can't tell you how much fun it is to go to work with your ex-girlfriend every day."

Timothy Hutton

Hutton won an Oscar for best supporting actor at age twenty (the youngest ever) for his role as a troubled teen in *Ordinary People*. It's hard to top that, but he tried, with numerous films including *Taps*, *The Falcon and the Snowman*, and *Sunshine State*.

Jackson dated his second *Dawson's Creek* costar after breaking up with Katie Holmes. When asked about dating on the job, he wisely observed, "When you're surrounded by beautiful women it seems difficult and foolish not to."

John Corbett
Actor from *Northern Exposure*

Brittany Daniel
American model and actress

2001

Debra Winger

Winger was nominated for Oscars for *An Officer and a Gentleman*, *Terms of Endearment*, and *Shadowlands*, but her debut role was in the sexy (if you're into pajamas) *Slumber Party '57*.

1998–1999
1995–1996
1986–1990
1990–1992

Mary-Louise Parker NEXT ▶

Keenen Ivory Wayans

Keenen got his start writing, producing, directing, and acting for *In Living Color* and his *Scary Movie* is the highest grossing film ever directed by an African American. He also directed *White Chicks*, which was nominated for five Razzie awards including Worst Director and Worst Actresses (for Shawn and Marlon Wayans, who played the chicks).

After reaching a divorce settlement with his ex, Daphne Polk, Wayans got together with Daniel, whom he directed in *Little Man*.

2006–2007

Joshua Jackson

Jackson got his break as team captain in all three *Mighty Ducks* films, but he's best known for his role as slacking, English-teacher-seducing Pacey Witter on *Dawson's Creek*.

1998–1999
1999–2000
2002

Kruger started seeing Jackson in 2006 after divorcing her husband of five years. Despite a short split in 2007, he moved into her New York apartment in 2008, but he had to make some sacrifices. "Half of [my] wardrobe, I lost. I'm in the smile-and-nod department of the nesting faculty in the Jackson/Kruger household!" said Jackson.

♥ 2006–

Diane Kruger

German model-actress Kruger portrayed the hottest girl in the world in 2004's *Troy* (no pressure) but *Maxim* ranked her at number fifty the next year—still, not too shabby. She got her start modeling as a finalist in Elite's "Look of the Year" competition and appeared in some French films before crossing over to Hollywood.

Adam Duritz p. 108

Duritz wrote the Counting Crows song "Butterfly in Reverse" for Parker, cleverly disguising his subject by calling her "Maryann" in the lyrics.

In possibly one of the biggest asshole moves in Hollywood relationship history, Crudup broke up with his long-term girlfriend, Parker, when she was seven months pregnant with their son to hook up with Claire Danes (pg. 112), his costar in *Stage Beauty*.

Crudup may have learned his unusual relationship etiquette from his parents, who divorced when he was in junior high and got remarried, to each other, a few years later.

Claire Danes p. 112

Billy Crudup
Crudup splits his time between stage and screen and is probably best known for his role as the lead rocker in Cameron Crowe's *Almost Famous*.

1996–2003

2003–2006

Hutton and Parker dated after starring together in *Prelude to a Kiss* on Broadway, a play in which Parker's character's soul is transferred into the body of an old man (and vice versa).

◀ BACK **Timothy Hutton**

1995–1996

Mary-Louise Parker
Not only did Parker study drama at the North Carolina School of the Arts, but she also got her start on stage (in Broadway's *Prelude to a Kiss*), providing her enough actor cred for a lifetime. Roles in *Boys on the Side* and *Angels in America* led to her biggest hit (get it) to date, the Showtime series *Weeds*.

2007–2009

Alexandra Hedison
Photographer

In 2004, the couple appeared together on the cover of the *Advocate*, just days before they broke up.

James Tupper
American actor

Heche met her *Men in Trees* costar Tupper while still married to Coley Laffoon. Tupper (also married at the time) cryptically said, "In that friendship, we kind of discovered we saw the world in a somewhat similar way," after which they ditched their spouses and had a son in 2009.

1990–1992

After her bad breakup with Martin, Heche acted out by claiming that she had literally "heard voices" throughout their relationship. Martin acted out by parodying Heche in his film *Bowfinger*, in which Heather Graham (pg. 47) played an actress from Ohio who sleeps around to get ahead and ends up dating a woman. Coincidence?

Heche met Laffoon on the set of her girlfriend's comedy special, dumped said girlfriend (Ellen DeGeneres), and married Laffoon just in time for their son, Homer, to be born a few months later.

Coleman "Coley" Laffoon
Cameraman

2001–2007

2007–

Ellen DeGeneres
Since coming out on her sitcom in 1997, Ellen has evolved into the lesbian America loves—even the reddest states can't get enough of her syndicated talk show. Her wedding to Portia de Rossi, held before California's Proposition 8 banned gay marriage, was covered by every media outlet, even conservative Fox News.

2001–2004

2004–

◀ p. 157 **Steve Martin**

1995–1997

Heche met Buckingham on a flight and had no idea he was a famous musician. She asked if he was going to Los Angeles to try his luck, and if he had "ever play[ed] with anyone I might have heard of?" But when you look like Heche does, lines like that work just fine.

Lindsey Buckingham
Fleetwood Mac guitarist

1992

Anne Heche
Heche got her start playing angel-and-devil twin sisters on the soap *Another World* and her career took off in the 1990s with big pictures starring Johnny Depp (pg. 114) and Harrison Ford (pg. 121). But her relationships have always overshadowed her acting.

Hollywood's most powerful same-sexers at the time appeared on Oprah Winfrey's show to chit chat about their relationship the day after Ellen came out on her eponymous sitcom. Oprah's ratings went through the roof.

1997–2000

Weeds costars Parker and Morgan split up and reconciled countless times during their relationship—at one point their relationship was in the "on" position long enough to get engaged. They're no longer together, but who knows what's in store?

The gay team (and dorky comedians everywhere) high-fived awkwardly when gorgeous, blonde de Rossi revealed her relationship with Ellen and went on to marry her in 2008. The wedding took place in their Beverly Hills home, despite a semigenuine invitation from Jenna Bush on Ellen's show to hold the nuptials at the Bush family ranch.

Jeffrey Dean Morgan

Morgan's characters were killed off on three different television series at the same time: Judah Botwin on *Weeds*, John Winchester on *Supernatural*, and Denny Duquette on *Grey's Anatomy*. He died on the big screen as The Comedian in *Watchmen*, so if your script has a death scene, you know who to call.

Portia de Rossi

The actress made a name for herself (literally as she changed her name from Mandy Rogers at fifteen) playing sexy but shallow women on shows like *Ally McBeal*, *Arrested Development*, and, more recently, *Better Off Ted*. In real life though, the Australian actress seems real smart.

Tony Romo p.109

2006–2007

153

Mike Fisher
NHL Player

2008–

Carrie Underwood

When Underwood sang her rendition of 1980s Heart hit "Alone" on *American Idol*'s fourth season, Simon Cowell (pg. 105) correctly predicted not only that she would win but also that she would be the best-selling *Idol* winner of all time. Of course, it didn't hurt that she was also the hottest *Idol* winner of all time.

2007–2008

Chace Crawford p.119 ▶

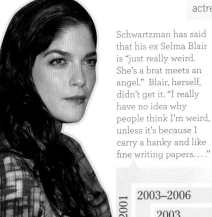

Schwartzman has said that his ex Selma Blair is "just really weird. She's a brat meets an angel." Blair, herself, didn't get it. "I really have no idea why people think I'm weird, unless it's because I carry a hanky and like fine writing papers...."

Jason Schwartzman

Coppola cousin Schwartzman launched his career as the star of *Rushmore*. If you look closely, you can see him as Gag Halfrunt, the private brain care specialist of Zaphod Beeblebrox in *The Hitchhiker's Guide to the Galaxy*.

❥ 2003–2005

After dating briefly in high school, Deschanel and Schwartzman reconnected, with the help of his *I Heart Huckabees* costar Dustin Hoffman, who set them up.

Married in a traditional Jewish ceremony at Carrie Fisher's (pg. 49) estate, the couple sped up their divorce proceedings three years later by waiving any claims for spousal support.

Zooey Deschanel

Deschanel has become Hollywood's go-to girl for deadpan, doe-eyed characters, like those she played in *Yes Man*, *The Happening*, and *(500) Days of Summer*.

Deschanel's band, She & Him, toured with Gibbard's Death Cab for Cutie in 2008 and the couple got engaged at the end of the year. By 2009, music reporters had noticed a transformation in Gibbard's style—he grew his hair, shaved his stubble, and generally hotted up thanks to her feminine touch.

2008–

Ben Gibbard
Lead singer for band Death Cab for Cutie

2001   2003–2006

2003

Blair and Perry met on the set of *Friends*. She was playing a guest role as a coworker who hit on Chandler when he was stuck in Tulsa on Christmas.

Matthew Perry p.123 ▼

Ahmet Zappa p.39 ▼

Selma Blair

Best known for her bi-curious kiss with Sarah Michelle Gellar (pg. 35) in *Cruel Intentions*, Blair claims she hasn't kissed a girl since. She has a BFA in photography, which might explain why she takes such great shots.

Barry Diller

Reportedly the richest member of the "Velvet Mafia" (Hollywood's gay cabal), Diller was the twenty-seven-year-old head of programming when he launched ABC's Movie of the Week in 1969, bringing us classics like *Gidget Gets Married* and *Skyway to Death*.

Von Furstenberg tried to quash rumors that her 2001 marriage to probably-gay billionaire Diller was a sham by telling a reporter that she and Diller were lovers "in a way that has been very strong . . . because it was so unexpected."

In her autobiography, *Diane: A Signature Life*, von Furstenberg reveals that she was so desperate to look sexy and thin on her date with O'Neal that she took a diuretic before dinner and spent most of the meal in the john.

Von Furstenberg has the dubious honor of having once had sex with Warren Beatty and Ryan O'Neal on the same day (we assume at different times).

Ryan O'Neal *p. 56*

Warren Beatty *p. 140*

🔒 2001– 💔 1975 💔 1978

◄ p.79 **Val Kilmer** 1996 💔

Crawford described Kilmer as brilliant and "almost too deep." The pair once got into a fight when she wore a hat advertising a bar whose owner Kilmer disliked. Celebrity endorsements can be tricky.

Cindy Crawford

She was the world's most famous supermodel, with the world's most famous mole. These days she is trying her hand at furniture design, a talent she may have picked up while pouting on couches from Milan to Tokyo.

Egon von Furstenberg
Prince and fashion designer

Prince Egon von Furstenberg's parents objected to his marrying Diane Simone, who was Jewish, but the prince defied his parents, making her a real live princess. The marriage lasted three years, but the multisyllabic name lived on.

1969–1973 🔒

Diane von Furstenberg

Born in Belgium to a middle-class Jewish family, Diane scored a title (and a name for her signature wrap dresses) when she married Prince Egon von Furstenberg in 1969. After they split, she went through men like Kleenex in allergy season saying, "I [wanted] to live like . . . a guy. And I absolutely enjoyed it."

Hooking up with Crawford was a big score for Gere, but one of Crawford's model friends explained why they split: "Gere's a boring fucking Buddhist."

Gere partied with von Furstenberg at the global epicenter for sex, drugs, and unimaginable debauchery in the 1970s—Studio 54.

🔒 1991–1995 💔 1976

Peter Brant
Publisher and paper company billionaire

Brant and Seymour began an ugly divorce battle in 2009 in which he alleged that she had a Vicodin addiction and he should get sole custody of their three kids because she submitted "invalid" urine samples for drug tests.

After sixteen years of marriage, Kelley has not cast his actor-wife Pfeiffer in any of his shows. "She's a bit controlling with her career . . . I like to be senior management and that never, never happens in her company." 'Nuff said.

David Kelley
Television producer

1993–

Gere and Lowell were married in 2002 but dated for many years prior. As long as Tibet isn't free, they will have a united purpose, as they are both devoted supporters of preserving the culture of Tibet.

Fisher Stevens
Actor

1988–1991

Richard Gere

Everyone's favorite China-boycotting Buddhist and whore-hiring corporate raider (wait, that was in *Pretty Woman*) got his start as Danny Zuko in a 1973 London production of *Grease*. A year later he was fired from the set of *The Lords of Flatbush* for feuding with Sylvester Stallone (pg. 138), who says Gere blames him for starting the gerbil rumor— you know the one we're talking about.

🔒 2002–

Peter Horton
Actor and director

Pfeiffer and actor-director Horton were an item for much of the eighties, and he directed her in the classic 1985 ABC special, *One Too Many*, in which she played a girl whose high school boyfriend (played by Val Kilmer, pg. 79) was a raging alcoholic.

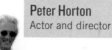

Carey Lowell
Actress

💔

◄ p.55 **Carole Mallory** 1970–1975

▲ Warren Beatty p.140

John Casablancas
Elite Model agency founder

Her relationship with John Casablancas, the head of Elite Model Management, began when she was just sixteen and Casablancas was forty-four (cringe factor: high).

Axl Rose

The Guns N' Roses idol may be one of rock's all-time greatest front men, but Rose is not an easy man to get along with. Just ask Kurt Cobain, whom he challenged to a fight.

Seymour's relationship with Axl Rose ended badly. How badly? Each alleged in court that the other was physically abusive, and for Seymour, speaking with Rose is out of the question.

"Would I ever have a conversation with him again? God no. I can't believe I lived through that."

According to Everly, Rose proposed to her by showing up at her house and threatening to kill himself if she did not marry him. The marriage lasted only a month, and Rose continued to hound her for more than a year after.

1994–2009 🔒 1991 ❣ 1984 ❣   1991–1993 ❣   🔒 1990–1991

Stephanie Seymour

The **übersexy** lingerie model made her mark as one of the original bodies for Victoria's Secret. Seymour published a book entitled *Stephanie Seymour's Beauty Tips for Dummies*, which taught readers how to get the right look for less money—because obviously she knows about shopping on a budget, being a supermodel and all.

Erin Everly

Daughter of country singing legend Don Everly, Erin is the inspiration for many of Guns N' Roses's greatest songs, including the anthem "Sweet Child of Mine." Axl Rose offered her half his share of the royalties for the track, saying he couldn't have written it without her. Amazingly, she declined.

❣ 1993–1994 **David Arquette** NEXT ▶

David Arquette NEXT ▶

Michelle Pfeiffer

During the filming of *Batman Returns* Pfeiffer had to be vacuum sealed into her costume. She might not have been able to breathe, but she was voted one of the most beautiful people in the world by *People* magazine six times.

❣ 1981–1988 🔒 1985–1986

If Keaton and Pfeiffer had particularly good chemistry as Batman and Catwoman, it was because they had dated years before. Keaton was effusive in his praise of his *Batman Returns* costar: "I'm such a fan ... I think she has more range than anybody."

Cox fell for Keaton, to whom she was later engaged, after seeing him play a drug addict in the film *Clean and Sober*. "I'm not afraid of that side of any man," said Cox. "My brother and my father are extremely manic, and I'm manic. That's what I call 'having a lot of energy.'"

1989–1995 🗲

Michael Keaton

Keaton (whose real name is Michael Douglas, oddly enough) became an actor after trying his luck as a stand-up comic. He embarked on a successful partnership with director Tim Burton (pg. 157), who cast him as a gross ghoul in *Beetlejuice* and later as the Dark Knight himself in *Batman*.

🔒 1999–   ❣   1995–1997

Courteney Cox

Born and raised in Alabama, Cox worked hard to lose her accent when she moved to New York City to start modeling. Her big break as the girl who got pulled onstage in Bruce Springsteen's "Dancing in the Dark" video led to roles in *Family Ties* (she was Michael J. Fox's girlfriend, pg. 88) and in a tampon commercial before she broke out in *Friends* in 1994.

▼ Adam Duritz p.108

Kilmer was once asked which of his past loves would have the worst things to say about him and his immediate response was Ellen Barkin, but he refused to reveal why!

▲ 2° to Lucy Liu
▲ 3° to Michael Bolton
▲ 4° to Jenny McCarthy

George Clooney p.125

◀ p.79 **Val Kilmer**

1984

1997–1998
Julia Ormond
British actress

Gabriel Byrne
The Irish actor didn't cross the pond until he was thirty-seven, but that didn't stop him from being named one of the "Sexiest Men Alive" by *People* magazine.

1988–1993

2006

2007

Naomi Campbell p.54

❤ 1998

Hugh Laurie
British actor

Fiennes dumped his wife of twelve years to get with Annis, who had played his mother in a production of *Hamlet*. Eleven years later, Annis suffered a similar fate at the hands of his lover, Romanian singer Cornelia Crisan.

Francesca Annis
British actress

Ellen Barkin

Barkin broke out in the movie *Diner* alongside "sex degrees" icon Kevin Bacon (pg. 85). The beautiful actress had this to say about blind dates after her second divorce, "You think, 'Why am I here? . . . Let's first see if the sex thing works, and then we could go have dinner.'"

2000–2006

Barkin said of her billionaire husband Perelman, "Ronald thinks he's compromising if we have one cook instead of three." When they split, she got $60 million and an additional $20 million by selling the jewelry he had given her during their marriage.

Ronald Perelman
Billionaire investor

Barkin pounced on Arquette when he was twenty-two and she was thirty-nine on the set of *Wild Bill*.

1994–1995

2007

1995–2006

2005

Gina Gershon
Big-mouthed beauty and gay icon Gershon was romantically linked to president Bill Clinton by *Vanity Fair*. With hot roles in *Bound*, *Showgirls*, *Palmetto*, and more, it's clear why she appeals to gays and presidents alike.

1983–1995

Qantas stewardess Robertson says she flirted with Fiennes, let him sit in the crew jumpseat with her, and then "reached down for his hand and told him to follow me." She led him to the restroom, and they had unprotected sex before the plane landed in Mumbai, where Fiennes was headed for an AIDS conference.

Ralph Fiennes

Fiennes, or "He-Who-Cannot-Be-Named" given the unusual pronunciation (rāf) of his seemingly simple first name, broke out with his creepy portrayal of Commandant Amon Goeth in 1993's *Schindler's List*. But it was his role as the mummified geographer in *The English Patient* that made him a (mispronounced) household name.

◀ BACK **Erin Invicta Everly**

1993–1994 ❤

Other than making the line "Do you like scary movies?" famous, the *Scream* trilogy also brought Cox and Arquette together. They have been married since 1999 and have a daughter named Coco.

David Arquette
Arquette comes from a family of actors so his success on the screen comes as no surprise. More impressive is his WCW World Heavyweight Champion belt which he won in 2000.

2004–2006

Crisan says that when she first met Fiennes at a London party she had no idea who he was. "Only much later I realized he'd been in the film *Maid in Manhattan*," she said.

Cornelia Crisan
Romanian singer

2007

Lisa Robertson
Qantas stewardess

◀ BACK **Courteney Cox**

1999–

Thompson and Laurie dated at Cambridge University, where they were both members of the Cambridge Footlights Revue (otherwise known as the drama geeks).

1980–1982 💔

Emma Thompson

Thompson's first big film role was *The Tall Guy*, which featured a rambunctious sex scene with Jeff Goldblum (pg. 142). But we know her best for her Oscar-winning turns in costume dramas like *Sense and Sensibility* and *Howards End*.

Alexandra Kingston

Kingston gained fame on this side of the pond with her portrayal of Dr. Elizabeth Corday, who married Anthony Edwards's (pg. 144) Dr. Greene on *ER*.

Fiennes left Kingston after twelve years of marriage for his *Hamlet* costar, older actress Francesca Annis. Kingston was nearly suicidal and once got into a bathtub with a knife, intent on killing herself.

Burton met his creepy counterpart Carter on the set of his *Planet of the Apes* remake—the star's beauty must have shown through despite the primate makeup because he dumped Lisa Marie to move near Carter (they share adjoining townhouses in London).

Branagh and Thompson shared on- and offscreen romances when they married in 1989, just as their film careers were lifting off. But the marriage was plagued with rumors of affairs, which proved true.

1989–1995 🔒

Carter brought divorce to Branagh and his wife Emma Thompson after she met him on the set of *Frankenstein*.

1994–1999 💔 2000 💔

Helena Bonham Carter

Kooky beauty Bonham Carter comes from a long line of Bonham Carters, going back to great-grandfather H. H. Asquith, prime minister of the U.K. right before World War I. She broke out in *A Room with a View* in 1986.

2001– ♥

Tim Burton

Burton was plucked from the depths of Disney by Paul Reubens to direct *Pee-Wee's Big Adventure* after Reubens saw his twisted short *Frankenweenie*, about a frankensteined dog.

Kenneth Branagh

Shakespeare is good and all, but could Irish actor-director Branagh be a little obsessed? (See *Henry V*, *Much Ado about Nothing*, *Hamlet*, *Love's Labour's Lost*, *As You Like It*, and *Othello*, if you must.)

Carter and Martin had an on-set romance when she was his patient on the set of dental thriller *Novocaine*. After her breakup with Kenneth Branagh and his with Anne Heche (pg. 152), a relationship built on oral surgery might have seemed painless in comparison.

Bernadette Peters

Peters, who took her stage name from her father's first name, started off in theater (she played Dainty June in *Gypsy*, a show she revived years later, in 2003) before heading off to star in film comedies with Mel Brooks and Steve Martin.

1977–1981 💔

Peters and Martin got intimate during *The Jerk*, in which their dimwitted couple sang a ukulele-accompanied duet of "Tonight You Belong to Me" (Peters wraps with a surprise trumpet solo).

Graham and Burns were set to move into John F. Kennedy Jr.'s (pg. 11) twenty-four-hundred-square-foot Tribeca loft together but split before they had the chance. Burns reportedly blamed the split on the fact that "she didn't want to get married and have children."

1998–2000 💔

1991–2001 ☊

Heather Graham p.47

Lisa Marie p.142

Steve Martin

He strutted as King Tut, he was a wild and crazy guy on *Saturday Night Live* (he was never a cast member but had hosted a record fifteen times by 2009), and his banjo playing won him a Grammy in 2002 on an Earl Scruggs track. But Martin may now be best known for his family films like *Father of the Bride* and for dating and marrying women whose father he could be.

Ed Burns

Burns was a production assistant at *Entertainment Tonight* when he wrote, directed, produced, starred in, and paid for his debut feature *The Brothers McMullen*. He managed to sneak the film to Robert Redford, and it went on to win the Grand Jury Prize at Sundance.

2003– Christy Turlington NEXT ▶

Burns said, "Friends of ours had tried to fix us up. We both live in New York, we're both pretty low-key, both heterosexual, but she was like, 'Uh, not really interested.'" The attacks of 9/11 postponed their Italian wedding, and they broke up briefly before marrying in 2003.

Jason Patric p. 102 ▲

Christian Slater p. 22 ▲

1995–2000

1994

2003– 🔒

Christy Turlington

Turlington rejected the label of super-model ("It's over, it's over, it's over") in 2007, but not the millions she had earned as precisely that, modeling for Maybelline, Calvin Klein, and Chanel since 1984.

◀ BACK **Ed Burns**

Turlington was engaged to actor Wilson, and they married in a "symbolic" ceremony in Thailand. She got his initials tattooed on her ankle—never a good move. The "marriage" became a "breakup," and the initials became a rose.

1987–1991 🔒

Roger Wilson
Actor in *Porky's* and *Porky's II*

Lisa Ann Russell
Model

Gosselaar says it was his policy "not to date guest stars or day players" on *Saved by the Bell* (regular cast members were fine), but when Revlon model Russell appeared in a cameo, he hooked.

1996–1997

After Wilson dumped her for Elizabeth Berkley, McManamon was arrested for threatening them both with death. Here's an excerpt from her phone message: "I'm going to cut you. I know where you live . . . I'm going to kill you both."

Kat McManamon
Model

1997–1999 💋

Leonardo DiCaprio (pg. 73) hit on Berkley after meeting her at a premiere. The catch was that she was already dating Wilson. The wronged Wilson tracked down DiCaprio at a New York restaurant, gave him a black eye (DiCaprio missed the 1998 Oscars because of it), and got beaten up by DiCaprio's posse.

Lark Voorhies
Voorhies, Jermaine Jackson's niece, found fame as Screech's love interest on *Saved by the Bell*. After graduating from the fictional Bayside High, she sued the *National Enquirer* for a 2006 story that quoted a friend saying she had a "terrible drug problem."

Gosselaar dated Voorhies (along with all the other women on the cast) and said, "*Saved by the Bell* was like high school for us, so we ended up going out with each other."

1993–1994 💋

Martin Lawrence
Comic actor Lawrence is known for his antics: donning a fat suit for *Big Momma's House*, brandishing a pistol on L.A.'s Ventura Boulevard, and falling into a three-day coma after jogging in heavy clothing in 100-degree weather to lose weight in 1999.

Lawrence was engaged to *Saved by the Bell* starlet Voorhies but left her to marry Miss USA runner-up Patricia Southall.

1996–1992 🔒

Mark-Paul Gosselaar

Gosselaar built a career on his portrayal of Zack on the series *Saved by the Bell*. Despite that character's slicked-back, Vanilla Ice (pg. 103) hairstyle, Gosselaar starred on *NYPD Blue* and *Raising the Bar*.

Tiffani-Amber Thiessen
American actress from *Beverly Hills, 90210*

1993

Thiessen and Gosselaar shared only a brief relationship off camera. "Y' know it's kinda hard not to [date], working with these beautiful women for six years," said Gosselaar.

1993–1995

💋 1993

The entire cast of *Saved by the Bell* dated each other, but Gosselaar had a special relationship with Berkley and wasn't happy about *Showgirls*. "There were scenes I didn't watch. I couldn't stand to see Elizabeth that way," he said.

Brian Austin Green p. 79

Elizabeth Berkley
Berkley played the smart feminist Jessie on *Saved by the Bell* for four years, and her character would have begged her not to take the part of dancing stripper Nomi Malone in the NC-17 campy megaflop *Showgirls*.

Benjamin Bratt
American actor from *Law & Order*

Bratt and Roberts may have fallen victim to the "Oscar Curse" (just ask Reese Witherspoon, pg. 18, Halle Berry, pg. 34, or Hilary Swank). They split mere weeks after she won her little golden man for *Erin Brockovich*. It was either that or, as Bratt later put it, her "unbearable ego."

Danny Moder
Cameraman

When asked about dating costars, Roberts said, "I've done nothing but work, film after film, since I was seventeen. I don't know who people think I'm going to meet, except actors." She met another option in cameraman Moder on the set of *The Mexican*.

Sutherland left his wife and kids to get engaged to Roberts after meeting her on the set of *Flatliners*. His reward? She dumped him three days before the wedding and ran off to Ireland with his *Lost Boys* friend and costar Jason Patric (pg. 102).

Kiefer Sutherland
Sutherland was so compelling in his role as Jack Bauer on *24* that the U.S. government took torture tips from his performances. After his breakup with Julia Roberts, he took a break from acting to launch a successful rodeo career.

Lyle Lovett
American country singer and actor

Hawke and ex-nanny Shawhughes married in a quiet ceremony one month before she delivered their child, daughter Clementine Jane Hawke.

Ryan Shawhughes
Nanny

When he asked her out in 1995, Perry "assumed [Roberts] wouldn't even take the call." But she was impressed by his chutzpah (apparently, everyone is afraid to ask her out). After she dumped him, Perry began a descent into drugs and drink, for which Roberts continues to blame herself.

Clooney's "close friendship" with Roberts on the set of *Ocean's 11* (culminating in a steamy dance at the wrap party) may have sparked her split from Benjamin Bratt. Clooney enticed Roberts to costar in the film by referring to her $20 million *Erin Brockovich* paycheck in a letter that read, "I hear you now work for twenty" with a $20 bill enclosed.

Liam Neeson p.115 ▲
Jason Patric p.102 ▲

Matthew Perry p.123 ▶
George Clooney p.125 ▶
Dylan McDermott p.131 ▶
Daniel Day-Lewis p.16 ▶

1998–2001
1987–1988
1991–1993
1995–1996
2001–
1990–1991
1993–1995
2001
1988–1990
1994–1995
1994
1994
1998–2004
2005–

Julia Roberts

Although preceded by bigger-haired roles in *Mystic Pizza* and *Steel Magnolias*, Roberts's hooker-in-love portrayal in *Pretty Woman* made her a megastar. A mere ten years later, she was the top-paid actress in Hollywood.

Only a few months into her marriage with Lyle Lovett, Roberts was photographed dancing and eating out with Hawke. Her PR team insisted that they were talking about a project, but Lyle said he "couldn't bear talking about" their relationship issues.

Ethan Hawke

Hawke's character's betrayal of a radical educator played by Robin Williams in the poetry-drenched boy drama *Dead Poets Society* was nothing compared to his public betrayal of gorgeous wife Uma Thurman (pg. 54) years later.

Uma Thurman p.54 ▶

When it comes to married celebrities, the nanny is more likely to do it than the butler. Such was the case for Thurman and Hawke—he married their former nanny three years after their divorce was finalized.

Acknowledgments

Mapping out the vast terrain of celebrity relationships is not unlike untangling a thousand iPod headphones that have been in your bag for a week, and I couldn't have done it without the help of these wise people. Gary Grossman was there at the beginning and built the database that makes *Sex Degrees* possible. Thanks goes to my writing assistants Sam Rodriguez, Stephen Morse, and Emily Faye. Jennifer de la Fuente turned an unhealthy obsession into an actual deal, and Christina Amini and Carey Jones at Chronicle Books honed the madness into this very book. Designing a fun, readable map was an insane challenge, and I must thank Karen Hsu, Julie Cho, and Alice Chung at Omnivore design and Suzanne Lagasa at Chronicle Books for making it awesome. Thanks to Kim Romero, Zipi Eyal, Chantelle Aspey, and Christine Jensch. And most of all, I have to thank my wife, Jessica Baumgardner, for her support and advice, and for raising our kids by herself for the last year or so.

Library of Congress
Cataloging-in-Publication Data:

Eyal, Irad.
    Sex degrees of separation : the ultimate guide to celebrity relationships / by Irad Eyal.
        p. cm.
    ISBN 978-0-8118-7180-8
    1. Celebrities—Biography. 2. Unmarried couples—Biography.
    3. Married people—Biography. I. Title.
    CT105.E93 2010
    305.5'2—dc22

                                2009051378

Manufactured in China
Designed by Omnivore

10 9 8 7 6 5 4 3 2 1

Chronicle Books LLC
680 Second Street, San Francisco, California 94107

www.chroniclebooks.com
www.sexdegrees.net

Are you a celebrity or did you get with one? Did we miss your relationship or mess up the details? Let us know! Seriously! Just send an e-mail to irad@sxdgs.com with the correct information. Please include some verification that you are who you say you are, and we'll make sure it's right in the next edition. Who says celebrities never get anything for free!